Domestic Violence Context

Domestic violence does not discriminate and is prevalent throughout the world regardless of race, age or socio-economic status. Why, then, do reactions and responses differ so widely throughout the world? While some countries work diligently to address the matter through prevention and training, others take a 'hands-off' approach in their response. This book is one of the first to investigate domestic violence on a global scale and provides best practices gleaned from various countries around the world to paint a detailed picture of how police response to domestic violence is currently being conducted and provide training bodies with up-to-date information to enhance current curricula.

Domestic Violence in International Context brings together expert scholars native to thirteen different countries to examine the history and scope of domestic violence and how it is being addressed, repressed or ignored in their respective countries. Their specialised knowledge and unique data come together to create a series of snapshots that will guide nations, societies and communities worldwide in formulating effective strategies to prevent, intervene and combat this epidemic, and examine partnerships and programmes already in place.

This book is essential reading for practitioners, policy makers and human rights organisations, as well as students and scholars of criminology, social work, sociology and law.

Diana Scharff Peterson is Professor of Criminology at the University of Texas of the Permian Basin, USA.

Julie A. Schroeder is Professor at the School of Social Work, Jackson State University, USA.

Routledge Studies in Crime and Society

Domestic Violence in International Context

Edited by
Diana Scharff Peterson
and Julie A. Schroeder

Routledge
Taylor & Francis Group

LONDON AND NEW YORK

First published 2017 by Routledge

2 Park Square, Milton Park, Abingdon, Oxfordshire OX14 4RN

52 Vanderbilt Avenue, New York, NY 10017

Routledge is an imprint of the Taylor & Francis Group, an informa business

First issued in paperback 2019

British Library Cataloguing in Publication Data
A catalogue record for this book is available from the British Library

Library of Congress Cataloging in Publication Data
Names: Scharff Peterson, Diana, editor. | Schroeder, Julie A., editor.
Title: Domestic violence in international context / edited by Diana Scharff Peterson and Julie A. Schroeder.
Description: 1 Edition. | New York : Routledge, 2017. | Series: Routledge studies in crime and society ; 27 | Includes bibliographical references and index.
Identifiers: LCCN 2016030756 | ISBN 9781138669642 (hardback) | ISBN 9781315618098 (ebook)
Subjects: LCSH: Family violence. | Victims of family violence. | Police–Attitudes.
Classification: LCC HV6626 .D6686 2017 | DDC 362.82/92–dc23
LC record available at https://lccn.loc.gov/2016030756

ISBN: 978-1-138-66964-2 (hbk)
ISBN: 978-0-367-22644-2 (pbk)

Typeset in Times New Roman
by Wearset Ltd, Boldon, Tyne and Wear

Contents

Figures

Tables

Contributors

Editors

Diana Scharff Peterson, PhD, has nearly 20 years of experience in higher education teaching in the areas of research methods; comparative criminal justice systems; race, gender, class, and crime; statistics; criminology; sociology; and drugs and behavior at seven different institutions of higher education. She has been the chairperson of three different criminal justice programs over the past 15 years and has published in the areas of criminal justice, social work, higher education, sociology, business, and management. Her research interests include issues in policing (training and education) and community policing, assessment and leadership in higher education, family violence, and evaluation research, and program development. She has published over 30 articles in areas of criminal justice, sociology, social work, business, management, and higher education and is the Liaison and Representative for the International Police Executive Symposium (IPES) (consultative status) for quarterly annual meetings at the United Nations meetings in New York City, Geneva, and Vienna including the Commission on the Status of Women in NYC, New York. She chaired and organized the 25th Annual Meeting of the IPES entitled, *Crime Prevention & Community Resilience: Police Role with Victims, Youth, Ethnic Minorities and Other Partners*, in Sofia, Bulgaria, July 27 to August 1, 2014 (27 countries and 43 presenters). She is the Managing Editor of *Police Practice and Research: An International Journal*.

Julie A. Schroeder, PhD, is a professor in the Jackson State University School of Social Work where she teaches at the Master's and doctoral level. She teaches both qualitative and quantitative research methods, program and practice evaluation, psychopathology, forensic social work, and social policy. She was co-principal investigator of Not on Our Campus funded by the Department of Justice Office on Violence against Women and has published on a variety of criminal justice issues including domestic violence. She earned her PhD in Social Work from Tulane University in New Orleans, Louisiana.

Contributors

Christiaan Bezuidenhout, PhD, is a professor in the Department of Social Work and Criminology, University of Pretoria. He teaches psycho-criminology, criminal justice, and contemporary criminology on an under-graduate and postgraduate level. During his academic career he has published numerous scientific articles in peer-reviewed journals and chapters in books. He has also acted as editor-in-chief for different scholarly books. He has participated in national and international conferences and has been actively involved in various community projects focusing on crime prevention and has assisted the South African Government in the development of different crime prevention initiatives. He holds the following degrees: BA (Criminology), BA Honors (Criminology), MA (Criminology), DPhil (Criminology). He also holds an MSc degree in Criminology and Criminal Justice from the University of Oxford.

Esperanza Bosch-Fiol, PhD, is a university lecturer and Director of the Gender Studies Research Group at the University de las Islas Baleares, Palma, Spain. Her area of research interest is violence against women.

Laetitia Coetzee obtained the degrees BA Law, BA Hons Criminology (*cum laude*), MA Criminology (*cum laude*), and DPhil Criminology from the University of Pretoria in South Africa. The title of her Master's dissertation is "An evaluation of existing measures aimed at restricting the use of the Internet as an avenue to initiate sexual activities with adolescents" and the title of her doctoral dissertation is "Victim empathy in youth sex offenders." She has been lecturing in the Department of Social Work and Criminology at the University of Pretoria since 2005 and her fields of speciality are youth misbehavior and victimology. She has published articles and book chapters and presented papers at national and international conferences focusing on sexual offending, youth misbehaviour, and victims of crime.

Irwin M. Cohen, PhD, is a faculty member in the School of Criminology and Criminal Justice at the University of the Fraser Valley, the holder of the University Senior Research Chair, RCMP for Crime Reduction, and the Director of the Centre for Public Safety and Criminal Justice Research. He received his PhD from Simon Fraser University for his work on the disutility of state torture. He has also published many scholarly articles and book chapters, delivered many lectures, conference papers, and workshops, and written policy reports on a wide range of topics including policing issues, restorative justice, serious and violent young offenders, Aboriginal victimization issues, and terrorism. He has been the co-principal investigator on dozens of research projects on a wide range of policing, youth, public policy, and Aboriginal issues. For his research into binge drinking, he received the 2007 Mothers against Drunk Driving (MADD) Citizens of Distinction Award for Research Prevention/Education.

Louise Cotrel-Gibbons is a non-profit management and communications professional currently living and working in Hanoi, Vietnam. She completed her undergraduate and Master's studies at the University of York and has field experience in Sri Lanka, Liberia, and Vietnam. Her research interests are strongly centered on concepts of power, empowerment, and gender equality for communities in developing regions.

Maximillian Edelbacher was born in 1944 in Vienna, Austria. He graduated from Vienna University (Mag. Jur.) and was Hofrat of the Federal Police of Austria. He served as the chief of the Major Crime Bureau, and as an international expert for the Council of Europe, OSCE, and UNO. He also chaired the Austrian Antifraud Insurance Bureau and lectured at several universities including the Vienna University of Economics and Business Administration, Danube University in Krems, and still lectures at the Vienna University, Department of Sociology. In 2015 he was appointed as Vice-President of the Vienna Liaison Office, of the Academic Council on the United Nations, and some years earlier as Director of the International Police Executive Symposium (IPES). He is the author of a number of books and journal articles.

M. Tugba Erdem, MA, is a research assistant at the Turkish Military Academy. Her area of research interest is crime and urban culture.

Victoria A. Ferrer-Pérez, PhD, is a university lecturer and a member of the Gender Studies Research Group at the University de las Islas Baleares, Palma, Spain. Her area of research interest is violence against women and, particularly, the analysis of its causes from a psychosocial point of view.

Suheyl Gurbuz is a PhD student of Sociology at the University of North Texas. His area of research interest is delinquency and comparative criminology.

Gerald Dapaah Gyamfi holds a PhD in Higher Education Administration from the University of Phoenix, Arizona, and an MSc in Human Resource Development from the University of Manchester. He is a fellow of the Institute of Chartered Secretaries and Administrators, UK, and Dean of the Weekend School at the University of Professional Studies, Accra, Ghana. He lectures risk management and operations management courses and has taught many police officers in these courses at the University of Professional Studies, Accra. He and his family own a private business, Geraldo Travel & Tours Ltd, in Accra. For over 10 years, he was the proprietor of ICSA (Institute of Chartered Secretaries and Administrators) Study Center in Ghana. He served as Session Clerk (four years) and Director of Human Resources and Administration (another four years) at a local congregation of the Presbyterian Church of Ghana. He has written many articles and books in the area of management and security and presented conference papers at many international conferences in different parts of the world, including United Nations Conference Side Events.

Josef Hörl (= Hoerl) was born in 1947 in Vienna, Austria. He graduated from Vienna University and from 1997 to 2012 he served there as Associate Professor of Sociology. He has authored more than 100 scientific publications focusing on social gerontology (particularly on elder abuse and neglect) and family sociology. He is a senior consultant with the Austrian Ministry of Social Affairs and co-author of the federal government's charter of the rights and responsibilities of older people. Until 2012 he served as president of the Austrian section of the International Network for the Prevention of Elder Abuse.

Mervyn Jackson, PhD, is a senior lecturer in the psychology discipline at RMIT University with research and teaching interests in all areas of social psychology including gender issues, pathological gambling, and tourist crime victimization.

Eray Karlidag is a PhD student in Public Administration at Virginia Commonwealth University (VCU). His area of research interest is violence and terrorism.

Miranda Lai is a lecturer and trainer in interpreting and translating at RMIT University, Melbourne, Australia. She is undertaking her PhD research into the PEACE police interviewing model mediated by interpreters. Her research interests include investigative interviewing in multilingual settings, public service translation and interpreting, and the intersection of security and communication.

Amanda V. McCormick is an associate professor in the School of Criminology and Criminal Justice at the University of the Fraser Valley where she teaches courses related to social policy, young offenders, and mental health issues related to crime. She is also a research associate with the Centre for Public Safety and Criminal Justice Research and the UFV Centre for Safe Schools and Communities. Her research interests focus on policing strategies, at-risk youth, and mental health issues among serious and violent young offenders. She received her PhD from Simon Fraser University where she completed her dissertation on personality disorders and serious and violent young offenders.

Bruno Meini, PhD, holds a doctorate in Criminology from the University of Bologna, an MA in criminal justice from the School of Criminal Justice at Rutgers University, and a Master's degree in research methods in the social sciences from the University of Florence. His research interest lies in the areas of policing, crime prevention, penology, social dimensions of HIV, and crime and security-related issues. He is Executive Assistant to the International Police Executive Symposium President, and Production Editor for *Police Practice and Research: An International Journal.*

Sedat Mulayim is a program director and lecturer, translating and interpreting, in the School of Global, Urban and Social Studies, RMIT University, Melbourne, Australia. His current PhD research is examining language barriers and social exclusion. His main publications and research activities focus on communication in diverse contexts, security, ethics, and social exclusion.

Susumu Nagai, MA, has over 30 years of experience in higher education teaching in the areas of clinical victimology; trauma and recovery; understanding of and assistance to victims of crime; counseling and psychotherapy for victims of crime; educational counseling; and educational psychology at five different public institutions and six different institutions of higher education. He is currently Dean of the Graduate School of Victimology, Tokiwa University in Japan with research interests including issues in understanding of and assistance to victims of crime, trauma recovery process, self-help groups of crime victims/survivors, surviving families of homicide cases, victims of domestic violence, and child abuse issues. He has published a book on counseling psychology, another on psychology of and assistance to victims of crime, and over 90 articles, book chapters, and papers in the areas of victimology, victim assistance, police stress, counseling psychology, developmental and cross-cultural psychology, etc. He chaired, from April 2006 through March 2008, the Cabinet Office Committee on Coordination for Victim Assistance, and chairs the Committee of Critical Incident Stress Network, Third Region, and Japan Coast Guard.

Huong Thu Nguyen, PhD, is a lecturer at the Department of Anthropology of Vietnam National University, Hanoi, and is currently affiliated with the Department of Gender Studies of Lund University as a Postdoctoral Research Fellow. Her research interests center on the intersection of sexual violence, gender diversity, ethnicity, and politics in Vietnam and the Philippines. Her recent work has appeared in *Culture, Health and Sexuality, Journal of Asian History, Sojourn,* and *Journal of Vietnamese Studies.*

Safiya Omari, PhD, is Associate Vice President of Research and Sponsored Programs and Associate Professor of Social Work and Public Health at Jackson State University in Jackson, Mississippi. She has grant funding from the Department of Justice Office on Violence against Women. She has worked in the areas of community mental health and domestic violence for most of her career. She earned her PhD in Social Psychology from North Eastern University in Boston, Massachusetts.

Olga Osby, PhD, is the new Associate Dean of the School of Social Work at Barry University in Miami Shores, Florida. She received her Master of Social Work and Doctor of Social Work degrees from Howard University in Washington, DC. Her research interests include African American women in rural communities, poverty and economic inequality, and kinship care among African American grandfathers. While on faculty at Jackson State University in Jackson, Mississippi, she was awarded the 2013–2015 Distinguished Professor Endowed Chair Award through Delta Sigma Theta Sorority, Inc. for $220,000, to fund her research on African American grandfathers. She has served two terms on the Commission on Faculty Development and Conference Planning for the Council on Social Work Education. While in Mississippi she served on the State Board of the American Civil Liberties Union (ACLU) for 5 years, and was elected to represent the state chapter as the representative to the National Board.

Mike Perkins, PhD, is a senior lecturer in Management at the British University Vietnam, based in Hanoi, where he leads a wide variety of management modules. He carried out his undergraduate and PhD studies in Management at the University of York, UK, and his thesis explored the factors underlying public confidence in policing. His primary research interests include performance management in public and private organizations, and how local law enforcement can influence public perceptions of police forces. He is also expanding his research into issues of gender equality, and transparency and integrity within emerging markets.

Darryl Plecas, PhD, is Professor Emeritus at the School of Criminology and Criminal Justice, University of the Fraser Valley. He is the author or co-author of more than 200 research reports and publications addressing a broad range of criminal justice issues. He holds two degrees in criminology from Simon Fraser University, and a doctorate in Higher Education from the University of British Columbia. He is currently the Member of the Legislative Assembly for British Columbia representing Abbotsford South and Parliamentary Secretary for Crime Reduction to the Minister of Justice.

Stephanie L. Reardon, LLB, is responsible for the operational management and delivery of services at LimeCulture Community Interest Company, a specialist sexual violence training and development organization in the UK. Through her background in the civil service and the various posts she held in central government, she has specialist knowledge around sexual violence policy development and service delivery and implementation. Formerly, she was the Delivery Manager for the Department of Health's National Support Team for Response to Sexual Violence (2009–2011) where her work improved the provision of Sexual Assault Referral Centre (SARC) services across the UK. She was the National Delivery Manager for the Improving Access to Psychological Therapies (IAPT) Programme (2007–2009), where she co-ordinated the delivery of new psychological therapies services across the NHS as part of a £173 million national program. From 2005 to 2007, she was the National Programme Manager for the Violence and Abuse Prevention Programme – a complex policy and research program focusing on the effects of domestic and sexual violence and abuse. She was also seconded to the Serious Organised Crime Agency (SOCA) Child Exploitation and Online Protection (CEOP) Centre between 2007 and 2008. She has a legal background and is also a qualified project manager and holds the Prince 2 Practitioner-level qualification.

Heidi Selenius, PhD, is Assistant Professor of Criminology at Örebro University in Sweden, where she collaborates with the Centre for Criminological and PsychoSocial Research. She has a background as a remedial teacher and received her PhD in Psychology from Stockholm University. She has participated in projects on dyslexia among offenders, child witnesses of homicidal violence and risk assessment of female offenders admitted to forensic psychiatric care. Currently her research is conducted within the Swedish police and with focus on risk assessment and risk management for intimate partner violence.

Özgür Solakoğlu, PhD, is a professor at the Turkish Army War College in Istanbul/Turkey. He earned his PhD in Sociology from the University of North Texas. His dissertation title is "Can Akers' social learning theory explain delinquent behavior among Turkish adolescents?" His primary research interests include quantitative method, globalization, and comparative criminology.

Susanne Strand, PhD, is an associate professor of Criminology at Örebro University in Sweden, where she collaborates with the Centre for Criminological and PsychoSocial Research. She is also an adjunct Associate Professor at the Centre for Forensic Behavioural Science at Swinburne University of Technology in Melbourne, Australia. She researches risks of violence in different contexts, with applied criminology and psychology as the academic base. Her work has been conducted within the police, where policing family violence and stalking were in focus, and within forensic psychiatric care, where risk for violence, female perpetrators, and psychopathy were studied primarily. The focus of her current research is to understand how the police work with risk assessment and risk management of domestic violence and stalking.

Kylee Trevillion is a post-doctoral research fellow at the Institute of Psychiatry, Psychology & Neuroscience, King's College London. She specializes in women's mental health research, conducting research on the mental health impacts associated with violence and abuse and practice and policy responses on violence against women. She is currently a program manager on a National Institute for Health Research-funded grant examining the effectiveness and cost-effectiveness of perinatal psychiatry services. Her previous work includes interviewing trafficked people about their healthcare needs and health service use, conducting systematic reviews to investigate the relationship between domestic violence and mental disorders, and piloting an intervention of domestic violence advocacy within community mental health services.

Foreword

by Lois Herman, WUNRN

I Got Flowers Today

I got flowers today.
It wasn't my birthday.
And he said a lot of
cruel things that really hurt.
I know he must be sorry
Because he gave me flowers today.

I got flowers today.
My mother-in-law tried to take them.
She says I am lazy and deserve to be hurt.
But, he did give me flowers today.

I got flowers today.
Last night he beat me worse than other times.
I cannot take the children and leave him.
I have no place to go, no money, just shame.
But he did give me nice flowers.

I got flowers today.
Today was a very special day.
It was the day of my funeral.
Last night he killed me
If only I had asked for help.
So, I got flowers today.
For the last time!
    WUNRN (Women's UN Report Network)
       adaptation of a poem by Paulette Kelly

Violence against women and girls is the most widespread human rights violation in this world. The World Health Organization indicates that about 1 in 3 women worldwide has experienced some form of gender-based violence in her lifetime.

The irony is that most of this violence is intimate partner violence or from a person the woman has known in some form of personal relationship. In reality, LOVE CAN HURT, and then the pain reaches us as women in a most profound personal way. It is further shocking that globally as many as 38 percent of murders of women, femicide, are committed by an intimate partner.

Despite current international frameworks such as: the Universal Declaration of Human Rights and its two Conventions; the UN Declaration on the Elimination of Violence Against Women; the CEDAW Committee General Comment No. 19 indicating that "States may also be responsible for private acts if they fail to act with due diligence to prevent violations of rights or to investigate and punish acts of violence"; the EU Istanbul Convention on Violence Against Women; and many other regional and national legislations to prevent, punish, and end violence against women, domestic violence, intimate-partner violence, in its multiple forms, domestic violence continues to be a scourge on society, and rampant in the family, whatever form of family, causing women to be victims of abuse, and eroding their dignity and self-worth. The hidden nature of domestic violence, the shroud of shame that accompanies it, and the under-reportage that prevails, make efforts to eliminate domestic violence exceedingly challenging. There is also pervasive impunity of abusers.

The dynamics of intimate partner violence can be very much impacted by culture, patriarchy, traditions, religious interpretations, and family values. Domestic violence truly reaches all generations. It is an intersectional issue that can be compounded by poverty, isolation, disabilities, serious dependency on a partner, and more. The reality that many women do not have economic independence keeps them from reporting repeated partner violence. But, assuredly, interpersonal and domestic violence occur at all income levels of society.

It is so very important for women, and girls, to learn and recognize the early signs of intimate partner violence. The complexities of child marriage, forced marriage, polygamous marriages, barter marriages, can make women and girls so very vulnerable to violence in the dynamics of interpersonal relationships.

There is also the sad repeated cycle of family violence when children see their mother being abused and normalize that abusive behavior, extending such a pattern into their adult lives.

Further, we live in a world with protracted conflict, war, militarization, that discriminate against women and accentuate male power. Women are the most victims of conflict, the most displaced persons and refugees. This volatility and uprooting of women can add to their vulnerability to interpersonal violence.

We also need to acknowledge the feelings associated with being abused and hurt, physically, mentally, emotionally, in so many ways, and the "system" needs to be sensitized to our female experiences. No woman can be "owned," and thus forced to comply with male demands or be abused. She has a human right to be her own person, free, unharmed, even autonomous.

This book is quite unique as it includes writers with extensive law enforcement background. Ultimately, the State is to be held responsible for acts of violence, whether perpetuated by State *or* non-State actors. The State needs to provide prevention, laws for protection, prosecution, and redress in defined and enforced ways for accountability and punishment. Law enforcement training and implementation is a vital part of breaking the cycle of intimate partner violence. But, there has been, throughout history, hesitance for law enforcement to move from the public sphere to the private sphere (of family).

There continue to be inadequate and culturally sensitive support services for women victims of violence. There need to be Orders for Protection, but these can be complex such as in rural areas and in male dominant cultures. Women victims of violence still want to stay home, not go to a shelter. They want to be safe and secure. So, how can this happen more often?

There is a program focused on having an eventual Violence Against Women International Convention. But, Conventions require ratification, monitoring, and accountability, both of which are problematic for UN Member States.

There is a problem of lack of data on domestic violence because of its invisibility and low reportage. The current UN Special Rapporteur on Violence Against Women is calling for national and local data collection on violence against women, knowing that data can, indeed, drive policy forward. She also plans to promote a Femicide Observatory to track the tragic killings of women by intimate partner violence.

Law enforcement can play a prominent role in building the trust of citizens, of women who are abused, that they will be taken seriously, that they will not be blamed for instigating or provoking the violence, or for deserving the abuse. Such assertive action by law enforcement can be part of the education that intimate partner violence will have serious and sustained repercussions on abusers. Women experiencing domestic violence must know their rights, must have access to the mechanisms of justice, and also support for restitution and healing. Women often help each other move from victimization to strength and self-confidence; but it is the legal action, the justice, that forms a basis to stop domestic violence and break the cycle of abuse that destroys relationships, families, and communities. Women in law enforcement, and training in sensitivities of domestic violence for all police, can result in abused women experiencing fairer treatment, and less compounded victimization by the civil system.

In countries where there are plural law systems, such as civil, religious, tribal, and village law, efforts must be made to educate women about their rights and bring the civil system to even the most remote areas. This is a challenge for States, but can be part of a defined program to prevent interpersonal violence, and to follow up with justice in the courts. The goal of gender harmony can still prevail!

In examining the root causes of intimate partner violence, we must examine gender stereotypes, male controls and assumed privilege; and with women and girls, men and boys, promote changes in attitudes and behaviors that can lead to building bridges and addressing gaps in the current systems.

This book reveals realities of domestic violence around the world, but also good practices, and multi-sectoral solutions to prevent intimate partner violence and create trust, support, and less violence, more peace, for all levels of society.

Sisterhood of Women

Women of the world, girls of the planet,
Domestic and partner violence must end.
We call for a world where we feel safety, trust.
Justice and rights, oppression and empowerment
Are part of woman's challenge for equality, for dignity,
For we are bonded in the female spirit.
We deserve to not be victims of violence and abuse,
But to be honored, cherished, loved.
Local to global, rural and urban, near and far,
Now is our time!

Lois A. Herman
Coordinator of WUNRN

Preface

This book is the product of the collaborative effort of 30 scholars from around the world, who have worked together to build a global bridge in their scholarship, striving to demonstrate the best practices in managing – and ultimately preventing – interpersonal violence (IPV). We all strongly agree that domestic violence and interpersonal violence are issues of worldwide concern, and we stand together as we offer practical solutions, along with cases of men and women across the world as they seek justice. As noted, many countries lag far behind in the fight to end domestic and interpersonal violence; thus, readers will encounter examples of grievous human suffering throughout the following twelve chapters.

Now is the time to take this issue to the world stage. Violence can no longer be tolerated in any corner of the world, whether in interpersonal or familial relationships. This unique collection of chapters, coupled with statistics from countries around the world, cannot be found elsewhere; the cosmopolitan makeup of the book's contributors provides a wider-ranging perspective than previous publications, proffering concepts and suggestions that represent every corner of our world. Primarily, this work aims to bring increased knowledge and awareness of this epidemic to a global stage, bolstered by reliable statistics and realistic solutions. We hope this book will shine a light on a problem that must come out of the dark. Truly, some parts of the world are making great strides in combating IPV; we hope others will listen. This project was born at the Commission on the Status of Women (CSW-56) when the Istanbul Convention was announced in 2012 in New York City, New York.

Acknowledgments

First of all, we'd like to thank our children Landon Peterson, Colten Peterson, Hayden Bruns, Arolsen Bruns, Courtney Schroeder, and Logan and Melanie Schroeder. We could not have done this without your support. It is our hope that victims of interpersonal violence around the world will, in some way, benefit from our efforts. Therefore, thank you for giving up your time with us over the past year. We would also like to thank all of our authors and their families for their efforts and speedy work. We believe you all are rock stars. This was truly a global effort. However, there are two who must receive honorable mention and gratitude, Dr. Steven Gaede and Dr. William Lutton for managing my (Diana's) hydrocephalus. I could not have finished without both of you, as you gave me my life back. Also, thanks to Dilip and Ana Das, who started our international adventures with the International Police Executive Symposium (IPES). Lastly, the Criminal Justice/Criminology and Social Work undergraduate and graduate students at the University of Texas, Permian Basin, Southeast Missouri State University, and Jackson State University – your help with this project has been priceless to us. May you all be guiding lights in the future of protecting those suffering from violence and crime. Thank you for believing our global effort to address violence against women, and for your everlasting patience with our progress to make it to the finish line. Adam Mortimer – thank you for help and efforts; without you, this project could not have been completed. Dina Deligiorgis and the staff at UN Women – thank you for your on-going support, as you helped us with our foundation to build this book of scholars from around the world. Finally, our gratitude to Thomas Sutton and Hannah Catterall of Routledge. Thank you for believing in our global effort to address violence against women, and for your everlasting patience with our progress to make it to the finish line.

Diana Scharff Peterson and Julie A. Schroeder

Introduction

International response to domestic violence

Julie A. Schroeder, Diana Scharff Peterson,
Safiya Omari and Olga Osby

While domestic violence is a common crime all over the world, police response differs widely. Even more disconcerting, an EBSCOhost search revealed very few academic publications on this topic since 2005. Only 17 research articles were included in one of the largest academic search engines in the world. This is cause for concern. As domestic violence continues to occur, our police departments are not benefiting from outcome research and enhanced, specialized training conducted on this very serious issue. The book will investigate domestic violence on a global scale and provide best practices gleaned from various countries around the world in an effort to inform interested parties in how response to domestic violence is currently being conducted and provide training bodies with up-to-date information to enhance current curricula.

It is clear that domestic violence is a worldwide problem that is grossly under reported. A 10-country study revealed that 55 percent to 95 percent of women who had experienced intimate partner violence had not reported the incident (s) to the police or any non-governmental social service entity (Domestic Violence Statistics, 2012). Prevalence studies reveal one in three girls and women will experience interpersonal gender-related violence over the course of their lifetimes (UNODC, 2010; World Health Organization, 2005). One half of women who die violent deaths do so at the hands of a domestic partner (UNODC, 2010). The Centers for Disease Control (CDC) 2005 data found that medical costs and work productivity lost as a result of violence against women costs the United States approximately $8.3 billion per year. More current data suggests that number has climbed to $16 billion (Pearle, 2013). Domestic violence does not discriminate. It is an equal opportunity destroyer that appears regardless of age, race, socioeconomic status, occupation, or level of education (Kouremetis, 2012). While these commonalities exist, reactions and responses differ widely across the globe.

Governmental entities throughout the world have very different responses to domestic violence. While some countries work diligently to address the matter through prevention and training, others take a "hands-off" approach in their response. Research suggests that gender roles, stereotypes, patriarchy appear to play prominent roles in the cause of domestic violence in many countries and it is amplified as a result of cultural beliefs and practices, as well as a lack of disapproval or tacit consent that domestic violence is an acceptable practice (Postmus & Hahn, 2007). Additionally, researchers have concluded that problems also stem from policing agency policy and officers who do not understand cultural differences and are complicit or tolerate traditional practices. Some States and countries have not criminalized traditional acts of violence toward women, or offer poor protection of women in various cultures (UNODC, 2010).

Prior to the 1980s, police in the United States also viewed domestic violence as a private matter and lacked understanding of the power and control perpetrators had over victims (Bruns, 2014; Stark, 2007). During that time police held four distinct views of domestic violence situations including: (1) oversimplification of the situation where police viewed the situation as less complex than it actually was; (2) blaming the victim believing the victim held partial responsibility for the incident; (3) patriarchal attitudes toward women; and (4) presuming that victims will, in the end, change their minds about pressing charges (Bruns, 2014).

Theoretical perspective

The vast majority of individual chapters in this book reflect the assumptions of postmodern and postcolonial thought whereby the critical interpretation of the lived experience and the impact of postcolonial rule can be explored alongside transnational feminist theory's responsive and politically engaging ideas around gender equality and oppression (Hegde, 1998; Hesse-Biber, 2013). This book allows the reader a peek into the structures that produce and reproduce patriarchy.

This chapter will provide a global snapshot of some countries dealt with in the book, providing in-depth analyses of others.

A global snapshot

Ammar, Orloff, Dutton and Aguilar-Hass (2005) found that interactions between Hispanic immigrants and police in the United States were disrupted due to language barriers and resulted in victims feeling that their reports were not taken seriously. In addition, victims reported feeling that police officers mistakenly believed that domestic violence was a part of the immigrants' culture overlooking their safety concerns. These researchers also found that reporting patterns differed for immigrant women based on the amount of time they had been in the country. Women who had spent more time in the United States were more likely to contact the police if they had been abused and particularly if their children had been exposed to the violence. Yet when officers responded to these calls, they were more likely to address the abuser and not the victim; often requesting that the abuser translate his partner's responses if the victim spoke limited English. Overall, arrests were made less than 30 percent of the time.

A large body of research is emerging finding that immigrant women in the United States are at a greater risk of abuse, and remain with their partners longer than non-immigrant women who are battered. These women sustain more physical and emotional injuries, have few resources, speak little English, and lack the awareness of their legal options and protections. Male immigrants use their wives' and children's immigrant status as a means of power and control. The constant threat of deportation keeps these women living in fear and willing to take the abuse rather than face deportation (Aguilar-Hass, Dutton & Orloff, 2000; Dutton, Orloff & Aguilar-Hass, 2000; Orloff, Dutton, Aguilar-Hass & Ammar, 2003; Ammar, Orloff, Dutton & Aguilar-Hass, 2005). Researchers have also found that female immigrants married to or living with American-born citizens face the same issues as those married to immigrants. There appears to be no significant difference between the rates of intimate partner violence or the reasons why women stay in these relationships (Raj & Silverman, 2002; Raj, 2006).

While the United States, through the Violence Against Women Act (VAWA) 1994, has made progress in protecting women, ongoing debate in Congress over the 2012 reauthorization of the Act resulted in a year of legislators bickering largely over the protection of undocumented immigrant women with the Democrats supporting a plan where protections would be put into place, allowing for a path to citizenship for victims of domestic violence. Any woman who cooperates with the authorities during the investigation of the crime would be offered a temporary visa. The Democrats believe that women may never come forward due to threats of deportation, thus the violence continues. Republicans argue, "the citizenship provision is akin to amnesty for illegal immigrants" (Grant, 2012). Sadly, the reauthorization was held in limbo until after the 2012 election, as it became an election year issue. The Act was not reauthorized until 2013.

The United States is not the only country with victims of domestic violence who are attempting to immigrate into their country. The UK has recognized the threats women face while attempting to gain citizenship through their partners. As a result, there is now an exception allowing immigrants to stay in the country when a relationship with an established citizen ends due to domestic violence. This exception is also in place for women from some parts of India and Pakistan as well due to the realization that women who return home following the end of a marriage are scorned and often face the possibility of being killed by a male family member to restore the family's honor. These are known as honor killings. However, few women are taking advantage of this exception. Sundari (2008) suspects that this is due to lack of knowledge of the provision as well as fear of involving the police.

Germany has recognized the need for increased protection for migrant women who are victims of domestic violence, particularly women of Turkish heritage and women from Eastern European countries who currently live in Germany, as research suggests that these women suffer domestic violence at higher rates than German women. Authorities are concerned specifically about young women who are subjected to forced marriages. These women are also at high risk for being victimized through human trafficking for sexual and labor exploitation as well as genital mutilation.

There has also been greater focus on women with disabilities, as they are at increased risk of becoming victims of domestic violence. They are also at risk of sexual abuse by caregivers. Numerous agencies are called upon to assist in combating domestic violence through enhanced service provision (Second Action Plan, 2007).

European response

In a 2002 report from the Council of Europe, Recommendation (Rec 2002) 5 was approved and adopted in efforts to combat gender-based violence. Recommendation 5 calls for an analysis of the implementation process and evaluation of ways by which to combat domestic violence and its impact across Europe. This evaluation investigates the activities conducted by each member state to combat domestic violence and the coordinated effort by member states to provide some uniformity in the implementation of policies and legislation. In efforts to do so, many member states developed a "Plan of Action" to specifically address domestic violence against women that is not only systematic and concrete, but also inclusive, showing evidence of strategic planning. This represents significant effort by member states to work together to eliminate domestic violence against women. While strides have been made by penalizing abuse through both legislation and prosecution, a lack of consistency still exists among member states in terms of recognizing certain acts as indications of domestic violence (Bohn & Hagemann-White, 2007).

Great Britain, Austria, Sweden, Spain, and Italy all provide detailed chapters in this book. Accounts of domestic violence and responses in other countries in the European Union are discussed below.

Northern Ireland

The Government of Northern Ireland feels strongly that domestic violence is not acceptable under any circumstances and it has had a devastating impact on families living in Northern Ireland (Northern Ireland Department of Health, Social Services and Public Safety, 2005). Police spend a great deal of their time responding to domestic violence incidents resulting in a government that saw the necessity of increasing efforts to curb such violence. As a result, the government passed the Domestic Violence, Crime and Victims Act 2004. This Act increases protection for victims, and gives the police greater power allowing them to arrest perpetrators.

The Women's Aid in Northern Ireland has worked diligently to raise awareness, but calls for more, including strategies implemented in a 5-year plan focusing on domestic violence prevention, protection, justice and support. Goals include increasing general awareness about domestic violence, holding perpetrators accountable, and facilitating the development of quality and coordinated responses among multiple agencies.

France

Crumley (2010) investigated efforts in France to ban psychological abuse in marriages. While the French recognize that domestic violence impacts many marriages, this country previously attempted to tackle the issue largely through public awareness and education. This legislative bill would outlaw "conjugal abuse of a psychological nature." The legislation in question targets verbal and mental abuse as well as humiliation that may lead to physical abuse. Though the effects of physical abuse can often scar someone for life, supporters of this legislation argue that mental abuse is just as dangerous and leaves victims injured on the inside, where the abuse can remain invisible.

Germany and the UK

There have been some recent developments in both German and English legislation and law enforcement (Kury & Smartt, 2006). While domestic violence has existed for centuries, it is only recently that Germany has recognized domestic violence as a criminal act. In addition, these researchers report that approximately one million children in the UK could be in a household that condones domestic violence. This research has heightened interest in the subject in the UK, creating discussions about the costs associated with domestic violence. As a result, these authors call for a multi-level approach as the collateral damage caused by domestic violence requires costly resources and the revelation that the police cannot fight the problem alone.

The Czech Republic

This country promulgated The Domestic Violence Act, which went into effect on January 1, 2007. This Act was put into place as an attempt to prevent violent attacks against women while also providing victims with needed assistance from community agencies and local government. In efforts to implement the Act the Czech Republic established 15 intervention units charged with aiding all victims of domestic violence. The Ministry of the Interior has used the Act to coordinate efforts and to establish a system of cooperation among other governmental entities including the Ministry of Justice, the Ministry of Labour and Social Affairs, the Ministry of Health and the police agencies of the Czech Republic (Czech Republic Final Report, 2009).

Norway

The Norwegian government's Ministry of Justice and Police, through the Action Plan Against Domestic Violence, states that domestic violence is unacceptable and makes it clear that domestic violence is a public responsibility. In the plan, the government calls for coherent policy introducing measures to combat domestic violence including improved training for police officers and increased support services for victims. The Norwegian government is determined to continue to monitor local law enforcement to ensure a more informed police force regarding all aspects of domestic violence in order to combat this serious problem. The government is committed to providing victims with support and protection and has outlined specific measures regarding continued implementation of the Action Plan (Ministry of Justice and the Police, 2011).

The Middle East

Turkey

Turkey is at a crossroads, trying desperately to become a part of the European Union; however, this patriarchal muslim-inspired government has been referred to as the "number one enemy of women" (Bilifski & Ersu, 2012), where honor killings have occurred for centuries. A detailed chapter on Turkey's efforts to stem the tide of domestic violence is included in this book.

The Islamic Republic of Iran

Esfandiari (2003) argues that violence against women in Iran is taking place regardless of whether abuse is accepted as a cultural norm. Iranian women have few rights and limited standing in the legal system. Iranian men are allowed four permanent wives and unlimited temporary wives. Legislation passed in early 2010 allows men to have additional wives without the knowledge of their other wives. Yet in light of these laws, women are often told to sacrifice themselves and to tolerate abuse, as marital rape is not illegal in Iran. A woman who cheats on her husband (she is allowed only one), is considered to have committed a capital offense, where punishment takes place in public with the woman usually being hung from a large crane (Michele, 2012). Fathers can arrange marriages for their daughters who are younger than 13 if they so desire. Despite these deplorable views toward and abuse of women, Iran has been given membership to the UN Committee on Women's Rights (America's Pro-Israel Lobby, 2010). Religious interpretation of the rights of women contributes to the idea that abuse is acceptable, a widely held belief that law enforcement is doing little to dissuade. Members sitting on this UN Committee include the Iranian Police Chief who advocates arrest for women with suntans, and clerics who believe that women who dress indecently are the cause of earthquakes.

Grassroots organizations are beginning to take shape and are educating Iranian citizens who are slowly beginning to recognize that abuse of women is neither normal nor acceptable. Public awareness campaigns are beginning to gain traction, yet many men do not consider their behavior as violent, but rather as a right (UNWomen, 2012).

Iraq

Gender-based violence is institutionalized throughout Iraq's legal system, where the government openly discriminates against girls and women. They have no recourse in response to abuse from relatives or spouses. Their rights are subjugated to the rights of men. In Iranian society, women are not allowed to live independently, resulting in dependency on males for socioeconomic support. Abused girls and women face an uphill battle due to cultural traditions and societal influences whereby violence at the hands of men is tacitly reinforced, where honor trumps safety in that those who seek support bring dishonor to their families. Even if women do file charges, the legal system is biased, where acts of domestic violence, human trafficking, and genital mutilation are largely ignored and insufficiently criminalized (Minwalla, 2011).

Police in Iraq realize the need for increased efforts to protect against domestic violence but have received little support from the government. In 2005 Iraq's Government made an effort to denounce domestic violence by adding Article 19 to the permanent Iraqi Constitution, stating, "all forms of violence and arbitrary treatment in the family, schools and society are prohibited." This article does not define the forms of violence to which it refers, although the legislative intent includes all forms of physical, psychological and sexual violence (UNSG, 2012).

In attempts to address domestic violence in the various regions of the country where acts of violence against women are occurring in vast numbers of cases, particularly in Kurdistan, the 2008 Act 15 was passed to include language directed at the Province/State level where Article 19 was being loosely enforced. This is an attempt to rein in jurisdictions where the law was being ignored or changed. According to Act 15, domestic violence law cannot be amended without consensus at the federal level (UNSG, 2012).

Saudi Arabia

In the largest study to date on violence against women and children, the National Guard Health Affairs National Family Safety Program (NFAP, 2012) interviewed professionals and employees of six institutions covering all parts of the country. These institutions included: male and female public schools, major hospitals, police departments, and Courts of the Ministry of Justice, and charitable organizations, including women's charitable organizations, and the Ministry of Social Affairs.

While results suggest that nearly three-quarters of Saudi men and women interviewed believe that domestic violence occurs in the country, just 49 percent believe it is a widespread problem. Sixty-eight percent of participants believe that Saudi Arabia needs to develop regulations protecting women from domestic violence. Ninety-seven percent of respondents reported receiving no training on domestic violence, with 69 percent indicating a desire to attend such trainings.

Only 22 percent of respondents stated that their agency had policies and procedures in place to deal with cases of domestic violence in their workplace. Of that 22 percent only 41 percent of employees reported seeing or reading these policies with 68 percent reporting that they had not seen these policies. Over three quarters (77 percent) said that there were no procedures in place that they knew of in their agencies (NFAP, 2012).

These researchers put forth a variety of recommendations for ways in which to improve response to domestic violence and child abuse including:

- Establish and implement a national comprehensive public awareness program partnering with the media to spread awareness.
- Establish training centers to ensure all helping agencies are aware of current workplace policies or work to develop such policies if they are missing from an organization.
- Establish a social protection safety net for women and children in need of services.
- Develop a single independent agency responsible for advocating for prevention programs, monitoring implementation until rules and regulations are promulgated and provide its own funding and logistical support.
- Develop and implement a reporting plan for all agencies to be used to develop civic registries to avoid duplication of services.
- Provide support for an annual conference where international researchers and experts in the field can report on their efforts and promote discussion of domestic violence-related issues. The conference could also be a means of increasing public awareness via the media.
- Call for more research and studies conducted in Saudi Arabia to further understand intimate partner violence and child abuse and neglect.

Afghanistan

Efforts to address domestic violence and forced marriage began in earnest with the development of the Women's Ministry Affairs in 2001. The next year the Ministry supported the Elimination of Violence Against Women Commission (EVAWI). The commission's mission was to work with other social service agencies to identify and analyze information, with the goal of eliminating all forms of violence against women (EVAWI, 2004). It began as a one-day workshop for strategic planning and met again in 2004 to discuss its ongoing progress. However, a research report published in 2008 (Nijhowne & Oates, 2008), using 2005 data found that:

- 87 percent of Afghan women reported at least one form of abuse or forced marriage
- 62 percent reported multiple forms of abuse
- 52 percent reported physical violence at the hands of their spouse
- 39 percent reported being hit by their husband in the past year
- 17 percent reported sexual violence
- 11 percent reported experiencing rape.

This research suggested that living in violent areas increased the chances of women experiencing domestic violence. Women living in high-conflict areas (war torn) experienced high levels of domestic abuse. Other risk factors include:

- experiencing violence increases the odds that it will happen again
- being in a forced marriage
- being single due to widowhood and divorce
- being in a polygamous marriage
- being under age 15 and married
- living in rural or southeastern or eastern border provinces due to war and Taliban strongholds.

Afghan women reported that they received abuse not only at the hands of their husbands (30.6 percent) but their mothers-in-law (23.7 percent) as well. Sadly, domestic violence is entrenched in the Afghan culture. Many women reported satisfactory relationships even though they experienced violence at home. It appears that women do not talk among themselves about domestic violence as only 18 percent reported knowing another woman in a violent relationship. Urban women are thought to be better protected in certain areas with better-organized governmental bodies and police forces. Rural women who are close to military conflict and in strongholds of the Taliban are at greater risk for violence due to oppressive ideology.

It appears that Afghanistan is attempting to make strides including women into various types of legislation. In 2005 the federal government established a protocol to end forced marriages. Violence against women and girls has also been included in the country's strategic planning process with the Afghanistan National Development Strategy 2008–2013, and a National Plan for the Women of Afghanistan 2007–2017 (UNSG, 2012).

Asia

India

India has an extensive list of legislation that has been passed in defense of the safety of women with the Immoral Traffic Act of 1956 outlawing the trafficking of migrant women, and the Dowry Prohibition Act of 1961 attempting to control violence based on the size of a family's dowry or dowry negotiations. There were few attempts made to protect the rights of women until the late 1990s when the national government developed the National Action Plan to Combat Trafficking and Commercial Sexual Exploitation in 1998. The National Policy on Empowerment of Women (2001) allowed for the inclusion of violence against women in other national strategies. Unfortunately, the national government has been, and still is, in their strategic planning mode, most recently with the Eleventh Five-Year Development Plan (2007–2012). However, in 2010 the national government gave police additional mechanisms to protect victims of domestic violence. Currently through a local court order police can now provide protection to victims during any part of the court process. Victims may request a personal security officer (PSO) who will remain with the victim, providing protection of her person and her property at her residence at any stage of the court process (UNSG, 2010).

According to UNSG (2012), national statistics on violence against women from the Commission on Violence Against Women in 2010, the commission had received a total of just over 11,000 complaints from April to November 2009. The commission collects data on a variety of forms of violence including domestic violence, sexual harassment, sexual violence, stalking, acid attacks, dowry-related violence/death, maltreatment of widows and female infanticide. These are governmental self-reported data which, considering the size of the country's population, is quite possibly under reported.

Buncombe (2009) addresses the plight of women in Kashmir who have had very few options or resources when they fall victim to domestic violence. In efforts to address the issue of women in need, women from the Hindu and Muslim cultures have come together and developed a charitable organization called Peace Direct. Peace Direct's goal is to provide victims with support and a voice to speak out against domestic violence. In addition to Peace Direct, activists from both the Hindu and Muslim communities have united to provide victims with legal assistance and to push for the adoption of anti-domestic-violence legislation.

China

Xu et al. (2005) conducted a large study interviewing Chinese women to determine the prevalence of and risk factors for domestic violence. They found that the lifetime prevalence of being a victim of domestic violence was 43 percent with 26 percent of respondents reporting abuse at the hands of their partner within the previous year. This information was gathered from women who actually sought medical treatment. These researchers believe prevalence rates are under reported throughout the country based on the cultural belief that women should not discuss issues around intimate partner violence outside of the family.

Risk factors included the male partner being in control of the couple's finances and holding the expectation that wives turn over their earnings to their husband for drinking and gambling. Cultural values surrounding extramarital affairs were evident in both partners. Women and their husbands believe that women should be punished if found to be having an extramarital affair.

While women reported that they desired equality in the marketplace, the majority of subjects interviewed did not hold the same desire for equality within their marriages. This belief in traditional cultural values was highly correlated with the likelihood of additional abuse.

While the Chinese government has been in the process of promulgating laws and regulations in provinces, autonomous regions and centrally administered municipalities since 1996, they have yet to pass domestic violence legislation. Tay (2012) reports that the Chinese Parliament may be close to "actually agreeing" to consider domestic violence legislation.

Currently, the police academy in Beijing offers training specifically addressing domestic violence. Judges and prosecutors are being trained in social gender theory and combating domestic violence. There have also been training programs developed, such as pilot projects on medical intervention for victims of domestic violence (UNSG, 2009).

Africa

Ford (2012) reports that domestic violence is the single largest threat for women living in West Africa. The International Rescue Committee (IRC) recently released the results of a 10-year study conducted in Sierra Leone, Liberia and Ivory Coast reporting that domestic violence is the "most urgent, pervasive and significant protection issue for women in west Africa." Domestic violence is still considered to be a private matter, but the IRC calls for humanitarian efforts to stem the tide of violence against women, which is considered to be the single most important public health concern. They also argue that empowerment of women presents a huge obstacle in post-war African countries.

Sierra Leone passed domestic violence statutes in 2007; yet prosecutions are few due to lack of access to police, and expensive medical and legal hurdles. Liberia and Ivory Coast have yet to pass legislation to counteract violence against women. The lack of funding is the primary reason for stalled efforts to protect victims of domestic violence.

The 2005 World Health Organization study on domestic violence in Africa found that domestic violence affects millions of African women each year. Prevalence rates of domestic violence found in Tanzania and Ethiopia's rural areas were 50 percent and 71 percent respectively. Amnesty International reports that in South Africa a woman is killed by her husband or boyfriend every six hours. Additionally, 60 percent of murder cases tried in Zimbabwe are related to domestic violence. In 2003, 47 percent of all homicides were domestic violence related.

Law enforcement and the protection of victims of domestic violence vary greatly across the country. While some countries have made police and courts "female friendly," in many other countries the police are not willing to intervene unless physical evidence exists, thus, ignoring many calls for men to be removed from their homes. Rwanda has implemented "gender desks" at police stations where women can meet with trained female staff when coming forward to report being victimized. The officer that meets with the woman is responsible for investigating the case and ensuring that necessary paperwork and other evidence is available for court proceedings. This appears to be working. In 2006 1777 rape cases were remanded to trial with 803 convictions. Gender desks are being given credit for "improved reporting and response to these crimes" (Kimani, 2007).

The WHO (2005) study reported not only the need for changes in the criminal justice system but changes in social attitudes as well. For example, 80 percent of women living in rural Egypt believed that beatings were justifiable if a woman denied sex to her husband. In Ghana more women than men believed beatings were justifiable in the above situation.

The police and courts in Uganda prosecute perpetrators of domestic violence using assault and homicide charges as a means by which to convict men of domestic violence, since the country has no domestic violence statutes. Unfortunately no such practices take place in Nigeria and domestic violence is grossly under reported. Yet Moroccan laws have changed as a result of support services being established to assist victims of violence. In 2004 Moroccan laws changed dramatically when, due to activism in that nation, the minimum age girls were considered marriageable was raise from 15 to 18. The legal obligation for women to obey their husbands was abolished and laws were put into place permitting women to contract their own marriages as well as more easily divorce their abusive spouses. In-depth chapters on the Congo and Ethiopia are presented in this book.

Australia

Australia has been at the forefront of domestic violence research and policy. Australians recognize the fact that the single biggest health risk factor for Australian women aged 15 to 44 is domestic violence. Access Economics commissioned the study that investigated domestic violence between intimate partners, and the increasing costs of dealing with domestic violence in the country. Researchers were surprised by the health impacts of domestic violence since traditional health risk factors often focus upon smoking, suicide, depression, and cancer (Australian Domestic Violence, 2005).

Nelson (2007) places domestic violence in a historical perspective dating back to World War I. The effects of war, in those days referred to as "shell shock," further exacerbated violent acts against women who, prior to the war, had a history of domestic violence. Men used their time spent on active duty as an excuse for acts of domestic violence. While some of these explanations for such behavior may have been warranted, many of the returning war veterans had mental health issues unrelated to domestic violence. Early twentieth century data gathered by scholars from personal interviews, court documents and military records were used to understand the circumstances and outcomes of various domestic violence cases in Australia. While many men were justly convicted of incidents of domestic violence, many escaped conviction on the false premise that the impact of the war had caused them to react violently to their spouses.

Significant progress in the response to domestic violence has evolved since the 1980s. At that time, the majority of states and territories were conducting investigations. In addition, the seemingly widespread support by the government, along with the continuous pressure from feminists, fueled the funding of intervention and other programs to support victims of domestic violence. While the movement ignited positive change, policy makers realized issues related to domestic violence could not be sustained by feminist groups and that men were also needed to change the minds of many and promote awareness of the seriousness ramifications of domestic violence and the importance of supporting measures to promote gender equality (Nancarrow & Struthers, 1995).

Researchers have not ignored the impact of domestic violence on indigenous populations. Wendt (2009) understands the complexities that exist when attempting to understand domestic violence in rural settings, particularly in the Barossa Valley, one of Australia's premier winegrowing areas. The pressure of many to overlook domestic violence results from the need to maintain family as well as family businesses in order to maintain the ability to survive and prosper. Wendt clearly understands why solutions for domestic violence in urban areas will not necessarily work in rural areas such as the Barossa Valley due to social constructions of rural culture.

Bhandari (2003) emphasizes the impact of domestic violence on women of Aboriginal origin who already face stigma in Australian society. Statistics suggest that Aboriginal women are 45 more times likely to be victims of domestic violence than other Australian women. The government is taking an interest in the suffering of Aboriginal women at the hands of their spouses. Historically, outsiders have regarded intimate partner violence in Aboriginal tribes as being down played; however, researchers are now arguing that this reluctance to discuss these issues is not necessarily due to the marginalization of this group both socially and economically. Domestic violence among this group will require long-term solutions to a very serious problem.

Oppermann and Bronitt (2006) address the issue of orders of protection for victims of domestic violence. Historically, domestic violence has not been taken very seriously in Australia. Yet, a 1993 study revealed that 34 percent of women who had been in an intimate relationship had at some point experienced intimate partner violence. The problem lies in that, for many years, men could legally punish their wives without fear of consequences or repercussions. While orders of protection are available, the lack of resources and enforcement of such orders makes it difficult to successfully combat family violence. In addition, a lack of support from the courts and police has further compounded an already large problem.

Researchers in Australia are interested in the elements that play the largest role in how officers respond to domestic violence calls. Prior to this study, little was known about how Australian officer's judgments influenced the ways in which they responded to domestic violence calls. To learn more about this, researchers used risk-assessment tools to investigate responding officers' decision-making processes when assessing danger during domestic violence calls. When studying police responses, the data often suggest that officers view their interaction as inadequate and inefficient, particularly in domestic violence situations. Results suggest that responding officers may have difficulty determining whether an event rises to the level of a domestic violence incident. This can ultimately determine their response to the situation. In addition, officers often reported that paper-based risk assessment forms were not helpful to them because they had to take multiple variables into consideration when assessing risk, including neighborhood characteristics, victim and perpetrator verbal cues, as well as their personal experiences based on previous domestic violence calls. Data analysis suggested that responding officers use only a few of the risk assessment items when making decisions about how they will respond to a situation. Instead, officers are more likely to base their decisions about risk-management strategies depending on the victim's level of fear. Future research should not only focus on empirically tested traditional assumptions regarding risk as presented on risk assessments, but also on how risk assessment tools might capture situational dynamics and how those dynamics factor into decision-making tasks (Trujillo & Ross, 2008). Research on South African police services and domestic violence data is included in a later chapter.

Best practices

The United Nations Office on Drugs and Crime (UNODC, 2010) has provided useful suggestions that have been gleaned from domestic violence interventions worldwide. These recommendations should be taken into consideration when planning prevention and response efforts.

- **Costa Rican** authorities have worked together to develop a protocol for use in high-risk situations where a women's life is in danger. Institutions who have signed on to use this protocol include: the Ministries of Security and Justice, the public health system, the judicial system, service providers and the National Institute for Women.

    Upon a threat being made the risk assessment is conducted and when the results trigger special measures to be taken for victims at high risk, the data is placed in a common database accessible by all institutions that agreed to use the protocol. The information is shared and tracked, orders of protection are monitored for violations or other acts or factors that increase the risk of homicide.
- **Argentina, Bolivia, Brazil, India, Peru, the Philippines** and **Uruguay** have set up special women's units for victims of domestic violence in police stations that are staffed by women in order to respond to the specific needs of these women. These units staffed by policewomen have increased the visibility of female police officers, attracting more women into the profession.
- The Organization for Safety and Cooperation in Europe had made concerted efforts to recruit and retain more female police officers. In **Kosovo** and **the Balkans** female participation in police academy training has reached unprecedented proportions. Domestic violence is treated as both a social problem and a crime in need of investigation and police academies have responded by offering specialized training.
- Bail hostels have been created in **the UK** and in **Northern Ireland** where alleged perpetrators must live until their trials. Hostels are different from jails in that perpetrators are able to continue working to support their families. This also allows for women and their children to remain safely in their homes. **Austria, Switzerland** and **Germany** all have removal laws. In these countries women are afforded community services that also include shelters, witness protection programs and anti-stalking/harassment laws.

- In addition to bail hostels, the **London** Metropolitan Police have set up three "safe havens" for sexual assault victims where they can receive confidential medical care, forensic examinations and the necessary social and support services. These women also have access to specially trained police officers who maintain contact with them throughout the investigation providing updates and information where evidence collected from their case has be linked to other crimes enhancing prosecutions of cases that might never have come to the attention of the authorities.

- In some areas of **the UK** police departments are allowed to take third-party information in cases where women are too scared to come forward on their own or refuse to make a formal complaint. "Cocoon Watches" encourage neighbors to report suspected perpetrators of domestic violence.

- The local police force in **Seville** has set up a specialist unit called the Diana Group. It is a cadre of specialists who deal with gender-based violence. While many of these women have reported incidents to police they report not being able to identify with the police process. The officers on this unit do not wear uniforms. The Diana Group assists the victim in ways to avoid secondary victimization. The group provides victims with ongoing care, case management, and social support, in order to help the client navigate the legal system and address specific issues they face during this difficult time in their lives.

- An organization created by the South African Regional Police Chiefs has developed comprehensive training materials that are delivered to all police in their respective regions and is currently being delivered across **South Africa**. The training materials include a training manual addressing issues related to domestic violence against women and children. These materials include curricula on various types of abuse that befall women and children including rape, incest, physical abuse, sexual harassment, human trafficking, types of violence that might be expected during armed conflict, and harmful traditional practices such as genital mutilation. This training includes both curricula and training manuals for each attendee.

- The United Nations has been working closely with the **Liberian and Rwanda** National Police in developing special protective units for women and children recognizing the need for specialized investigative and support services to encourage victimized women and their children in seeking assistance from the criminal justice system. Liberia now has these specialized units in all 15 counties assisting victimized women and children to seek safety and justice.

- The **Canadian** Government has taken measures in a number of provinces that enhance the education and training for their police force and victimized women and children.

  The Royal Canadian Mounted Police have developed a pocket-sized guide to assist field investigators with the 16 most common crime scenes they are likely to encounter as well as the types of evidence most commonly collected at these crime scenes. The guide goes on to instruct officers on the collection, preservation and handling of the 76 most common types of evidence they will likely encounter. The guide uses photographs and diagrams to ensure all key points in the investigation are covered.

In British Columbia officers are provided with a guidebook specifically designed for domestic violence investigations. This guide ensures that all evidence needed to assist with prosecution of each case is available and provides relevant information at bail hearings that might be useful in protecting victims from further violence. The risk assessment provides the court with an extensive social history on the alleged perpetrator addressing all areas of his life in depth in order to educate judges and prosecutors when making decisions about how to proceed with the case, all the while protecting the victims. The government in British Columbia has also developed and provides wallet-sized cards for officers to provide to women who are victims of domestic violence. These cards include tips, planning and emergency phone numbers in the event of an attack.

The British Columbia Institute against Family Violence created the Aid for Safety Assessment and Planning (2006), a manual setting forth guidelines for those providing services to women and children when conducting assessments and in developing individualized safety plans to protect them from further abuse. This manual provides the most current best practices found in academic and agency research.

In Alberta, government officials have collaborated with police departments, social service agencies, academic experts, family law specialists, and prosecutors in developing the Alberta Relationship Threat Assessment and Management Initiative. The goal of this initiative is to actively and effectively address potential threats in high-risk relationships and in stalking incidents.

Canadian authorities use a battery of screening instruments from all around the globe. The *Brief Spousal Assault Form for the Evaluation of Risk* (B-SAFER) (Kropp, Hart & Belfrage, 2004) was developed by Canadian researchers for use in criminal justice settings as a means to assess future risk of spousal assault. The *Ontario Domestic Assault Risk Assessment* (ODARA) is a general violence assessment addressing recidivism and is coupled with the *Danger Assessment Instrument* (2007), assessing incidence and patterns of violence in intimate partner relationships and is used as a safety planning tool (Campbell, 1995). Finally, the MPS Domestic Violence Risk Assessment Model (2003), developed by the London Metropolitan Police (in the UK) is a tool that assesses the workload and demands placed upon investigators guiding administrative decisions to ensure that victims are protected by police who are physically and mentally able to conduct their jobs to the best of their ability.

Conclusion

Over the past 10 years many countries have developed statutes (Ammar et al., 2005; Postmus & Hahn, 2007), and the 2012 Istanbul Convention ratified the first formal statement regarding violence against women. While there is still a great deal to be done, countries all over the world are incorporating unique ways in which to assess for risk, provide services for victims, properly investigate, and prosecute perpetrators in efforts to stem the tide of domestic violence.

References

Aguilar-Hass, G.A., Dutton, M.A., & Orloff, L.E. (2000). Lifetime prevalence of domestic violence against latina immigrants: Legal and policy implications. *Domestic Violence: Global Responses. Special Issue of the International Review of Victimology*, 7(1/2/3), 93–113.

America's Pro-Israel Lobby. (2010). *Near East Report*. Retrieved March 22, 2013 from www.aipac.org

Ammar, N., Orloff, L.E., Dutton, M.A., & Aguilar-Hass, G. (2005). Calls to police and police response: A case study from the Latina immigrant women in the U.S. *Journal of International Police Science and Management*, 7(4), 230–244.

Australian Domestic Violence. (2005). *CPJ: Counseling & Psychotherapy Journal*, 16(3), 29.

Bhandari, N. (2003). Aboriginal violence against women. *Contemporary Review*, 283(16), 353–355.

Bilifski, D., & Ersu, S. (2012, April 25). Women see worrisome shift in Turkey. *New York Times*. Retrieved March 22, 2013 from www.nytimes.com/2012/04/26

Bohn, S., & Hagemann-White, C. (2007). Protecting women against violence: Analytical study on the effective implementation of recommendation Rec(2002)5 on the protection of women against violence in Council of Europe member states. Strasbourg.

Bruns, D. (2014). Perspectives of women victims of wealthy batterers: Is justice served? *Global Journal of Human-Social Science: C Sociology and Culture*, 14(2), 1–21.

Buncombe, A. (2009). Independent appeal: Safe haven for women beaten and abused in Kashmir. *The Independent*. Retrieved March 22, 2013 from www.independent.co.uk/news/world/asia/independent-appeal-safe-haven-for-women-beaten-and-abused-in-kashmir-1851473.html

Campbell, Jacquelyn C. (Ed.). (1995). Assessing dangerousness: Violence by sexual offenders, batterers, and child abusers. Interpersonal violence: The practice series. Thousand Oaks, CA, US: Sage Publications.

CDC. (2005). Data and statistics: Violence prevention. Retrieved March 22, 2013 from www.cdc.gov/ViolencePrevention/data_stats/index.html

Crumley, B. (2010). Fresh bid to ban marital abuse that is psychological. *Time*. Retrieved March 22, 2013 from www.time.com/time/world/article/0,8599,1952552,00.html

Czech Republic. (2009). Final report of the Czech Republic on the national activities within the *Council of Europe campaign to combat violence against women, including domestic violence*. Czech Republic.

Domestic Violence Statistics. (2012). Retrieved March 22, 2013 from http://domestic violencestatistics.org/domestic-violence-statistics/

Dutton, M.A., Orloff, L., & Aguilar-Hass, G. (2000). Characteristics of help-seeking behaviors, resources, and service needs of battered immigrant Latinas: Legal and policy implications. *Georgetown Journal of Poverty, Law and Policy*, 7, 30–49.

Esfandiari, G. (2003). World: Violence against women in Iran, abuse is part of the culture. Retrieved March 22, 2013 from www.payvand.com/news/03/nov/1159.html

EVAWI. End Violence Against Women International. (2004). Retrieved March 23, 2012 from *www.evalwintl.org*

Ford, T. (2012, May, 22). Domestic violence is biggest threat to West Africa's women, IRC says. *Guardian*. Retrieved March 22, 2013 from www.guardian.co.uk/global-development

Grant, D. (2012, May 16). House passes Violence Against Women Act, grudgingly. *Christian Science Monitor*. Retrieved March 22, 2013 from www.CSmonitor.com

Hegde, R.S. (1998). A view from elsewhere: Locating difference and the politics of representation from a transnational feminist perspective. *Communication Theory*, *8*(3), 271–297. DOI: 10.1111/j.1468–2885.1998.tb00222.x

Hesse-Biber, S. (2013). Advanced topics: Transnational Feminism. [Syllabus]. Department of English Boston College.

Kimani, M. (2007). Taking on violence against women in Africa. *African Renewal*, *1*(2), 4.

Kouremetis, D. (2012). Bruises hidden from view: Spousal abuse knows no social class. Retrieved March 22, 2013 from http://voices.yahoo.com/topic/32629/spousal_abuse.html?cat=5

Kropp, P.R., Hart, S.D., & Belfrage, H. (2004). *The Brief Spousal Assault Form for the Evaluation of Risk* (B-SAFER). Psychological Assessments Australia. Retrieved from March 22, 2013 www.psychassessments.com.au

Kury, H., & Smartt, U. (2006). Domestic violence: Recent developments in German and English legislation and law enforcement. *European Journal of Crime, Criminal Law and Criminal Justice*, *14*(4), 407.

Michele, J. (2012). Iran: Execution of women and children. A report by Safe World for Women. Safe World International. Retrieved from March 22, 2013 www.asafeworldforwomen.org

Ministry of Justice and the Police. (2011). *Turning Point. Action Plan Against Domestic Violence*. Norway.

Minwalla, S. (2011). Institutionalized violence against women and girls in Iraq. Law and Practices in Iraq. Heartland Alliance for Human Needs & Human Rights 2011. Retrieved March 22, 2013 from www.scribd.com/doc/49420024/

Nancarrow, H., & Struthers, K. (1995). The growth of domestic violence responses in Australia: A "flash in the pan" or a sustainable program for change? *Social Alternatives*, *14*(1), 44–48.

Nelson, E. (2007). Victims of war: The First World War, returned soldiers, and understanding of domestic violence in Australia. *Journal of Women's History*, *19*(4), 83–106.

Nijhowne, D., & Oates, L. (2008, July 4). A national report on domestic abuse in Afghanistan Global Rights: Partners for Justice. Section 1.ca. Retrieved March 22, 2013 from http://section15.ca/features/news/2008/07/04/afghan_women/

Northern Ireland Department of Health, Social Services and Public Safety. (2005). Tackling violence at home: A strategy for addressing domestic violence and abuse in Northern Ireland. Retrieved March 22, 2013 from www.nio.gov.uk

NFAP. (2012). Study: Domestic violence child abuse and neglect in Saudi Arabia. National Family Safety Program: National Guard Health Affairs. Retrieved March 22, 2013 from www.nfsp.org.sa/index.php/component/

Oppermann, M., & Bronitt, S. (2006). Protection orders and family violence. *Legaldate*, *18*(3), 6–7.

Orloff L., Dutton, M.A., Aguilar-Hass, G., & Ammar, N. (2003). Battered immigrant women's willingness to call for help and police response. *UCLA Women's Law Journal*, *13*(1), 43–100.

Pearle, R. (2013, December). Domestic violence: The secret killer that costs $8.3 billion annually. *Forbes*. Retrieved March 22, 2013 from www.forbes.com/sites/robert-pearl/2013/12/05/domestic-violence-the-secret-killer-that-costs-8-3-billion-annually/#3519b7543c13

Postmus, J.L., & Hahn, S.A. (2007). Comparing the policy response to violence against women in the United States and South Korea. *International Social Work*, *50*(6), 770–782.

Raj. (2006, April, 24). Men's IPV perpetration and sexual risk behaviors: Data from Hispanic and Black men from a single urban health center in Boston. Cited in: Aguilar-Hass, G., Ammar, N., & Orloff, L. Battered immigrants and U.S. citizen spouses. *Legal Momentum*, 1–10. Retrieved March 22, 2013 from http://action.legalmomentum.org/site/DocServer/dvusc.pdf?docID=314

Raj, A. & Silverman, J. (2002). Violence against immigrant women: The roles of culture, context, and legal immigrant status on partner violence. *Violence Against Women*, 8(3), 367–398.

Second Action Plan. (2007). Second action plan of the federal government to combat violence against women. *Federal Ministry for Family Affairs, Senior Citizens, Women and Youth* – BMFSFJ 11018 Berlin. Online: www.bmfsfj.de

Stark, E. (2007). *Coercive control*. Oxford University Press: New York.

Sundari, A. (2008). Neither safety nor justice: The UK Government response to domestic violence against immigrant women. *Journal of Social Welfare & Family Law*, 30(3), 189–202.

Tay, H.F. (2012, May, 30). China may enact domestic violence law. ABC Radio Australia.

Trujillo, M., & Ross, S. (2008). Police response to domestic violence. *Journal of Interpersonal Violence*, 23(4), 454–473.

UN Secretary General's Database on Violence Against Women. (2009). Policy academy of the Beijing public security department training curriculum on domestic violence. Retrieved March 22, 2013 from http://sgdatabase.unwomen.org

UN Secretary General's Database on Violence Against Women. (2010). Police protection of violence victims. India. Retrieved March 22, 2013 from http://sgdatabase.unwomen.org

UN Secretary General's Database on Violence Against Women. (UNSG). (2012). Act 15 of 2008. Retrieved March 22, 2013 from http://sgdatabase.unwomen.org

UNODC. (2010). *Handbook on effective police responses to violence against women*. Criminal Justice Handbook Series. Vienna, Austria.

UNWomen. (2012). Law to protect family and prevent violence against women. The UN Secretary General's Database on Violence Against Women. Retrieved March 22, 2013 from http://sgdatabase.unwomen.org

Wendt, S. (2009). *Domestic violence in rural Australia*. Sydney: Federation Press.

World Health Organization. (2005). Violence against women in Africa. Cited in: World Health Organization. *WHO multi-country study on women's health and domestic violence against women: Summary report of initial results on prevalence, health outcomes and women's responses*. Geneva.

Xu, X., Zhu, F., O'Campo, P., Koenig, M.A., Mock, V., & Campbell, J. (2005). Prevalence of and risk factors for intimate partner violence in China. *American Journal of Public Health*, 95(1), 79–85. Retrieved March 22, 2013 from doi/pdf/10.2105/AJPH.2003.023978.

1 Intimate partner violence in Canada

Policies, practices, and prevalence

Amanda V. McCormick, Irwin M. Cohen,
and Darryl Plecas

Introduction

The United Nations defines violence against women (VAW) as "any act of gender-based violence that results in, or is likely to result in, physical, sexual or psychological harm or suffering to women, including threats of such acts ..." (UN, 1993). A common form of VAW is the threat or infliction of physical, sexual, emotional, or financial harm in the context of interpersonal relationships; known broadly as domestic violence and, more specifically, as intimate partner violence (IPV) (Provincial Office of Domestic Violence, 2014). For many years, IPV was considered an issue to be dealt with in private; more recently, however, there has been broader recognition at a policy and practice level that IPV is a public concern that affects society as a whole (Ministry of Children and Family Development, 2014). This chapter provides an overview of prevalence rates for victimization by an intimate partner, examines the paradigm shift in Canadian society toward IPV, highlights some innovative strategies adopted across Canada, and concludes with a summary of key remaining challenges in effectively preventing and responding to IPV.

The nature and extent of intimate partner violence in Canada

Though consistently rated highly on the Organisation for Economic Co-Operation and Development's (OECD) Better Life Index (www.oecdbetterlifeindex.org/countries/canada/), IPV is a common occurrence in Canada, with nearly one in ten Canadian adults reporting recent physical and/or sexual intimate partner violence victimization (Brennan, 2011a; Gannon & Mihorean, 2005; Mihorean, 2005; Patterson, 2003), costing an estimated $7 billion or more per year in direct and associated costs (Zhang, Hoddenbagh, McDonald & Scrim, 2012). The rates of emotional and financial abuse are even higher; however, the Canadian General Social Survey does not consider these as forms of IPV. Given that physical/sexual IPV, and emotional and financial victimization appear highly correlated (e.g., Brennan, 2011b), the national victimization statistics likely underestimate the extent of spousal victimization in Canada.

Domestic violence is a highly gendered occurrence. While domestic violence can be perpetrated by a female against her male or female partner, the vast majority of domestic violence police calls for service in Canada involve heterosexual couples where the male partner is accused of engaging in violence against a female partner (Zhang et al., 2012). Further, the violence perpetrated by male partners against their female victims is often considerably more serious, often involving choking and physical beatings (Brennan, 2011a, 2011b; Sinha, 2013).

Of note, the rates of IPV are substantially higher for Aboriginal women in Canada. In 2009, twice as many Aboriginal women (15 percent) compared to non-Aboriginal women (6 percent) reported having been victimized by a spouse in the previous five years. In addition, over half (59 percent) of the Aboriginal victims reported being injured, compared to less than half (41 percent) of non-Aboriginal victims (Brennan, 2011b). There are many underlying factors that explain the increased risk of Aboriginal women to domestic violence, many of which originate from the negative effects of the Indian Act in 1876, which transformed many matriarchal Aboriginal cultures into patriarchal systems. One of the most damaging policies that has had a consequential ripple effect over many subsequent generations of Aboriginal families was the practice of removing Aboriginal status from an Aboriginal woman who married a non-Aboriginal man, forcing these women to become economically and emotionally dependent on their male spouses (Alberta Justice and Solicitor General & Alberta Crown Prosecution Service, 2014). Many Aboriginal peoples also suffer from ongoing direct and multi-generational traumas as a result of the policy decision to place Aboriginal children in residential schools in an attempt at assimilation. This practice led to wide-ranging traumas resulting from routine neglect, as well as the infliction of physical, sexual, emotional, and spiritual abuse, and has directly contributed to the high rates of post-traumatic stress disorder found in many Aboriginal communities that is often self-medicated through substance abuse, and which permeates society through the infliction of violence against loved ones (Royal Commission on Aboriginal Peoples, 1996). Thus, whereas historical Aboriginal responses to VAW might include confrontation by peers, followed by banishment, castration, and death, many Aboriginal communities in Canada today have become numb to this trend, with some communities reporting victimization rates upward of 70 percent (Bopp, Bopp & Lane, 2003).

In terms of people coming to Canada from other countries, approximately 5 percent of immigrant women in Canada report IPV (Sinha, 2013). Often, this trauma is compounded by concerns regarding sponsorship security, ineligibility to obtain social services, and barriers to social and professional help resulting from language difficulties, shame, economic dependence, and cultural norms (MacLeod & Shin, 1993; Bhuyan, Osborne, Zahraei & Tarshis, 2014). Given that one-fifth of Canadians identify as "foreign-born" (Statistics Canada, 2011), violence against immigrant women is a pressing concern for Canadian society.

Unfortunately, the most recent Canadian victimization study found that less than one-quarter (23 percent) of female IPV victims reported their victimization to the police (Brennan, 2011a). Of note, this reporting rate was a substantial decrease from a decade ago when 37 percent of female victims of IPV reported their victimization to the police (Ogrodnik, 2006). These rates may be even lower among immigrant populations in Canada, especially among Indo-Canadian and Muslim women where patriarchal notions concerning a woman's position in the family play a dominant role in acceptance of engaging in VAW (Ammar, Couture-Carron, Alvi & San Antonio, 2014; Baobid, 2002; MacLeod & Shin, 1993). Similarly, there are relatively low rates of reporting domestic violence to the police among Aboriginal populations, despite the greater likelihood for violence to be inflicted against Aboriginal women by their partners (e.g., Brennan, 2011a; Malcoe & Duran, 2003; Sinha, 2013; Tjaden & Thoennes, 2000). Given Canada's longstanding undertones of discriminatory attitudes toward its Aboriginal citizens, this underreporting may be the byproduct of poor quality police response to previous calls for service.

For Aboriginal and immigrant women, fear of being ostracized by one's community and fear of shaming the family are additional reasons that detract from the likelihood of calling the police in response to intimate partner victimization, as well as perceptions that the police will give their cases less attention than non-ethnic women (Ammar et al., 2014; Campbell, 2010; Epstein, 1999; Jiwani & Buhagiar, 1997; MacLeod & Shin, 1990; Martin & Mosher, 1995; McGillivray & Comaskey, 1999; Miedema & Wachholz, 1998; Native Women's Association of Canada, 1994; Wolf, Ly, Hobart & Kernic, 2003). There may also be a preference to deal with the issue first using the family, church, or larger community (Baobid, 2002; Miedema & Wachholz, 1998; El-Khoury et al., 2004; Wolf et al., 2003). Additional issues that make the decision to call the police more complex for immigrant women include a fear of deportation upon conviction (for the partner, as well as for herself), language barriers, and social and economic dependence on their partner, which is also an important reason for why Aboriginal women infrequently report victimization by their partner to the police (Baobid, 2002; Chambers, 1998; Dosanjh, Deo & Sidhu, 1994; Gillis et al., 2006; Jiwani & Buhagiar, 1997; MacLeod & Shin, 1990; Martin & Mosher, 1995; McDonald & Cross, 2001; Miedema & Wachholz, 1998; Native Women's Association of Canada, 1994; Wolf et al., 2003). An additional significant barrier to immigrant women's involving the police is a general lack of awareness about rights and the law. In fact, 15 years ago, Miedema and Wachholz (1998) conducted focus groups with nearly 50 women who had immigrated to New Brunswick, Canada, many of whom reported subsequent victimization at the hands of their husband. Consistently, the women believed they would be deported if their husband (sponsor) was arrested or convicted of domestic violence. A second set of false beliefs centered on divorce and the fear that they would lose custody of their children, as well as be denied the right to claim any household property or other material gains (Miedema & Wachholz, 1998).

The underreporting of IPV to police explains why spousal victimization composes 32 percent of Canadian victimization data on all violent crimes, but only 11 percent of police-reported violent crime in Canada (Zhang et al., 2012). This is unfortunate, given Ogrodnik's (2006) observation that, in a significant percentage of cases (57 percent), the level of spousal violence decreased following police intervention. However, the reduced recidivism following police intervention could also be a consequence of a more severe criminal justice system response, as victims reported that they were more likely to call for police assistance when the abuse was more severe, they feared their partner would kill them, there was a previous history of abuse, or there was the use of a weapon or alcohol in the incident (Bonomi, Holt, Martin & Thompson, 2006; Brewster, 2001; Chambers, 1998; Dutton, Goodman & Bennett, 1999; Gillis et al., 2006; Ogrodnik, 2006; Sinha, 2013; Wiist & McFarlane, 1998).

Still, it is notable that police intervention can have a positive effect on reducing recidivism among domestic violence offenders, but that Aboriginal and immigrant women are less likely to benefit from this intervention, as Canadian statistics also show that, not only is intimate partner violence homicide highly gendered (Campbell et al., 2007; Ontario Domestic Violence Death Review Committee, 2008; Taylor-Butts & Porter, 2011), but Aboriginal women are disproportionately at risk of experiencing lethal domestic violence (Sinha, 2013). Of note, intimate partner homicides are relatively rare in Canada, with one-fifth (18 percent) of all solved homicides in Canada involving intimate partners (Beattie, 2005). However, the rates of IPV ending in homicide tend to be slightly higher in the western provinces than the rest of Canada, with British Columbia slightly above the national average. Still, in general terms, the rate of IPV ending in homicide has remained relatively stable over the past decade (Dauvergne, 2005; Kowalski, 2006; Provincial Office of Domestic Violence, 2014; Taylor-Butts & Porter, 2011). The remainder of this chapter will focus on the increasing politicization of IPV in Canada, while acknowledging ongoing challenges with effectively managing this complex phenomenon.

Responses to IPV in Canada

Consistent with the experiences of many other nations, IPV has not always been regarded as a public issue in Canada. When, in 1982, the Canadian government introduced a motion that police lay charges in domestic violence assaults against women, the immediate response from the floor was "laughter and jeers" (Sweetman, 1982, as cited in Alberta Justice and Solicitor General & Alberta Crown Prosecution Service, 2014).

For many years, the Canadian criminal justice system failed to recognize and respond to this form of VAW. Research conducted only two decades ago concluded that police officers did not perceive intimate partner violence as a legal problem and wanted to avoid domestic violence calls. In fact, victims were seen as weak, unreliable, uncooperative, or to be disbelieved (Hannah-Moffat, 1995; Stephens & Sinden, 2000). These attitudes have, for the most part, shifted substantially over the last two decades as policies and practices geared toward acknowledging and eliminating violence against women have been developed, leading to new police practices, including the development of specialized units to respond to both perpetrators and victims involved in intimate partner violence and the adoption of mandatory arrest policies to take much of the police discretion around appropriate response away.

Division of political responsibility

Canada has ten provinces and three territories. The British North America Act of 1867 and the Constitution Act of 1982 set in place a federal system of government, which divided lawmaking abilities into federal and provincial/territorial responsibilities. Whereas the Canadian federal government retained jurisdiction over the passage of criminal law, the provinces and territories were tasked with the actual administration of justice, as well as the administration of other social systems, including child welfare and the healthcare system. An unfortunate consequence of this policy decision is that, while national laws against assault, sexual assault, and financial victimization prohibit violence against women, the individual provinces and territories are responsible for devising individual policies and practices for their judicial system's response. Further, each province and territory operates different policing models, ranging from fully provincial police forces (e.g., Ontario Provincial Police) to a mix of municipal (e.g., Calgary, Vancouver, and Abbotsford) and municipally contracted Royal Canadian Mounted Police (RCMP) detachments. Complicating this arrangement further is the provision of certain governmental powers to Aboriginal groups. For instance, First Nations communities can negotiate self-governing powers, meaning they can accept responsibility for administering justice, health, and other matters of the welfare state. These policy decisions have resulted in a wide range of local or jurisdictional practices in preventing and responding to IPV. The following sections will describe some notable Canadian examples of IPV policy and practice.

Policy and practice in British Columbia

British Columbia is one of the provinces and territories with the highest rates of IPV. In 2010, the national average of spousal victimization was recorded as 363 victims per 100,000 persons, but British Columbia's victimization rate was 427 (Provincial Office of Domestic Violence, 2014; Sinha, 2012). Moreover, the province reported 147 spousal homicides in less than one decade, with the vast majority involving female victims (72 percent) and male perpetrators (84 percent) (British Columbia Coroner's Service, 2012).

Policies addressing violence against women have been in place in British Columbia for several decades, starting with the 1986 Ministry of Attorney General Wife Assault policy and transitioning to the 1993 Violence Against Women in Relationships (VAWIR) policy which, despite its name, focuses equally on victims of either gender (Ministry of Public Safety and Solicitor General, Ministry of Attorney General & Ministry of Children and Family Development, 2010). The VAWIR policy has been updated several times (1996, 2000, 2004, and 2010). The 2010 amendments were designed to improve coordination between agencies involved in responding to domestic violence, particularly those involved in justice and child welfare, after a high-profile death of several members of a family, including a child, that was attributed, in part, to the failure to communicate between justice and child welfare agencies (Representative for Children and Youth, 2009).

While the policy has been commended for promoting proactive arrests and the consideration of unequal power relations as a common source of violence against women, one unfortunate unintended effect of the policy was a substantial increase in the average amount of time police spent responding to a domestic assault call for service from approximately one hour to between 10 and 12 hours, given that the required number of investigative steps increased to 58 from 36 (Malm et al., 2005a, 2005b). The increasing complexities in investigating domestic violence files is one reason many jurisdictions have introduced specialized units dedicated to handling domestic violence offenders.

The VAWIR policy established the respective roles of police and other stakeholders (e.g., Ministry of Children and Family Development, Corrections, WorkSafe BC) in responding to and reducing domestic violence (Ministry of Public Safety and Solicitor General et al., 2010). For instance, the policy requires that all police in British Columbia take "training on conducting evidence-based, risk-focused domestic violence investigations and on assessing domestic violence risk with a focus on safety planning" (Provincial Office of Domestic Violence, 2014, p. 14). Police should also have 24-hour access to the Protection Order Registry, which should contain information on all provincial civil and criminal protection orders. A report of domestic violence, regardless of how long after the incident occurred, must always be investigated by a police officer and should be considered a priority file (Ministry of Public Safety and Solicitor General et al., 2010). In the process of their investigation, police are guided to arrest – when appropriate – only the primary aggressor, considered the most dominant member in the incident, regardless of who initiated the incident. The police should also make a victim referral to a community-based or police-based victims service provider, and should arrange safe transportation, if need be, to a shelter or other temporary residence. Given the dynamic nature of domestic violence cases, the policy states that police are also supposed to monitor the offender's compliance with conditions and review the offender's risk status should they violate a condition, as well as communicate with the victim to review whether they are participating in safety planning (Ministry of Public Safety and Solicitor General et al., 2010).

The 2010 policy update introduced the Protocol for Highest Risk Cases, which provides for information sharing among the various partners (i.e., police, Crown Counsel, corrections, victim service workers, child welfare) to facilitate offender management and the provision of victim safety in those instances involving perpetrators of domestic violence who are most likely to re-offend and inflict serious harm or even death on the victim (Ministry of Public Safety and Solicitor General et al., 2010; Provincial Office of Domestic Violence, 2014). As stated in the VAWIR policy, this designation is assigned by the police when warranted by a formal risk assessment. Essentially, when police are faced with a situation that they believe may qualify as highest risk, the policy states that they should immediately request a B-SAFER risk assessment be completed and notify their protocol partners. If the risk assessment is conducted in time, it should be included in the Report to Crown Counsel for the offender's bail hearing along with other investigatory details, a discussion of safety and protection concerns to the victim and others, and an opinion on risk and possible need for detention. Of note, the policy strongly advises against releasing high-risk suspects on an Undertaking or Promise to Appear. During this initial investigation, police and their partners are expected to regularly communicate relevant information, including the safety of the victim and, if applicable, her children, the status of the suspect, including court conditions and release status, and to update with new relevant information, such as contacts with the victim or other forms of condition violations (Ministry of Public Safety and Solicitor General et al., 2010).

Specifically, the protocol states that information, including the results of risk assessments, court outcomes/conditions, breaches of conditions, and "other relevant information pertaining to the accused/offender or victim," should be shared in a timely manner (Provincial Office of Domestic Violence, 2014, p. 7).

A recent change in British Columbia's approach to preventing and reducing domestic violence was the establishment of the Provincial Office of Domestic Violence in 2012. This was in response to another report by the Representative for Children and Youth on the death of three children as a result of a family violence situation (see the Representative for Children and Youth, 2012). In 2014, the office announced their three-year Provincial Domestic Violence Plan, which allocated nearly $6 million toward the creation of more specialized domestic violence police units, funding for offender treatment, improved access to several types of services needed by victims, and specialized programming for Aboriginal families, immigrants and refugees, and women with disabilities (Provincial Office of Domestic Violence, 2014; Woodin, 2014).

Alberta's Integrated Threat and Risk Assessment Centre (I-TRAC)

A decade ago, the government of Alberta, with support from the federal Canadian government, established Alberta's Law Enforcement Response Teams (ALERT). ALERT is a unique organization in Canada in that it integrates the efforts of the province's municipal and RCMP agencies in investigating organized and serious crimes. The model removes the jurisdictional restrictions imposed by Canada's regional policing and also facilitates information sharing across sectors, including mental health and child welfare (Sharpe, 2011). Within this model, the Integrated Threat and Risk Assessment Centre (I-TRAC) is specifically assigned to conduct risk assessment and develop risk reduction plans for victims of domestic violence and stalking, as well as to provide training to agencies managing these cases. In the 2013–2014 operating year, I-TRAC conducted nearly 200 requested threat and risk assessments that informed decisions relating to case management (ALERT, 2014).

Ontario's Domestic Death Review Committees

Death review committees employ a retrospective analysis whereby they conduct an inquest into previous cases of domestic violence to identify common factors, signs of escalating severity, and missed opportunities for prevention and intervention. The Office of the Chief Coroner of Ontario established a provincial Domestic Violence Death Review Committee in 2003, with the goal of identifying risk factors that predict the likelihood of lethal violence, and the creation of recommendations to prevent similar deaths from occurring (Federal-Provincial-Territorial Ad hoc Working Group on Family Violence, 2013).

The main conclusion drawn from these reviews was that most deaths resulting from domestic violence were both predictable and preventable. There were indications of escalating violence that often were not acted upon due to lack of information sharing between various sectors involved in responding to IPV. Overall, since its inception in 2003, this committee has identified 39 risk factors for domestic homicide (Jaffe, Dawson & Campbell, 2011). Unfortunately, despite the insights offered by regularly conducting death reviews, few provinces and none of the territories have adopted this practice (Jaffe, Dawson & Campbell, n.d.).

Specialized and integrated domestic violence units in British Columbia

Specialized domestic violence units are becoming increasingly common among RCMP and municipal agencies in Canada, particularly in British Columbia, where recent government funding has been allocated, in part, for the development of both specialized and integrated units. Specialized domestic violence units are typically staffed by a team of specially trained police officers and supervisors and, at times, civilian personnel tasked with victim services. While all police officers have basic training in investigating violence files, and are affected by specialized domestic violence policies, members of specialized units benefit from additional targeted training, such as on conducting risk assessments. While there are few available academic studies assessing the effectiveness of these units (see Whetstone, 2001 for one example), previous research has consistently found that victims reported greater satisfaction when their case was handled by a specialized unit compared to a general patrol officer (Apsler, Cummins & Carl, 2003; Grasely et al., 1999; Lane, Greenspan & Weisburd, 2004; Uekert et al., 2001; Weisz, Canales-Portalatin & Nahan, 2004; Whetstone, 2001). Specialized units often have the ability to focus on a more limited number of files, build greater rapport with the victim, and increase perceptions of support. Moreover, many victims reportedly appreciate the ability to connect with a police-based victim advocate, highlighting this service as one of the most essential in helping them continue with criminal justice system proceedings (Grasely et al., 1999; Whetstone, 2001).

An increasing trend in British Columbia has been the movement toward more integrated units. One successful example of an alternative model of integrated teamwork are the Domestic Violence Response Teams or DVRTs. Examples of these teams can be found in Vancouver, where the Vancouver Police Department (VPD) pairs its investigators with community counselors specializing in domestic violence (Rossiter, 2011). This team is both reactive – responding to calls for service involving domestic violence – and proactive – reaching out to victims in relationships with high-risk persons (Rossiter, 2011). New Westminster is another police department with a DVRT; however, this team appears to operate differently than VPD's as their services are more focused on the post-call for service period. Another example of an integrated team involves physically co-locating domestic violence police units with other agencies/services working in the area. For instance, New Westminster, Abbotsford, and Oak Bay police all have domestic violence units where police, victim services workers, and child protection workers are co-located (Rossiter, 2011) and able to offer a wide range of services without requiring the victim to travel to multiple locations.

Approximately 30 police agencies across the province participate in Interagency Case Assessment Teams (ICAT) where a cross-range of service providers meet to share information about the offender and engage in safety planning (Jackson & Martinson, 2015). The purpose and benefit of an ICAT is to enhance information sharing across the sectors working in areas related to domestic violence, including the police, court representatives, corrections, victims' services, and child welfare workers (Ending Violence Association of BC, n.d.). With an increasing need to share information in the instance of escalating violence in order to prevent lethal violence, the provincial Freedom of Information and Protection of Privacy Act was recently amended to indicate that "it is appropriate to collect, use and disclose information for the specific purpose of reducing the risk that an individual will be a victim of domestic violence if that violence is reasonably likely to occur" (Jackson & Martinson, 2015, p. 28). In all other situations, where the offender has not been labeled as highest risk, disclosure is made at the discretion of the person holding the information, and given challenges typically associated with information sharing (e.g., ownership over information, fears of violating privacy legislation, and lack of knowledge about what the information will be used for), more often than not, information sharing does not occur. As such, this amendment was critical to improving the criminal justice system response to serious cases of domestic violence. However, an outstanding issue remains with the lack of integration at the court level. While most other provinces and territories have successfully operated domestic violence courts going back two decades, British Columbia has yet to make this transition. That said, there are ongoing political discussions regarding the need to better merge the court systems; most notably, the way in which the criminal and civil systems deal with the related issues of domestic violence and child welfare (Jackson & Martinson, 2015).

Specialized domestic violence court systems in Canada

In Canada, few domestic violence cases proceed to court and, when they do, the offender often receives a light penalty, typically involving probation as opposed to a custodial sentence (Russell & Ginn, 2001; Gannon & Mihorean, 2005; Beaupré, 2015). Court practices for processing domestic violence cases vary by province. An increasingly common process in Canada is to utilize some version of a domestic violence court that may range from specially trained criminal justice system personnel to an entirely separate court process and procedure (Ministry of Justice, 2014).

In 1990, Manitoba was the first Canadian province to introduce specialized courts and specialized Crown prosecutors and judges in the provincial capital city of Winnipeg (Gannon & Mihorean, 2005). Seven years later, the province of Ontario was the next to introduce a specialized prosecution and judicial team, as well as an early intervention stream where offenders pleading guilty at their first court appearance were referred to treatment as a release (bail) condition, and a Partner Assault Response Program (www.parprogram.ca; Ministry of Justice, 2014). In 2000, the Yukon introduced an early intervention stream where offenders would be regularly monitored by the court and judge throughout their bail and probationary period (i.e., judicial review, as opposed to police supervision; Ministry of Justice, 2014; Tutty & Ursel, 2008). Notably, a cost efficiency evaluation indicated that the average cost per case was $1,630 compared to nearly $2,000 per one-day trial in the traditional court system (Ministry of Justice, 2014). In addition, the Yukon developed a Spousal Abuse Treatment program with nearly 100 percent retention rates (Tutty & Ursel, 2008).

Also, in 2000, the province of Alberta began the trend toward domestic violence courts in eight of its major cities (Ministry of Justice, 2014). For instance, the city of Calgary introduced a domestic violence court that uses both an expedited docket system, as well as a trial system specifically for domestic violence. This means that first time domestic violence offenders can quickly be held accountable and can receive intervention, which enables the trial court to spend more time focusing on chronic domestic violence offenders (Tutty et al., 2011). The docket system works by staying the charges through use of peace bonds for low-risk offenders (no criminal record or a minor non-domestic violence record) who are willing to take responsibility for the incident. The peace bond conditions typically mandate participation in treatment (e.g., counseling, substance abuse). Probation officers then monitor the offender's compliance to these conditions for the duration of the peace bond (Tutty et al., 2011). Another element of Calgary's specialized response to domestic violence is the HomeFront agency that provides court support for victims through case workers who are formally mandated to work with victims both before and during the trial process. Specifically, case workers from the agency attend court with the victim or represent their interests, but also are responsible for updating victims with any changes in their partner's status (e.g., released from custody), work with the victim to develop safety plans, and coordinate access to community resources (Alberta Solicitor General, Calgary Rocky View Child and Family Services & HomeFront, 2002). Notably, the review by Tutty and colleagues (2011) reported a statistically significant difference in the percentage of domestic violence victims appearing at trial, from one-fifth (20 percent) to half (49 percent).

In 2003, the province of Saskatchewan established a domestic violence court in three major cities (Regina, Saskatoon, and North Battleford) (Courts of Saskatchewan, n.d.; Ministry of Justice, 2014). The central feature of this provincial program is the treatment option offered to those who agree to plead guilty. Specifically, offenders proceeding through the domestic violence court are given an opportunity to first complete treatment (weekly counseling for approximately 20 weeks and, potentially, substance abuse treatment) prior to being sentenced for their offence(s). Treatment completion is then factored into the subsequent sentence in that offenders who have completed the program will not receive any jail time and their sentence will be reduced. Offenders who choose not to participate in this stream are processed through the traditional court system (Department of Justice Canada, 2013). Of note, offenders with a pattern of previous domestic violence incidents and/or offenders who exerted a significant degree of violence are not eligible for participation. In effect, this program appears to be focused on early intervention.

The eastern provinces were the next to establish domestic violence courts and processes, starting with New Brunswick in 2007 in the capital of Moncton, followed by the province of Newfoundland and Labrador in 2009, and Nova Scotia in 2012 (Ministry of Justice, 2014). In 2011, the Northwest Territories also established a domestic violence court in the capital city of Yellowknife (Ministry of Justice, 2014). These models closely followed the Yukon's Domestic Violence Treatment Option court (Ministry of Justice, 2014).

Only one jurisdiction (Toronto, Ontario) has introduced integrated domestic violence courts that focus on the often co-occurring instances of domestic violence and family court issues (Ministry of Justice, 2014). Given the constitutional division of responsibility in Canada, no single court had simultaneously considered criminal and civil (family) matters. The subsequent lack of information sharing and often inconsistent, individualized judicial orders in response to criminal and civil issues occurring within the same domicile resulted in some severe instances of domestic violence, including the deaths of several women and children (Birnbaum, Bala & Jaffe, 2014; Campbell, 2010; Representative for Children and Youth, 2009, 2012).

Notably, given its tendency toward higher rates of domestic violence and recent experience with domestic violence homicides, British Columbia is one of only three provinces/territories[1] that has yet to establish a provincial system of specialized courts. However, five individual municipalities have recently established specialized processes that seek to improve information sharing and collaborative service provision from community, police, and court representatives (Ministry of Justice, 2014).

Overall, these courts have achieved substantial reductions in court processing times; attained increases in guilty pleas; made early intervention to first time offenders; connected offenders more quickly with treatment; concluded cases in court more rapidly; contributed to increased sentences in the form of more frequent incarceration and fewer conditional discharges; realized substantial and, at times, statistically significant reduced recidivism rates, and achieved greater victim satisfaction with the criminal justice system processing of their case (Alberta Solicitor General et al., 2002; Gannon & Mihorean, 2005; Ministry of Justice, 2014; Moyer, Rettinger & Hotton, 2000 as cited in Tutty & Ursel, 2008; Tutty & Ursel, 2008; Trainor, 2002).

Continuing issues in preventing and responding to IPV in Canada

In addition to the high rates of domestic violence in Aboriginal communities and the help-seeking challenges experienced by immigrant victims of IPV, additional ongoing Canadian concerns regarding IPV primarily are: (1) the lack of a national strategic response; (2) the wide variation in risk assessment practices; and (3) the difficulty with effectively collaborating criminal and civil responses to domestic violence issues.

National strategy for domestic violence

As a result of its federalist structure, Canada faces somewhat unique challenges in preventing and responding to IPV. Recently, there have been vocal calls for the establishment of national strategies to improve the efficiency and effectiveness of managing IPV. The Canadian Network of Women's Shelters and Transition Houses recently published *The Case for a National Action Plan on Violence Against Women*, as a result of their Mapping VAW Policy and Opportunities Project. Their project concluded that, whereas IPV was considered a gendered form of violence at the provincial/territorial level, it was not at the national level; VAW was defined inconsistently across federal and provincial/territorial policies; the lack of funding for supportive services put women's safety at risk; and there was a need for legal reform given the over-reliance on a criminal justice system response to a multi-sectorial issue, dual charging practices, and the lack of access to services and treatment (Canadian Network of Women's Shelters and Transition Houses, 2013). An additional consequence of the inconsistent policies and practices regarding IPV in Canada has been the proliferation of risk assessment tools.

Inconsistent risk assessment practices

Risk/threat assessment is completed at multiple levels and by multiple sectors, including police, Crown, and community services. Assessments of risk cannot only help professionals assess the threat posed by an offender and the corresponding response demanded by police and the larger justice system, but can also help victims more accurately recognize their own level of risk and put an appropriate safety plan in place (Campbell, 2010).

Given that there is no national standard for preventing and responding to domestic violence in Canada, there are unsurprisingly a wide variety of risk assessment instruments in use that focus on domestic violence, such as the Spousal Assault Risk Assessment used by Corrections and, for police, the Level of Service Case Management Inventory used in probation, the Violence in Relationship Checklist utilized by the RCMP, and the Aid to Safety Assessment Planning used in victim services. Unfortunately, usage seems to largely vary by province (Millar, 2009; Millar, Code & Ha, 2013). Specifically, Millar and colleagues noted that police agencies across Canada use the following tools: Violence in Relationship Investigative Checklist (RCMP in Newfoundland and Labrador); the Spousal/Partner Abuse, Assault Court Package Supplement (RCMP in Newfoundland and Labrador); the Domestic Violence Police Investigation Checklist (municipal police and RCMP in Prince Edward Island); the Court Information Package (municipal police and RCMP in Prince Edward Island); the Ontario Domestic Assault Risk Assessment (police in Ontario, RCMP and municipal police in Nova Scotia, the Integrated Threat and Risk Assessment Centre in Alberta, RCMP in the Northwest Territories, and police-based victim services in Saskatchewan); the Brief Spousal Assessment Form for the Evaluation of Risk (municipal police and RCMP in New Brunswick; municipal police and RCMP in British Columbia); the Spousal Assault Risk Assessment (police in Ontario, the Integrated Threat and Risk Assessment Centre in Alberta, the Vancouver Police Department, and the Yukon RCMP); the Victim's Statement of Risk (police in Ontario); the Bail Safety Program Interview Checklist (police in Ontario); the Domestic Violence Supplementary Report Form (police in Ontario); Stalking Assessment and Management (the Integrated Threat and Risk Assessment Centre in Alberta, the Vancouver Police Department, and the Surrey RCMP's Behavioural Sciences Unit); the Family Violence Investigation Report (municipal, First Nations, and RCMP police in Alberta); the HCR-20 (the Integrated Threat and Risk Assessment Centre in Alberta, the Vancouver Police Department, and the Surrey RCMP's Behavioural Sciences Unit); Threat Assessment Questions for Field Personnel (Vancouver Police Department); the Risk of Sexual Violence Protocol (the Integrated Threat and Risk Assessment Centre in Alberta); the Psychopathy Checklist (the Integrated Threat and Risk Assessment Centre in Alberta); the Static 99 (the Integrated Threat and Risk Assessment Centre in Alberta); and the Response Protocol for Quebec Police Services (police in Quebec) (see Millar, 2009 or Millar et al., 2013 for a summary of each risk assessment tool). While these tools have varying purposes, it is plausible that more stringent guidelines and their usage could result in a more consistent approach to risk assessment.

Conversely, one absent form of risk assessment that has been successfully applied in many American states is the assessment of the potential for lethal violence to occur using the Lethality Assessment Program (LAP) (http://mnadv. org/lethality/lap-nationally/). The LAP is used by first responders (typically police) to identify a victim's current level of risk and provide an instant connection with service advocates who can deliver services to mitigate the risk of lethal violence. The assessment of risk is made quickly at the scene using an 11-question screen based on the Danger Assessment measure by Campbell (Campbell et al., 2007).[2] The questions touch on known risk factors for elevated violence among intimate partners. If the victim's responses indicate a life-threatening level of risk, the police officer calls a victim advocate and then passes the phone to the victim to have a conversation about building a safety plan. If the victim refuses to speak to the advocate, the officer advises the victim that they believe they are in danger and that people in similar situations to the victim have been killed by their partner, and they advise the victim of what signs to be aware of that may indicate increasing levels of risk to their safety (Maryland Network Against Domestic Violence, n.d.). Importantly, in a recent Department of Justice assessment of LAP in Oklahoma, Messing et al. (2014) found that the LAP successfully discriminated between victims experiencing near fatal violence incidents within seven months. Use of the LAP was associated with a reduction in future violent victimization, increased use of protective actions on behalf of the victims, and greater satisfaction with the police (Messing et al., 2014). An evaluation of the program in Connecticut reported that investigating officers felt that the program helped them to "reach people [they] wouldn't have reached before," they were "more tuned into signs of potentially volatile situations," the program was "not a lot of work on the … front end for the police officers" and "would, if it hasn't already, save somebody's life," and that their relationships with community service agencies were strengthened (Dutton, 2015). However, to date, no police agency in Canada has adopted this protocol.

Information sharing challenges

A third ongoing challenge to effectively and efficiently preventing and responding to IPV are the challenges with information sharing between agencies managing the same clients. Information sharing is necessary for the successful mitigation of escalating risk of domestic violence, as without comprehensive and contextualized risk factors, agencies cannot fully protect women at risk of IPV.

One persistent barrier to successful information sharing is generated by the type of victims' services, and the corresponding rules around disclosure of information. According to Allen (2014), approximately one-third (36 percent) of Canadian victim services are police-based, and nearly one-quarter (24 percent) are offered by non-profit organizations in the community. This distinction is important because it affects disclosure rules around information that would be useful in assessing risk and engaging in safety planning. Essentially, whereas police-based victim services share information with their unit, disclosure rules prevent community-based victim services from sharing with police agencies, unless the victim requests or approves that the information is shared or, in the case of British Columbia, the case meets the highest risk designation. As previously discussed, the development of integrated networks, such as I-TRAC in Alberta and ICATs in British Columbia, have begun to reduce these information gaps, at least in cases involving high-risk offenders.

A second major barrier to information sharing is the inconsistent response offered by criminal (domestic violence) and civil (family matters) court decisions. In addition to threats of violence, women experiencing IPV may also be managing ongoing custody or separation agreements (Ursel, 2012). Often, these systems are unaware of any simultaneous proceedings (FPT Ad hoc Working Group on Family Violence, 2013). In fact, a review of the cases proceeding through the Integrated Domestic Violence Court in Toronto observed that one in ten family cases also experienced a criminal proceeding concerning domestic violence (FPT Ad hoc Working Group on Family Violence, 2013). Given the lack of awareness of each court system from the other, orders handed down by these respective courts may be in violation of each other, such as a supervised access agreement in family court and a no-contact order from criminal court, which can result in confusion regarding the priority of different or competing orders, or could contribute to an increased risk for victimization (FPT Ad hoc Working Group on Family Violence, 2013).

As noted, at least one court in Canada (Toronto, Ontario) has adopted an integrated model that seeks to simultaneously manage criminal and civil cases involving the same family, and the federal Department of Justice published a report entitled *Making the Links in Family Violence Cases: Collaboration among the Family, Child Protection and Criminal Justice Systems* (FPT Ad hoc Working Group on Family Violence, 2013). Thus, there does appear to be some positive movement toward developing more effective integrated legal responses to domestic violence.

Conclusion

Canada has made significant strides in the recognition of IPV as a social issue that affects all members of society. There are many innovative practices occurring across the provinces and territories, including ICATs in British Columbia, coordinated risk assessments in Alberta, domestic violence death review committees in Ontario, and a variety of domestic violence courts across Canada that offer both early intervention to low risk offenders and severe criminal justice system responses to higher risk offenders.

However, there are still several areas where Canada can improve its coordination to respond to IPV, and still much that can be done to prevent it from happening in the first instance. In some communities, IPV has become a normalized occurrence (Ministry of Children and Family Development, 2014) where patriarchal notions about a woman's roles and values dominate the shared community beliefs. Canada must undertake greater efforts to raise awareness about the damage caused by VAW, specifically to the women exposed to it, but also indirectly to broader society, and must do more to convey to its citizens that VAW will not be tolerated. Canada also needs to develop more integrated systems and consistent policies and practices. At the very least, developing a national framework from which to approach these issues would be a major first step towards developing efficient and effective prevention of VAW.

Notes

1 The others are Quebec, Nunavut, and Prince Edward Island. Of note, the program in Newfoundland and Labrador ended in 2013 due to a lack of funding (Ministry of Justice, 2014).

2 Go to http://mnadv.org/_mnadvWeb/wp-content/uploads/2011/10/LAP_Info_Packet–as_of_12–8-10.pdf for a copy of the screen.

References

Alberta Justice and Solicitor General & Alberta Crown Prosecution Service. (2014). *Domestic violence handbook for police and Crown prosecutors in Alberta*. Retrieved January 2016 from https://justice.alberta.ca/programs_services/families/documents/domesticviolencehandbook.pdf

Alberta Law Enforcement Response Teams. (2014). *2013–2014 ALERT annual report.* Retrieved January 2016 from http://issuu.com/alert_ab/docs/2013-14_alert_annual_report_-_final/1

Alberta Solicitor General, Calgary Rocky View Child and Family Services, & Home-Front. (2002). *Interagency Domestic Violence Protocol.* Retrieved March 2015 from http://homefrontcalgary.com/main/assets/files/Microsoft%20Word%20-%20Proba-tion%20-%20Child%20Welfare%20-%20HomeFront%20Protocol.pdf

Allen, M. (2014). *Victim services in Canada, 2011/12.* Ottawa, ON: Statistics Canada.

Ammar, N., Couture-Carron, A., Alvi, S., & San Antonio, J. (2014). Experiences of Muslim and non-Muslim battered immigrant women with the police in the United States: A closer understanding of the commonalities and differences. *Violence Against Women, 19*(12), 1449–1471.

Apsler, R., Cummins, M.R., & Carl, S. (2003). Perceptions of the police by female victims of domestic partner violence. *Violence Against Women, 9*(11), 1318–1335.

Baobid, M. (2002). *Access to woman abuse services by Arab-speaking Muslim women in London, Ontario: Background investigation and recommendations for further research and community outreach.* London, Ontario: Centre for Research on Violence Against Women and Children.

Beattie, K. (2005). Spousal homicides. In K. AuCoin (Ed.), *Family violence in Canada: A statistical profile 2005* (pp. 48–51). Ottawa, CA: Minister of Industry.

Beaupré, P. (2015). *Cases in adult criminal courts involving intimate partner violence.* Ottawa, CA: Statistics Canada.

Bhuyan, R., Osborne, B., Zahraei, S., & Tarshis, S. (2014). *Unprotected, unrecognized: Canadian immigration policy and violence against women, 2008–2013.* Migrant Mothers Project. Retrieved January 2016 from www.migrantmothersproject.com/wp-content/uploads/2012/10/MMP-Policy-Report-Final-Nov-14-2014.pdf

Birnbaum, R., Bala, N., & Jaffe, P. (2014). Establishing Canada's first integrated domestic violence court: Exploring process, outcomes, and lessons learned. *Canadian Journal of Family Law, 29*, 117–171.

Bonomi, A.E., Holt, V.L., Martin, D.P., & Thompson, R.S. (2006). Severity of intimate partner violence occurrence and frequency of police calls. *Journal of Interpersonal Violence, 21*, 1354–1364.

Bopp, M., Bopp, J., & Lane, P. (2003). *Aboriginal domestic violence in Canada.* The Aboriginal Healing Foundation.

Brennan, S. (2011a). Self-reported spousal violence, 2009. In *Family Violence in Canada: A Statistical Profile* (pp. 8–19). Ottawa, ON: Minister of Industry. Retrieved May 2015 from www.statcan.gc.ca/pub/85-224-x/85-224-x2010000-eng.pdf

Brennan, S. (2011b). Violence victimization of Aboriginal women in the Canadian provinces, 2009. *Juristat.* Catalogue no. 85–002-X. Ottawa: Statistics Canada. Retrieved May 2015 from www.statcan.gc.ca/pub/85-002-x/2011001/article/11439-eng.pdf

Brewster, M.P. (2001). Legal help-seeking experiences of former intimate-stalking victims. *Criminal Justice Policy Review, 12*, 91–112.

British Columbia Coroner's Service. (2012). *Intimate partner violence in British Columbia, 2003–2011.* Victoria, BC: Ministry of Justice. Retrieved July 2015 from www.pssg.gov.bc.ca/coroners/reports/docs/stats-domestic-violence.pdf

Campbell, M. (2010). *Threat assessment and risk management in domestic violence cases: An overview of Ontario justice and community collaboration for 2010 and future directions.* Centre for Research & Education on Violence against Women and Children.

Campbell, J.C., Glass, N., Sharps, P., Laughon, K., & Bloom, T. (2007). Intimate partner homicide: Review and implications of research and policy. *Trauma, Violence & Abuse, 8*(3), 246–269.

Canadian Network of Women's Shelters and Transition Houses. (2013). *The case for a National Action Plan on violence against women.* Retrieved January 2016 from http://endvaw.ca/wp-content/uploads/2015/10/The-Case-for-a-National-Action-Plan-on-VAW.pdf

Chambers, S.D. (1998). *An analysis of trends concerning violence against women: A preliminary case study of Vancouver.* Vancouver: Feminist Research, Education, Development and Action Centre (FREDA). Retrieved March 2015 from http://fredacentre.com/wp-content/uploads/2010/09/Chambers-1998.pdf

Courts of Saskatchewan. (n.d.). *Domestic violence court.* Retrieved March 2015 from www.sasklawcourts.ca/index.php/home/provincial-court/adult-criminal-court/domestic-court

Dauvergne, M. (2005). Homicide in Canada, 2004. *Juristat, 25*(6). Catalogue no. 85–002-XPE. Ottawa: Statistics Canada.

Department of Justice Canada. (2013). *Making the links in family violence cases: Collaboration among the family, child protection and criminal justice systems: Volume 1.* Retrieved January 2016 from www.justice.gc.ca/eng/rp-pr/cj-jp/fv-vf/mlfvc-elcvf/vol.2/p16.html

Dosanjh, R., Deo, S., & Sidhu, S. (1994). *Spousal abuse in the South Asian community.* Vancouver, India Mahila Association. Retrieved March 2015 from http://fredacentre.com/wp-content/uploads/2010/09/Dosanjh-et-al-1994.pdf

Dutton, L.B. (2015). *Evaluation of the Lethality Assessment Program.* Presented at the Academy of Criminal Justice Sciences, March 2015, Orlando, Florida.

Dutton, M.A., Goodman, L.A., & Bennett, L. (1999). Court-involved battered women's responses to violence: The role of psychological, physical, and sexual abuse. *Violence and Victims, 14*, 89–104.

El-Khoury, M., Dutton, M.A., Goodman, L.A., Engel, L., Belamaric, R.J., & Murphy, M. (2004). Ethnic differences in battered women's formal help-seeking strategies: A focus on health, mental health, and spirituality. *Cultural Diversity and Ethnic Minority Psychology, 10*(4), 383–393.

Ending Violence Association of BC. (n.d.). *Interagency case assessment team best practices: Working together to reduce the risk of domestic violence.*

Epstein, D. (1999). Effective intervention in domestic violence cases: Rethinking the roles of prosecutors, judges, and the court system. *Yale Journal of Law and Feminism, 11*, 3–50.

Federal-Provincial-Territorial (FPT) Ad hoc Working Group on Family Violence. (2013). *Making the links in family violence cases: Collaboration among the family, child protection and criminal justice systems.* Department of Justice Canada.

Gannon, M., & Mihorean, K. (2005). Sentencing outcomes: A comparison of family violence and non-family violence cases. *JustResearch, 12*, 42–51.

Gillis, J.R., Diamond, S., Jebely, P., Orekhovsky, V., Ostovich, E., MacIsaac, K., Sagrati, S., & Mandell, D. (2006). Systematic obstacles to battered women's participation in the judicial system: When will the status quo change? *Violence Against Women, 12*, 1150–1168.

Grasely, C., Stickney, J., Harris, R., Hutchinson, G., Greaves, L., & Boyd, T. (1999). *Assessing the integrated model of services for abused women: The consumers' perspective.* London, Ontario: Centre for Research on Violence Against Women and Children. Retrieved March 2015 from www.learningtoendabuse.ca/sites/default/files/pub_grasely1999.pdf

Hannah-Moffat, K. (1995). To charge or not to charge: Frontline officers' perceptions of mandatory charge policies. In M. Valverde, L. MacLeod, & K. Johnson (Eds.), *Wife assault and the Canadian criminal justice system* (pp. 35–46). Toronto, Canada: University of Toronto, Centre of Criminology. Cited in: Gillis, J.R., Diamond, S.L., Jebely, P., Orekhovsky, V., Ostovich, E.M., MacIsaac, K., Sagrati, S., & Mandell, D. (2006). Systematic obstacles to battered women's participation in the judicial system. When will the status quo change? *Violence Against Women, 12,* 1150–1168.

Jackson, M. & Martinson, D. (2015). *Risk of future harm: Family violence and information sharing between family and criminal courts.* Discussion Paper for the Canadian Observatory on the Justice System Responses to Intimate Partner Violence.

Jaffe, P., Dawson, M., & Campbell, M. (n.d.). *Multi-disciplinary perspectives on preventing domestic homicides: A discussion paper from a Canadian think-tank.*

Jaffe, P., Dawson, M., & Campbell, M. (2011). *Lessons learned from domestic violence tragedies: Emerging research, policies & practices to prevent domestic homicides.* Centre for Research & Education on Violence against Women and Children.

Jiwani, Y., & Buhagiar, L. (1997). *Policing violence against women in relationships: An examination of police response to violence against women in British Columbia, Executive summary.* FREDA Centre for Research on Violence Against Women and Children. Retrieved March 2015 from http://fredacentre.com/wp-content/uploads/2010/09/Jiwan-and-Buhagiar-1997.pdf

Kowalski, M. (2006). Spousal homicides. In L. Ogrodnik (Ed.), *Family violence in Canada: A statistical profile 2006* (pp. 52–57). Catalogue no. 85–224-XIE. Ottawa: Statistics Canada.

Lane, E., Greenspan, R., & Weisburd, D. (2004). The Second Responders Program: A coordinated police and social service response to domestic violence. In B. Fisher (Ed.), *Violence against women and family violence: Developments in research, practice and policy* (pp. III-2–1–III-2–11). Washington, DC: National Institute of Justice. NIJ number: 199701. Retrieved March 2015 from https://www.ncjrs.gov/pdffiles1/nij/199701.pdf

MacLeod, L., & Shin, M.Y. (1990). *Isolated, afraid, and forgotten: The service delivery needs and realities of immigrant and refugee women who are battered.* Ottawa, ON: National Clearinghouse on Family Violence. Retrieved March 2015 from http://publications.gc.ca/collections/Collection/H72-21-78-1992E.pdf

MacLeod, L., & Shin, M.Y. (1993). *"Like a wingless bird": A tribute to the survival and courage of women who are abused and who speak neither English nor French.* Retrieved March 2015 from http://publications.gc.ca/collections/Collection/H72-21-110-1994E.pdf

Malcoe, H. & Duran, B. (2004). Intimate partner violence and injury in the lives of low-income Native American women. *Violence Against Women and Family Violence: Developments in Research, Practice, and Policy.* Retrieved March 18, 2016 from http://ncjrs.gov

Malm, A., Pollard, N., Brantingham, P., Tinsley, P., Plecas, D., Brantingham, P., Cohen, I., & Kinney, B. (2005a). *A 30 year analysis of police service delivery and costing.* Report prepared for the Royal Canadian Mounted Police. Abbotsford, BC.

Malm, A., Pollard, N., Brantingham, P., Tinsley, P., Plecas, D., Brantingham, P., Cohen, I., & Kinney, B. (2005b). *A 30 year analysis of police service delivery and costing: "E" division.* Report prepared for the "E" Division Royal Canadian Mounted Police. Abbotsford, BC.

Martin, D.L., & Mosher, J.E. (1995). Unkept promises: Experiences of immigrant women with the neo-criminalization of wife abuse. *The Canadian Journal of Women and the Law, 8,* 3–43.

Maryland Network Against Domestic Violence. (n.d.). *Lethality Assessment Program: Maryland model for first responders.* Retrieved March 2015 from http://mnadv.org/_mnadvWeb/wp-content/uploads/2011/10/LAP_Info_Packet-as_of_12-8-10.pdf

McDonald, S., & Cross, P. (2001). Women's voices being heard: Responsive lawyering. *Journal of Law and Social Policy, 16,* 207–239.

McGillivray, A., & Comaskey, B. (1999). *Black eyes all of the time: Intimate violence, Aboriginal women, and the justice system.* Toronto: University of Toronto Press.

Messing, J.T., Campbell, J., Sullivan Wilson, J., Brown, S., Patchell, B., & Shall, C. (2014). *Police departments' use of the Lethality Assessment Program: A quasi-experimental evaluation.* NCJRS. Retrieved March 2015 from https://www.ncjrs.gov/pdffiles1/nij/grants/247456.pdf

Miedema, B., & Wachholz, S. (1998). *A complex web: Access to justice for abused immigrant women in New Brunswick.* Ottawa: Status of Women Canada.

Mihorean, K. (2005). Trends in self-reported spousal violence. In K. AuCoin (Ed.), *Family violence in Canada: A statistical profile, 2005* (pp. 13–32). Catalogue no. 85-224-XIE. Ottawa: Statistics Canada.

Millar, A. (2009). *Inventory of spousal violence risk assessment tools used in Canada.* Retrieved August 2015 from www.learningtoendabuse.ca/sites/default/files/Inventory%20of%20spousal%20violence%20risk%20assessment%20tools%20used%20in%20Canada.pdf

Millar, A., Code, R., & Ha, L. (2013). *Inventory of spousal violence risk assessment tools used in Canada: Updated 2013.* Department of Justice Canada. Retrieved August 2015 from www.section15.gc.ca/eng/rp-pr/cj-jp/fv-ff/rr09_7/rr09_7.pdf

Ministry of Children and Family Development. (2014). *Best practices approaches: Child protection and violence against women.* British Columbia.

Ministry of Justice. (2014). *Framework for domestic violence courts in British Columbia.* Retrieved January 2016 from www.pssg.gov.bc.ca/victimservices/shareddocs/dv-courts-framework.pdf

Ministry of Public Safety and Solicitor General, Ministry of Attorney General, & Ministry of Children and Family Development. (2010). *Violence against women in relationships policy.* British Columbia.

Moyer, S., Rettinger, J., & Hotton, T. (2000). *The evaluation of the domestic violence courts: Their functioning and effects in the first eighteen months of operation, 1998–1999.* A report to the Ministry of the Attorney General of Ontario, Toronto: Moyer and Associates. Cited in: L. Tutty, K.Wyllie, P. Abbott, J. Mackenzie, E.J. Ursel, & J.M. Koshan, (2008). *The justice response to domestic violence: A literature review.* Retrieved March 2015 from http://homefrontcalgary.com/main/assets/files/Justice%20Response%20to%20Domestic%20Violence%20Literature%202008.pdf

Native Women's Association of Canada. (1994). *Aboriginal women: Police charging policies and domestic violence.* Retrieved March 2015 from www.nwac-hq.org/reports/Police%20Charging%20Policies%20&%20Domestic%20Violence.pdf

Ogrodnik, L. (2006). Spousal violence and repeat police contact. In L. Ogrodnik (Ed.), *Family violence in Canada: A statistical profile 2006* (pp. 11–18). Catalogue no. 85–224-XIE. Ottawa: Statistics Canada.

Ontario Domestic Violence Death Review Committee. (2008). *Annual report to the Chief Coroner.* Toronto, ON: Office of the Chief Coroner.

Patterson, J. (2003). Spousal violence. In H. Johnson & K. AuCoin (Eds.), *Family violence in Canada: A statistical profile* (pp. 4–7). Catalogue no. 85–224-XIE. Ottawa: Statistics Canada.

Provincial Office of Domestic Violence. (2014). *British Columbia's Provincial Domestic Violence Plan.* Victoria, BC: BC Ministry of Children and Family Development.

Representative for Children and Youth. (2009). *Honouring Christian Lee. No private matter: Protecting children living with domestic violence.* Office of the Representative for Children and Youth.

Representative for Children and Youth. (2012). *Honouring Kaitlynne, Max and Cordon. Make their voices heard now.* Office of the Representative for Children and Youth.

Rossiter, K. (2011). *Domestic violence prevention and reduction in British Columbia (2000–2010).* The FREDA Centre for Research on Violence Against Women and Children.

Royal Commission on Aboriginal Peoples. (1996). *Looking forward, looking back: Report of the Royal Commission on Aboriginal Peoples, Volume 1.* Ottawa, ON: Communication Group Publishing.

Russell, D., & Ginn, D. (2001). *Framework for Action Against Family Violence.* Nova Scotia: Department of Justice. Retrieved March 2015 from https://novascotia.ca/just/publications/docs/russell/toc.htm

Sharpe, D. (2011). *Alberta Integrated Threat & Risk Assessment Centre (I-TRAC).* Retrieved January 2016 from www.victimsweek.gc.ca/symp-colloque/past-passe/2011/presentation/pdfs/Dellrae_Sharpe_eng.pdf

Sinha, M. (2012). Family violence in Canada: A statistical profile 2010. Ottawa, ON: Minister of Industry. Retrieved May 2015 from www.statcan.gc.ca/pub/85-002-x/2012001/article/11643-eng.pdf

Sinha, M. (2013). Measuring violence against women: Statistical trends. *Juristat.* Statistics Canada Catalogue no. 85–002-X. Ottawa: Statistics Canada.

Statistics Canada. (2011). Immigration and ethnocultural diversity. Government of Canada. Retrieved January 2016 from www12.statcan.gc.ca/nhs-enm/2011/as-sa/99-010-x/99-010-x2011001-eng.pdf

Stephens, J., & Sinden, P.G. (2000). Victims' voices: Domestic assault victims' perceptions of police demeanor. *Journal of Interpersonal Violence, 15*, 534–547.

Sweetman, K. (1982, May 13). Male MPs' guffaws at wife beating query enrage female MPs. *The Ottawa Citizen.*

Taylor-Butts, A., & Porter, L. (2011). Family related homicides, 2000 to 2009. In *Family Violence in Canada: A Statistical Profile* (pp. 32–41). Ottawa, ON: Minister of Industry. Retrieved May 2015 from www.statcan.gc.ca/pub/85-224-x/85-224-x2010000-eng.pdf

Tjaden, P. & Theonnes, N. (2000). Full report of the prevalence, incidence, and consequences against women: Findings from the national violence against women survey. Washington, DC: National Institute of Justice. Retrieved March 19, 2016 from *www.ncbi.nlm.nih.gov*

Trainor, K. (Ed.). (2002). *Family violence in Canada: A statistical profile.* Catalogue no. 85–224. Ottawa: Statistics Canada.

Tutty, L., Koshan, J., Jesso, D., Ogden, C., & Warrell, J.G. (2011). *Evaluation of the Calgary Specialized Domestic Violence Trial Court & monitoring the First Appearance Court: Final Report.* Retrieved January 2015 from www.ucalgary.ca

Tutty, L.M., & Ursel, E.J. (2008). Chapter Three: The court response to domestic violence. In L. Tutty, K. Wyllie, P. Abbott, J. Mackenzie, E.J. Ursel, & J.M. Koshan (Eds.), *The justice response to domestic violence: A literature review.* Retrieved March 2015 from http://homefrontcalgary.com/main/assets/files/Justice%20Response%20to%20Domestic%20Violence%20Literature%202008.pdf

Uekert, B.K., Miller, N., DuPree, C., Spence, D., & Archer, C. (2001). *Evaluation of the STOP Violence Against Women Grant Program: Law enforcement and prosecution components.* Alexandria, Virginia: Institute for Law and Justice. Retrieved March 2015 from https://www.ncjrs.gov/pdffiles1/nij/grants/189163.pdf

United Nations, General Assembly. (1993). *Declaration on the Elimination of Violence against Women.* A/RES/48/104.

Ursel, J. (2012). Chapter 7: Domestic violence and problem-solving courts. In K. Ismaili, J.B. Sprott, & K. Varma (Eds.), *Canadian criminal justice policy: Contemporary perspectives* (pp. 160–181). Oxford University Press.

Weisz, A.N., Canales-Portalatin, D., & Nahan, N. (2004). An evaluation of victim advocacy within a team approach. In B. Fisher (Ed.), *Violence against women and family violence: Developments in research, practice and policy* (pp. III-3-1-III-3-8). Washington, DC: National Institute of Justice. NIJ Number: 199701. Retrieved March 2015 from https://www.ncjrs.gov/pdffiles1/nij/199701.pdf

Whetstone, T.S. (2001). Measuring the impact of a Domestic Violence Coordinated Response Team. *Policing: An International Journal of Police Strategies & Management, 24,* 371–398.

Wiist, W.H., & McFarlane, J. (1998). Utilization of police by abused pregnant Hispanic women. *Violence Against Women, 4,* 677–693.

Wolf, M.E., Ly, U., Hobart, M.A., & Kernic, M.A. (2003). Barriers to seeking police help for intimate partner violence. *Journal of Family Violence, 18,* 2, 121–129.

Woodin, H. (2014). *Province unveils domestic violence plan at KPU conference.* Retrieved March 2015 from www.kpu.ca/news/province-unveils-domestic-violence-plan-kpu-conference

Zhang, T., Hoddenbagh, J., McDonald, S., & Scrim, K. (2012). *An estimation of the economic impact of spousal violence in Canada, 2009.* Department of Justice Canada.

2 The prevalence of severe intimate partner violence in Sweden

Susanne Strand and Heidi Selenius

Introduction

Intimate partner violence (IPV) is a serious global problem, which has been highly prioritised in Swedish society, specifically in the last two decades. The aim of this chapter is to investigate the prevalence of severe intimate partner violence against female victims reported to the police in Sweden.

Sweden is geographically located in Northern Europe; it is a fairly large country with a total landmass of 407,310 square kilometres. In 2015, the population of Sweden was 9,851,017, meaning that on average there were 24.2 individuals living per square kilometre (62.7 per square mile). This means that most of the country is considered to be rural and remote, with only three larger cities; Stockholm, Malmö and Gothenburg, that are considered to be urban cities. Hence, there are certain difficulties in handling cases of IPV. The report rate of IPV in rural and remote areas has been shown to be lower than in urban areas, and the protective actions, such as shelters, are much more difficult to offer and use in remote areas (Edwards, 2015).

IPV is here defined as one partner committing physical, psychological or sexual violence towards their partner. In Sweden the lifetime occurence rate of IPV is about 25.5 per cent for women and 16.8 per cent for men (Frenzel, 2014), compared to the lifetime occurrence rate for female victims of IPV in other countries in Europe and North America that have been found to be about 30 per cent (Garcia-Moreno et al., 2013). In the official Swedish report from 2014, conducted by the Swedish National Council for Crime Prevention (BRÅ), gender of the perpetrator is not separated, which means that the prevalence of same-sex IPV cannot be seen specifically, it is, however, included in the prevalence reported above. The most common IPV is with a male perpetrator towards a female victim. Although IPV is important to investigate in all relationships this chapter will focus on severe IPV committed by a male perpetrator towards a female victim in Sweden.

Definitions

This is a descriptive study conducted by reviewing the official offence statistics of Sweden. The majority of the statistics are from yearly statistics and reports, presented by the Swedish Crime Prevention Authority (BRÅ). The definitions of reported assaults and reported gross violation of a woman's integrity for this study is the offences reported to the police, being committed by a male perpetrator towards his female partner. The convictions are defined as those reported offences that have been sentenced in a court of law. Due to the fact that there is some time between the date of the report of the offence and the date of conviction, the numbers are not a specific follow-up for the specific case per se, it is rather overall statistics at group level. In practice this means that the convictions for 2009 may reflect some reported offences in 2008 and that the reported offences in 2014 have not been followed up entirely, due to still being in the criminal justice system. There are some limitations with using the reported statistics to measure IPV; the most difficult limitation that affects the validity of the data is that many victims do not report the offences to the police at all. For example, in 2012 7.9 per cent of victims of IPV reported that they had some kind of contact with the police, but only 3.9 per cent of them reported an offence (Frenzel, 2014). According to the national surveys on safety conducted every year in Sweden, there is an estimate that about 30 per cent of victims of IPV report the offences to the police (BRÅ, 2014). When investigating the reported offences of IPV one must have in mind that there are few victims who actually report IPV to the police and that the overall prevalence of IPV can be much higher.

Although severe violence is more frequently reported to the police than less severe violence, that could be due to its severity and the physical injuries that come with severe violence. Others, like extended family, friends, work colleagues, etc., report IPV to the police as well, and the police need to investigate the report. For severe IPV, where there has been an injury that required medical attention, there is an obligation for the healthcare facilities to report that to the police. Also social services have an obligation to report IPV to the police. This means that to follow up the severe violence by investigating the reported offences can be an indication of the awareness of the problem in society, which means that the problem can be dealt with to a larger extent.

The socio ecological model

The motives for the perpetrators and explanations of IPV can be said to be many; there is not a single cause and effect that can be said to fully explain this global problem. Heise (1998) has shown in her work with the socio ecological model as a theory of IPV, that IPV can be explained by integrating several aspects of a modern society. The socio ecological model shows that IPV can be understood by evaluating the individual perpetrator, the relationship, the community, and the society where the IPV is committed, and how these separate areas influence the perpetrators to commit IPV in different degrees. The perpetrator exercises his power over the victim and will by that method reach his goals to control her, and he will find support for his actions within the ecological framework. Different areas will be of different importance for the perpetrators where the ecological model gives an overall explanation of its complexity.

The normalisation process

One question that is often asked is 'why does a woman live together with an abusive and harassing man?' According to the normalisation process of violence by Lundgren (2012) such a question is irrelevant for women subjected to intimate partner violence, because their understanding of violence is redefined. Women subjected to violence may be well educated, and have social support from an extensive social network of friends and family, as well as not. They are gradually isolated both physically and psychologically by the perpetrator, and their only contact with people is with their partner. The man controls the woman in every aspect; how she should behave, what she may say, think, feel, and whom she meets. The violence emerges in the isolation and the man emotionally controls the woman. In the beginning the woman thinks the violent acts against her are unacceptable, but over time the boundaries between love and violence are eradicated, and the woman as a person is gradually blotted out. Besides being violent, the man is also loving and soothing after the abuse. Lundgren explains that the woman believes violence against her is a part of the loving acts, and something she both deserves and needs in order to be a better mother, partner as well as friend. In addition, the woman believes that she is the cause of the violence, because she thinks she is misbehaving, not pleasing the man, or not conforming to his desires. Her self-confidence and self-appraisal fades away, and the man has total control over her. Besides the control, the man can use the violence to get sexually aroused, and the physical violence can therefore also shift into sexual violence. Neither the woman nor the man identifies himself or herself as an abused or as an abuser. Consequently, the normalisation process might explain why some men who repeatedly abuse their partner are not reported to the police.

The only way out of this negative spiral is for the woman to seek help from others or that she realizes that the abuse might escalate into lethal violence or that her children are in danger. It is at this point she is most likely to leave an abusive man. In line with the normalisation process, women threatened and abused by an intimate partner are at an elevated risk of being victimised by more severe violence in the future (Kropp, Hart & Belfrage, 2010). Swedish research has shown that as many as 40 per cent of the women being killed by their partner or ex-partner have reported IPV to the police before their murder (Rying, 2007). It is of great importance to investigate the prevalence of IPV, specifically the more severe forms, in order to be better at managing the risk for further IPV.

Physical assault

In a Swedish survey of being a victim of IPV in 2012, lifetime prevalence of IPV was also surveyed (Frenzel, 2014). In this survey the physical, psychological and sexual offences towards the victim were investigated. The results showed that lifetime prevalence of physical violence was 15.0 per cent, when divided into categories 13.1 per cent reported less severe violence, 6.2 per cent reported severe physical violence, 5.1 per cent reported sexual offences, and 3.6 per cent reported severe sexual offences. Psychological violence was reported for 23.5 per cent of the victims. Divided into categories; 19.1 per cent reported violations, 11.1 per cent reported attempts to restrain the freedom of the victim, 12.2 per cent reported threats and 7.8 per cent reported harassment. In this survey 59.8 per cent reported that they had been the victim of more than one type of offence.

Between 2009 and 2014 the amount of assaults towards a female intimate partner were increasing from 11,605 reports in 2009 to 13,413 in 2014 (see Figure 2.1). Transformed into numbers of assault per 100,000 inhabitants, that increased from 125 assaults per 100,000 to 139 during the same time period. The majority of the perpetrators of assaults towards a female intimate partner were older than 21 years, which were almost the same during the time period (92.8 per cent–94.0 per cent). The reported perpetrators were suspected of committing several assaults towards their partners, which can be seen in Figure 2.1. The number of suspects increased slightly from 2,450 in 2009 to 2,961 in 2014. The clearance rate for assaults towards a female intimate partner was reported to be between 16 per cent and 23 per cent during 2009 to 2014.

The law 'gross violation of a woman's integrity'

In 1998 gross violation of a woman's integrity was included in the Swedish Penal Code. The law is applied when a woman's self-confidence is severely damaged due to repeated and systematic abuse as well as violation by her former or current partner. The acts cover assaults, threats, deprivation of liberty, coercions, sexual assaults or other molestations, as well as rape. Additionally, in 2013 offences

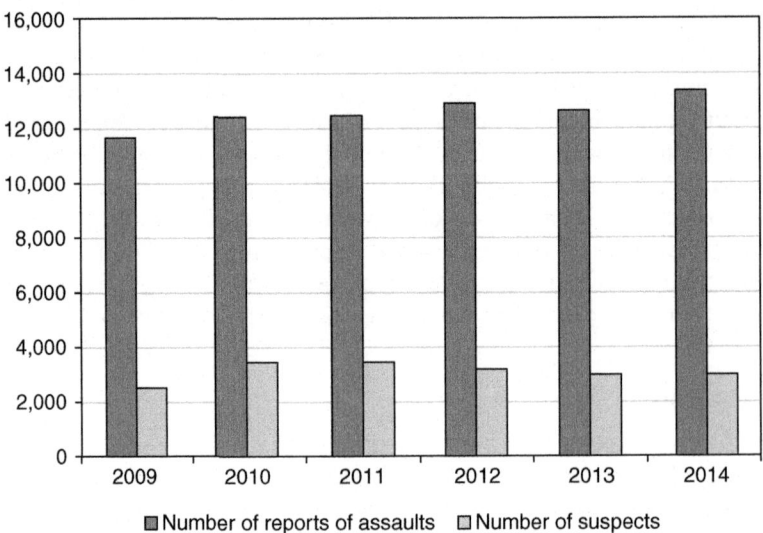

■ Number of reports of assaults   □ Number of suspects

Figure 2.1 Total number of reported assaults towards a female intimate partner and the number of suspects during 2009–2014.

inflicting damage and violation of restraining orders were included in the law. One offence against a partner not often considered serious enough for a prison sentence, but a row of offences against a woman by a current or former intimate partner is regarded as *one* serious offence, and it is, normally, punished with imprisonment. The law specifically addresses the issue that the woman has been normalised into the violence and that the violence is damaging the self-confidence of the woman.

Some women will talk about the repeated and systematic violence in police interviews and thereby the report of crime will be for gross violation of a woman's integrity, while some will have an initial police report of assault that, due to more information becoming available from the investigation, later will be reclassified as gross violation of a woman's integrity, meaning that the report of assault actually ends up being a prosecution of gross violation of a woman's integrity. When investigating the reports of this offence it is important to understand that there might be more cases of reports of this specific crime than can be seen when only using the report of the offences.

The Swedish government has decided to punish repeated and systematic abuse more severely than individual actions and, therefore, the gross violation of a woman's integrity was included in the Swedish Penal Code with a possibility for the court to sentence the convicted perpetrators to longer time in prison than the single offence might do. Offenders who are found guilty of this offence should be sentenced to between two and six years of imprisonment.

Gross violation of a woman's integrity is an offence of public prosecution in Sweden, which means that people other than the violated woman can report the violence to the police, so that the abusive man can be charged and sentenced. The police can start to investigate the offences without the approval of the woman, however, it is difficult for the police to provide evidence for prosecution without her participation in the investigation (Marklund & Nilsson, 2008). Some of the women report the violence to the police and will later withdraw the report, although it cannot be withdrawn since it is once reported and then the prosecutor will continue the investigation of the case and take it to court. The reasons women give for withdrawing their report can be many, such as, they say that 'he is usually not like this', or 'it was actually my fault, I started it', or 'I don't want him to go to prison, I just want it to end'. For example, when they are in an acute phase of IPV and need help from the police they will report the offence, and then withdraw the report when the police come to their assistance due to being afraid of the perpetrator and not wanting him to go to prison. This is a typical behaviour when victims of IPV are being normalised to the violence; when the acute danger is no longer present they feel sorry for the perpetrator instead of leaving him.

Yearly, on average 2,145 perpetrators have been reported for gross violation of a woman's integrity since the law was enacted in 1999 until 2014 (Range: 1,147–2,733), with a peak of reports in 2008 of 2,733 cases. During the first five years there was a steady increase of reported offences due to the implementation of the law. The conviction rate was, however, rather low, ranging from 5.1 per cent to 14.4 per cent, with an average of 11.1 per cent. However, if the perpetrator is not convicted for the offence of gross violation of a woman's integrity,

he can be convicted of any of the offences reported as the foundation of the prosecution, i.e. they can be sentenced for assault, harassment, unlawful threats etc.
(The Swedish National Council for Crime Prevention, n.d.).

In Figure 2.2 it can be seen that the number of reports of gross violation of a
woman's integrity decreased by 24.9 per cent from 2,657 cases reported in 2009
to 1,997 reported offences in 2014. The clearance rate for gross violation of a
woman's integrity has also decreased, from 27 per cent in 2009 to 18 per cent in
2014. A decrease can be seen for the convictions as well, where the conviction
rate decreased from 12.2 per cent in 2009 to 9.2 per cent in 2014.

Since 2009 the Swedish Crime Prevention Authority has yearly reported the
prevalence of assaults towards women committed by their partners. When comparing the development of the number of reported offences of assaults, it
increased by 5.3 per cent from 132 assaults per 100,000 inhabitants in 2009 to
139 in 2014, while the reported offences of gross violation of a woman's integrity decreased during the same time period, with 22.2 per cent from 27 reported
offences per 100,000 inhabitants to 21 (see Figure 2.3).

In Sweden the minimum punishment for assault is two years and the
maximum sanction is 10 years of imprisonment, and for gross violation of a
woman's integrity it varies between a minimum of two years to a maximum of
six years of imprisonment. For murder and manslaughter it is 18 years. Lifetime
imprisonment can be applied as a punishment for murder in cases with specific
conditions. Of those offenders convicted for gross violation of a woman's integrity during 2009–2014 most of them have been sentenced to imprisonment

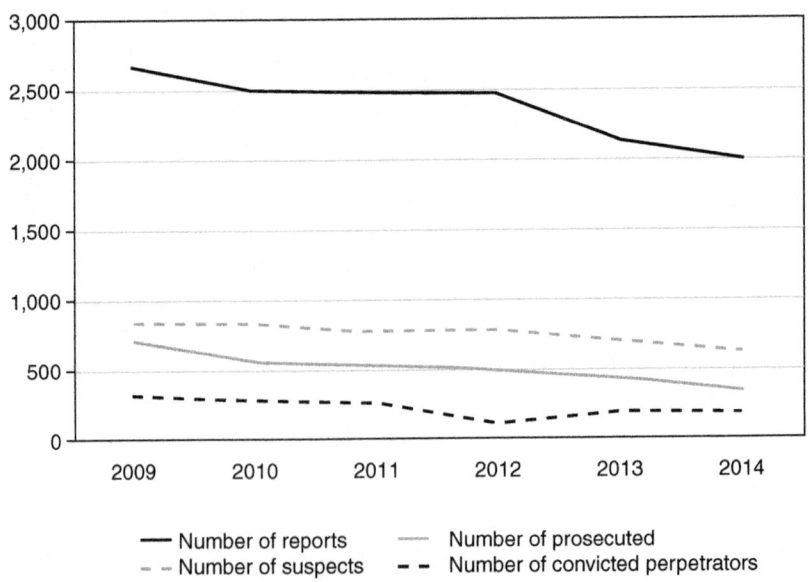

Figure 2.2 Number of reports, suspects, prosecuted and convicted offenders of gross
violation of a woman's integrity in Sweden during 2009–2014.

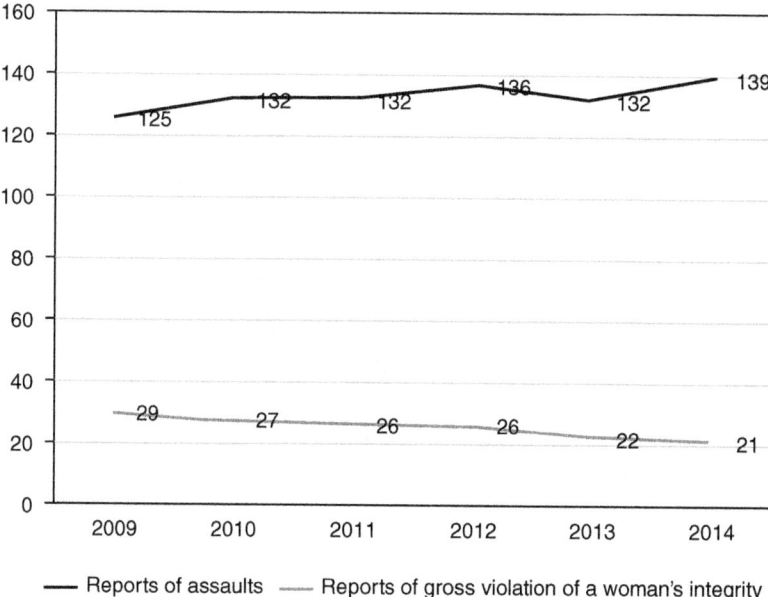

Figure 2.3 Number of reports of assaults and gross violation of a woman's integrity per 100,000 inhabitants in Sweden during 2009–2014.

(72–79 per cent prison, 0–3 per cent forensic psychiatric care), with an average prison sentence of 10–11 months. Some offenders have been sentenced to less than one month of prison, whereas others have been sentenced to four years of prison. Besides imprisonment, there are also offenders sentenced to probation (see Figure 2.4). A small number of offenders have also been sentenced to juvenile secure care, fines, or received a conditional sentence. Furthermore there are also a handful of offenders with abstention from prosecution.

Stalking

Stalking is a course of conduct in which one individual repeatedly intrudes upon another, causing fear or distress. The European studies to date have reported a lifetime prevalence of about 10 per cent in Germany, Sweden, and Austria (Dressing, Kuehner & Gass, 2005; Dovelius & Öberg, 2006; Stieger, Burger & Schild, 2008), which is lower than the 15–20 per cent prevalence in the UK and Australia (Budd et al., 2000; ABS, 2006). About 50–60 per cent of the stalkers are stalking a former partner. Stalking is a form of psychological terror that affects the victim severely. The perpetrator harasses the victim and can make their lives very difficult. Victims of stalking following a relationship where IPV was present, have explained that the fear of not knowing what the stalker, her

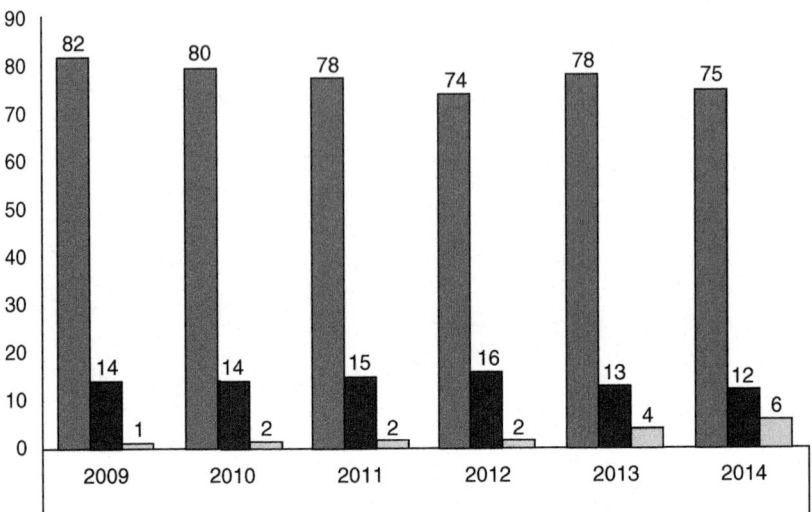

Figure 2.4 Frequency of offenders punished with imprisonment and probation due to gross violation of a woman's integrity during 2009–2014.

former partner, is going to do and when terrifies her more than living with him when she had some control over the situation. Some victims change their lives to such an extent that they tend to isolate themselves; they also show symptoms of post-traumatic stress. This is an offence of IPV that affects the victims severely, and it needs to be better understood in order to better help the victims (Kamphuis, Emmelkamp & Bartak, 2003).

In North America and Australia the first stalking laws were enacted in the early 1990s, while the European countries were to follow in the years to come. The Swedish stalking law was enacted on 1 October 2011, and followed the same outline as for the offence of gross violation of a woman's integrity. One of the aims with the stalking law was that cases of IPV that did not fulfil the criteria for gross violation of a woman's integrity or gross violation of a person's integrity could be handled within this new stalking law. An evaluation of the stalking law in Sweden for the first two years, 2012 and 2013, showed that 1,696 cases were reported and 263 cases were prosecuted, which is about 16 per cent of the reported cases. One hundred and twenty seven were convicted of stalking, which is 48.3 per cent of the prosecuted cases but only 7.5 per cent of the reported cases. About half (48.0 per cent) of the convictions were related to an ex-partner, where 70 per cent of the convicted ex-partners had a no-contact order issued upon them (Jerre, 2015).

Lethal violence

Lethal IPV is in Sweden defined as either: murder, manslaughter, or involuntary manslaughter. The prevalence of convicted perpetrators of lethal IPV towards a female victim during 1990–2004 was a total of 193 women, which was about 17 women per year. That was one woman being killed by her partner or former partner every third week. In 40 per cent ($N = 97$) of the cases, violence had been reported to the police prior to the deaths, and in 46 per cent ($N = 112$) of the cases prior threats were reported. All of these offenders were sentenced to imprisonment; 135 (70 per cent) were sentenced to prison, of which 32 (23 per cent) were sentenced to life imprisonment, and 58 (30 per cent) were sentenced to forensic psychiatric care (Rying, 2007).

A specific report on lethal violence in Sweden for the time period 1999–2014 showed that there has been a decrease of intimate partner murders, from being 17 a year for a rather long time, to 13 a year for the time period 2008–2013 (Granath, 2015). This 24 per cent decrease was mainly for victims in the ages of 30–49 years old and who lived outside the urban areas. In Sweden 21.7 per cent of the murders committed in Sweden in 2002–2013 were towards an intimate partner.

Repeated victimisation

International research has found recidivism of IPV to range from 15 per cent in a Spanish study (Loinaz, 2014) to 28 per cent in a US study (Goldstein, Cantos, Brenner, Verborg & Kosson, 2015). The recidivism of IPV was reported to be over 40 per cent, measured as repeated victimisation reported to the police over a time period of up to four years, in a study of IPV perpetrators in Stockholm (Belfrage & Strand, 2012). In Figure 2.5 the official statistics from Sweden show

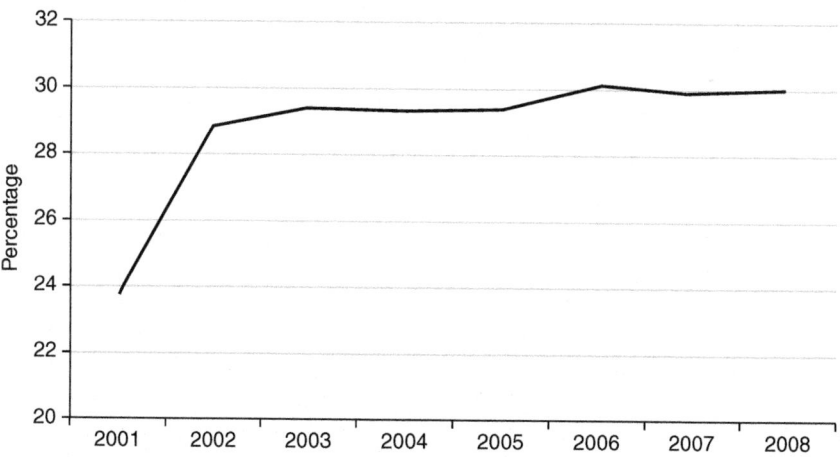

Figure 2.5 Percentage of reported recidivism of IPV within 12 months of the first report during 2001–2008.

that on average 28.9 per cent of women who reported that an intimate partner had committed an offence towards them reported a new offence within a 12-month period after the first report (Jönsson, 2010). The offences investigated were murder, attempted murder, assault, sexual offences, gross violation of a woman's integrity, harassment and unlawful threats.

Another important step that has been undertaken during the last decade to prevent revictimisation of IPV was the implementation of structured professional risk assessment procedures as a method for the police to assess the risk for future IPV, when IPV is reported to the police. This implementation has increased the police awareness of the importance of risk management in IPV cases in order to prevent recidivism. The Swedish National Police Board (2010) has recommended the police to perform risk analysis and risk assessments as part of their work to prevent future IPV. The Brief Spousal Assault Form for the Evaluation of Risk (B-SAFER; Kropp, Hart & Belfrage, 2010) is supposed to be used for cases of IPV where risk assessments are needed, and in 2014 the Swedish National Police Board stated that the B-SAFER should be used in all cases of reported IPV (Swedish National Police Board, 2014). The risk factors in the B-SAFER are regarded to be central in order to prevent future IPV. The violence risk assessment procedure includes the following steps: (1) gathering and analysing information in the case; (2) assessing the presence of the risk factors and the victim vulnerability factors; (3) using the results as the foundation of which the overall risk is assessed; and (4) making a risk management plan for the victim.

In order to reduce recidivism the performed violence risk assessment needs to be followed by a risk management plan, including what protective actions should be used for the victim. Research has shown that the Swedish police have been helped by the process of risk assessment to identify and match the level of risk to the level of risk management recommended, resulting in reduced recidivism (Belfrage, Strand, Storey, Kropp & Hart, 2012; Belfrage & Strand, 2012). The protective actions the police can use to manage the risk are, for instance, having a security talk with the victim, suggesting a restraining order, moving the victim to a shelter, getting an alarm package, contacting social services, helping the victim to get an attorney to represent them in court etc. The Swedish police have a victim support officer that is a contact person for the victim and will follow up on the outcome of the protective actions taken. A report on following up the work the police have been conducting to prevent IPV showed that, the better the police work with victim support, the more likely the victim was to report new offences of IPV (Jönsson, 2010). It is, however, very difficult to evaluate how effective the risk management is by only investigating new reported offences as a measurement of recidivism. The victim might, for many different reasons, not report the IPV if it happens again. A better measurement of revictimisation of IPV is to conduct interviews with the victims on any actions of IPV, reported or not reported, for at least one year after reporting the offences to the police. However, a result of using reported offences as a measurement of revictimisation is that it will be a measurement of the lower end of the scale of recidivism; it is not less than the reported numbers, it is more. When reported revictimisation is about 30 per cent, that is an indication that society needs to do much more in order to protect the women; the protective actions taken were not enough to prevent further IPV.

Conclusion

There has been a slight increase of reporting severe IPV over the last years in Sweden. The most common reported offence of severe IPV is assault, which increased by 15.6 per cent, while the offence of gross violation of a woman's integrity, which was one of the least common reported offences besides murder, decreased by 22.2 per cent. There is no evidence that concludes that there is an overall increase of IPV in Sweden; the statistics reveal more that the level is the same but that the hidden numbers are decreasing, and reporting IPV is increasing. This is encouraging, since by reporting the offences to the police, women being abused by their partner can get help to handle their situation. It is an indication that the confidence in the police to help is increasing. It is then of utmost importance that the police have the resources to follow up on the increase in the reports so that women can be helped in their situation. If there is a lack of resources and women who report IPV to the police do not get help, there might be a decrease of reports and women will then be on their own to handle their situation. The risk for revictimisation might increase without society knowing about it and then the help women can get would be more on a voluntary basis, like the women's shelter. When women seek help to handle their situation of IPV, society must step in and help them as much as possible. They need all the help and support we can give them in order to break the normalisation of the violence so that they can continue their lives without an abusive partner.

The most severe violence, murder, has decreased from 17 to 13 cases a year, which is very good. What this decrease is due to is difficult to say. But the police have worked more systematically with assessing risk for severe IPV, and one study has shown that the resources the police have had to protect victims of IPV had been used for the identified high-risk cases with very good results for those cases (Belfrage & Strand, 2012). It is, however, very difficult to investigate the outcome of preventive work in such a complex area. The police also work closely with social services and the women's shelter, which means that more resources are used from different parts of society. During the last decade IPV has been debated heavily in the media and IPV is today considered to a large extent to be more of a problem on society level, instead of being a problem on individual level, which is all in line with the socio ecological model by Heise. This debate has hopefully increased the legitimacy for authorities like the police and the social services for the victims, and might have influenced them to trust that they will get some help if they report the offences.

Overall, the police do a good job to protect and prevent IPV, although there is still a long way to go to reduce the high rate of reported revictimisation of 30 per cent. By working more systematically and using the tools and methods available they are on the right path. To be able to follow up on the repeated victimisation the police need to have more regular contact with the victim for a longer time after the reports of the IPV. This could be in line with the more systematic work that needs to be conducted by the police in order to reduce recidivism of IPV. Considering the high likelihood that the victim might be normalised and not able to break the vicious circle by herself, she needs a contact person who keeps in touch with her on a regular basis. That will give her the security that she needs to leave the abuser. The victim support officers within the police are doing this to some extent, but the lack of resources and personnel are some of the reasons why the police do not do this to a full extent. The Swedish police have the routines and the skilled police officers to do this work, but there are not enough personnel and there is a lack of resources to work with.

Sweden consists to a large extent of rural and remote areas. This means that the police need to be creative to find solutions for risk management that are not available in urban areas, as well as needing more police officers working with these questions. The distances can be very far, meaning that if an incident is reported it might take hours before the police arrive at the scene of the offence. Due to this, police officers have to prioritise acute situations before the preventive work, and it might simply not be possible to follow up in other ways than calling the victim on the phone. By having a closer cooperation with other authorities like the social services in the most remote areas this can be a way to handle the follow-up of the IPV. But then more resources are needed for the work to help victims of IPV.

Since the statistics of the severe forms of IPV show a slight increase of reports, there is a possibility that we must work even harder to protect those who report the offences and that resources must be increased for this work. If the resources increase it will be a signal to those 70 per cent of victims of IPV who are not reporting the offences that society will help them if they report. This will hopefully increase the reports, which should be seen as a sign of trust and confidence for the Swedish police rather than an increase of IPV.

According to the socio ecological method, the level of community and society have an influence on the occurrence of IPV, and by increasing resources and developing methods to prevent IPV will hopefully decrease IPV and make the work against IPV much more successful. More resources are therefore needed for the police and the social services, which to a large extent have the responsibility for risk management of victims of IPV. Extra resources specifically for preventing IPV have been given to authorities before with good results, but there are still not enough. A large increase of resources would be a good statement from society to say that any form of IPV will not be tolerated and it must be a prioritised area to work with prevention, in order to reduce the revictimisation of IPV.

References

Australian Bureau of Statistics (ABS). (2006). *Personal safety survey Australia 2005*.
Belfrage, H., & Strand, S. (2012). Measuring the outcome of structured spousal violence risk assessments using the B-SAFER: Risk in relation to recidivism and intervention. *Behavioral Sciences and the Law 30*(4), 420–430. DOI: 10.1002/bsl.2019

Belfrage, H., Strand, S., Storey, J.E., Gibas, A.L., Kropp, R., & Hart, S.D. (2012). Assessment and management of risk for intimate partner violence by police officers using the spousal risk assessment guide (SARA). *Law and Human Behavior. 36*(1), 60–67. DOI: 10.1037/h0093948

Brottsförebyggande rådet, (2014). Nationell Trygghets Undersökning, NTU 2013. *Om utsatthet, trygghet och förtroende. BRÅ Rapport 2014:1.* Stockholm: Swedish National Council for Crime Prevention.

Budd, T., Mattinson, J., Myhill, A., & Home Office Research, Development and Statistics Directorate. (2000). *The extent and nature of stalking: Findings from the 1998 British crime survey.* London: Home Office Research study 210.

Dovelius, A.M., & Öberg, J. (2006). *Stalkning i Sverige Omfattning och åtgärder. BRÅ Rapport 2006:3.* Stockholm: Swedish National Council for Crime Prevention.

Dressing, H., Kuehner, C., & Gass, P. (2005). Lifetime prevalence and impact of stalking in a European population. Epidemiological data from a middle-sized German city. *British Journal of Psychiatry 187*, 168–172.

Edwards, K.M. (2015). Intimate partner violence and the rural–urban–suburban divide: Myth or reality? A critical review of the literature. *Trauma, violence, & abuse. 16*(3), 359–373. DOI: 10.1177/1524838014557289

Frenzel, A. (2014). *Brott i nära relation. En nationell kartläggning. BRÅ-report 2014:8.* Stockholm: Swedish National Council for Crime Prevention.

Garcia-Moreno, C., Pallitto, C., Devries, K., Stöckl, H., Watts, C., Abrahams, N., & Petzold, M. (2013). *Global and regional estimates of violence against women: Prevalence and health effects of intimate partner violence and non-partner sexual violence.* Geneve: World Health Organization.

Goldstein, D.A., Cantos, A.L., Brenner, L.H., Verborg, R.J., & Kosson, D.S. (2015). Perpetrator type moderates the relationship between severity of intimate partner violence and recidivism. *Criminal Justice and Behavior.* Advance online publication. DOI: 10.1177/0093854815616841

Granath, S. (2015). *Det dödliga våldet i Sverige 1990–2014. En beskrivning av utvecklingen med särskilt fokus på skjutvapenvåldet. BRÅ Rapport 2015:24.* Stockholm: Swedish National Council for Crime Prevention.

Heise, L.L. (1998). Violence against women: An integrated, ecological framework. *Violence Against Women, 3*(4), 262–290.

Jerre, K. (2015). *Olaga förföljelse .Tillämpningen av den nya straffbestämmelsen. Rapport 2015:2.* Stockholm: Swedish National Council for Crime Prevention.

Jönsson, L. (2010). *Upprepad utsatthet för våld. Polisens och socialtjänstens arbete i nio län BRÅ Rapport 2010:19.* Stockholm: Swedish National Council for Crime Prevention.

Kamphuis, J.H., Emmelkamp, M.G., & Bartak, A. (2003). Individual differences in post-traumatic stress following post-intimate stalking: Stalking severity and psychosocial variables. *The British Journal of Clinical Psychology, 42*, 145–156.

Kropp, P.R., Hart, S.D., & Belfrage, H. (2010). *Brief spousal assault form for the evaluation of risk (B-SAFER), version 2: User manual.* Vancouver, Canada: ProActive ReSolutions Inc.

Loinaz, I. (2014). Typologies, risk and recidivism in partner-violent men with the B-SAFER: A pilot study. *Psychology, Crime & Law, 20*(4), 183–198.

Lundgren, E. (2012). *Våldets normaliseringsprocess och andra våldsförståelser.* Växjö: Riksorganisationen för kvinnojourer och tjejjourer i Sverige (ROKS).

Marklund, F., & Nilsson, A. (2008). *Polisens utredningar av våld mot kvinnor i nära relationer* [Police investigations of violence against women in intimate relationships]. *BRÅ Report 2008:25.* Stockholm: Swedish National Council for Crime Prevention.

Rying, M. (2007). *Utvecklingen av dödligt våld mot kvinnor i nära relationer. BRÅ Rapport 2007:6.* Stockholm: Swedish National Council for Crime Prevention.

Stieger, S., Burger, C., & Schild, A. (2008). Lifetime prevalence and impact of stalking: Epidemiological data from Eastern Austria. *The European Journal of Psychiatry,* *22*(4), 235–241.

Swedish National Police Board. (2010). *Riktlinjer för polisiära riskanalyser vid våld på individnivå [Guidelines for policing risk analysis to violence at the individual level].* Stockholm: Swedish National Police Board.

Swedish National Police Board. (2014). *Uppföljande inspektion av polismyndigheternas hantering av rutiner vid bl.a. riskanalyser. Tillsynsrapport 2014:9. [Follow-up inspection of police authorities handling procedures e.g. risk analyses. Supervision Report 2014:9.]* Stockholm: Swedish National Police Board.

The Swedish National Council for Crime Prevention. (n.d.). (Brottsförebyggande rådet, BRÅ). Website: www.bra.se/bra/bra-in-english/home.html

3 Responding to domestic abuse in England and Wales

Stephanie L. Reardon and Kylee Trevillion

On behalf of Limeculture Community Interest Company

Introduction

This chapter focuses on domestic abuse in England and Wales, looking specifically at how it is defined, the scale of the problem, and some of the civil and criminal remedies that are available for victims. This chapter also looks at the criminal justice, health and inter-agency responses to domestic abuse in England and Wales.

While the United Kingdom consists of four countries (England, Scotland, Wales, and Northern Ireland), the latter three have devolved administrations, each with varying powers. The UK Government's policy on domestic abuse is predominantly the responsibility of the Home Office, a Ministerial Department that focuses on policing. The remit of the Home Office is England and Wales only. Domestic abuse in Scotland and Northern Ireland are dealt with by their own devolved administrations.

Definition of domestic abuse

Currently, there is no universally agreed definition of domestic abuse. As a consequence, many countries across the globe have established different terminologies and legal frameworks to define this form of abuse. In March 2013 the Home Office introduced an extended definition of domestic abuse, to be used across government, in recognition of the practical limitations of the existing definition. The new UK definition captures the multi-dimensional nature of domestic abuse, which involves both physical and non-physical forms of abuse. It encompasses, but is not limited to, psychological, physical, sexual, financial and emotional abuse (Home Office, 2013a). The definition makes specific reference to 'controlling' behaviours, which are defined as acts to make a person subordinate and/or dependent through forms of isolation, exploitation, deprivation and close regulation of behaviour. It describes 'coercive' behaviours, which are defined as an act or a pattern of acts of assault, threats, humiliation and intimidation or other abuse that is used to harm, punish, or frighten (Home Office, 2013a). Stalking behaviours – defined as repeated and malicious following, harassment or threats – are also incorporated within the new working definition. The revised definition also lowers the age criteria from 18 years to 16 years – in response to increasing evidence of a high prevalence of violence among young adults (Smith, Osborne, Lau & Britton, 2012; Stöckl, March, Pallitto & Garcia-Moreno, 2014).

The UK definition is one of the few to include violence perpetrated by intimate partners and by adult family members (i.e. mothers, fathers, sons, daughters, brothers, sisters and grand-parents; those directly related or in-laws or step-families). It also acknowledges that domestic abuse is rarely a single incident (Dutton, 2007; Stark, 2007; Howard, Feder & Agnew-Davies, 2013a). Indeed, the intimate relationship between the perpetrator and recipient means that the violence is often more frequent and severe than other forms of victimisation (Kropp, Hart & Belfrage, 2005).

Scale of the problem in England and Wales

In common with all other countries around the world, it is impossible to know the true scale of domestic abuse in England and Wales. This is due to the nature of the abuse, which is surrounded in secrecy, and the unwillingness of victims for various reasons to come forward to report their abuse. However, while it is widely accepted that domestic abuse in England and Wales is significantly under-reported, police in the UK receive a domestic assistance call every minute (Stanko, 2000; Home Office, 2003). Despite the frequency of calls to the police for assistance, it is estimated that, on average, a woman is assaulted 35 times before her first call to the police (Jaffe & Burris, 1982). Two women are killed every week in England and Wales by a current or former partner (Office for National Statistics, 2015). That is, one woman killed every three days. Evidence from general population surveys in England and Wales indicates that 47 per cent of female homicides and 5 per cent of male homicides are perpetrated by a current partner or ex-partner (Smith et al., 2012).

In November 2009, Sylvia Walby of the University of Leeds estimated the total cost of domestic abuse to be £15.7 billion a year (Walby, 2009). This is broken down as follows:

- The costs to services (Criminal Justice System, health, social services, housing, civil legal) amount to £3.8 billion per year.
- The loss to the economy – where women take time off work due to injuries – is £1.9 billion per year.
- Domestic abuse also leads to pain and suffering that is not counted in the cost of services. The human and emotional costs of domestic abuse amount to almost £10 billion per year.

General population estimates

The most reliable estimates of the extent of domestic abuse in England and Wales come from the Crime Survey for England and Wales (CSEW), formerly the British Crime Survey (BCS). Each year in England and Wales the government commissions a survey of people's experience as victims of crime since the age of 16 and in the past year. Being a household survey, it picks up more crime than the official police figures, as not all crimes are reported to the police, let alone recorded by them. Two sets of figures are available from the CSEW: the first, collected from the survey's inception in 1981, comes from the results of face-to-face interviews; the second, available from 2004/2005, comes from self-completion modules which respondents complete in private by responding to questions on a computer. The new methodology added in 2004/2005 was in response to increasing evidence that disclosure of abuse is much higher for self-completion surveys than researcher-administered modules (Walby and Allen, 2004). The unwillingness of respondents to reveal experiences of domestic abuse to an interviewer means that the face-to-face assessments underestimate the extent of domestic abuse.

In the most recent survey – conducted between April 2014 and March 2015 – a representative sample of 35,000 households were asked to report on their experiences of domestic abuse using both researcher-administered and self-completed questionnaires. The CSEW estimates of domestic abuse are based on a relatively broad definition (which is not the same as the legal definition) covering male and female victims of partner or family non-physical abuse, threats, force, sexual assault or stalking. The latest statistics show that some 8.2 per cent of women and 4 per cent of men are estimated to have experienced domestic abuse in 2014/2015, equivalent to an estimated 1.3 million female and 600,000 male victims. The most common forms of past year abuse are non-sexual partner violence (6 per cent of women and 3 per cent of men) and stalking (5 per cent of women and 2 per cent of men) (Office for National Statistics, 2016).

Data revealed that overall, 27.1 per cent of women and 13.2 per cent of men have experienced some form of domestic abuse since the age of 16. These figures are equivalent to an estimated 4.5 million female victims and 2.2 million male victims between the ages of 16 and 59. Among women, the most frequent types of lifetime experiences of abuse (i.e. since the age of 16 years) are non-sexual partner abuse (20 per cent), stalking (20 per cent) and sexual assault (19 per cent). Among men, the most frequent types of abuse are stalking (10 per cent) and non-sexual partner abuse (9 per cent) (Office for National Statistics, 2016).

The UK Government claims that levels of domestic abuse in England and Wales have generally declined over the past decade. In the year ending March 2005 there were approximately 2.7 million victims compared to just under 2.0 million in the year span 2014/2015. This is a statistically significant reduction of 27 per cent. It should be noted that classification criteria are not consistent year by year, meaning that reports of declining numbers of incidents may not be reliable.

Criminal justice system estimates

Despite the claim that there have been reductions in the levels of domestic abuse in England and Wales, the number of reports to the police has increased. In relation to police data, the CSEW reviewed reports of domestic abuse cases among

43 of the 46 UK police forces. Such incidents are not published within a centrally collated crime series, and are therefore recorded at individual police force level. In February 2016, the Office for National Statistics (ONS) published an analysis of these data and found that the number of cases recorded by police has increased year on year from 2007/2008. In 2014/2015 the number of cases recorded reached 943,628 – this is a 43 per cent increase on 2007/2008 (Office for National Statistics, 2016).

In England and Wales, the Crown Prosecution Service (CPS) is the principal public prosecuting agency for conducting criminal prosecutions. The main responsibility of the CPS is to provide legal advice to the police and other investigative agencies during the course of criminal investigations. It is the CPS role to decide whether a suspect should face criminal charges following an investigation and to conduct prosecutions both in the magistrates' courts and the Crown Court. In 2014/2015, there were 122,898 domestic abuse cases referred to the CPS – an increase of 19 per cent on 2013/2014. Compared to 2008/2009 the number of cases referred to the CPS increased by 53 per cent (Crown Prosecution Service, 2015).

It should be noted that the number of cases referred to the CPS is not the same as the total number of people arrested for the offence. Between arrest and referral to the CPS the police may decide that no crime has been committed or that there is insufficient evidence to proceed. Of the cases referred to the CPS, the decision to charge was made in 68.9 per cent of cases. This is a slight fall in proportion from 2013/2014 when 70.3 per cent were charged. In 2014/2015 a total of 92,779 defendants were prosecuted in England and Wales, an increase of 19 per cent on 2013/2014 and a 38 per cent increase on 2008/2009. The number of offenders successfully convicted in 2014/2015 was 68,601. This represented 73.9 per cent of completed prosecutions – a slight fall on the 74.6 per cent obtained the year before (Woodhouse & Dempsey, 2016). It is important to interpret these findings with caution, however, as only a small proportion of cases are ever reported to the police and findings from the household surveys highlight the levels of under-reporting among those experiencing abuse.

Risk factors and impacts of domestic abuse

Findings from the 2014–2015 Crime Survey for England and Wales (CSEW) highlight that women are at least twice as likely as men to have experienced some form of domestic abuse within the past year and their adult lifetime. With respect to lifetime experiences of sexual assault, findings indicate that women are five times more likely to experience this form of abuse (including attempted assaults) compared to men; 19 per cent versus 4 per cent, respectively. Despite gender differences, it is important to note that men may also experience domestic abuse victimisation and both men and women should have access to appropriate support.

The annual England and Wales crime survey and other UK prevalence studies highlight additional risk factors for domestic abuse, alongside female gender. Women and men of a younger age (i.e. 16 to 24 years of age), women who are separated or divorced, and men and women with a long-term illness, physical disability or mental illness are found to be at increased risk of abuse (Richardson et al., 2002; Jonas et al., 2014; Khalifeh, Howard, Osborn, Moran & Johnson, 2013; Khalifeh, Oram, Trevillion, Johnson & Howard, 2015; Office for National Statistics, 2016). Indeed, recent reviews have found that, across all diagnostic categories, men and women with mental disorders experience a high prevalence and increased likelihood of domestic abuse compared to people without mental disorders (Trevillion, Oram, Feder & Howard, 2012; Bundock et al., 2013; Howard, Oram, Galley, Trevillion & Feder, 2013b). Evidence suggests that a bi-directional relationship exists between domestic violence and mental illness; domestic violence may lead to the development of mental illness and mental illness may increase a person's risk of entering in to unsafe environments and relationships (Howard et al., 2013a).

Domestic abuse is associated with both short- and long-term adverse health consequences, which may be present even after the abuse has ceased. Physical injuries as a direct result of violence are common, with more injuries sustained by women than men (Tjaden, 2000). Numerous mental health problems are associated with domestic abuse and are seen to be exacerbated by the frequency and severity of violence experienced (Golding, 1999; Trevillion et al., 2012; Bundock et al., 2013).

There are no distinct patterns of injury that reliably predict domestic abuse (Boyle, Robinson & Atkinson, 2004) and numerous physical and psychological impacts are reported. One of the most significant predictors is repeated attendance at healthcare services (Fanslow, Norton & Spinola, 1998). People experiencing domestic abuse have increased contact with healthcare services compared with the general population (MacMillan et al., 2006). Research estimates around 41 per cent of people in contact with general practices and at least one in every five people in contact with emergency services have experienced domestic abuse (Feder et al., 2009; Howard, Trevillion & Agnew-Davies, 2010). Furthermore, an estimated 30 per cent of female psychiatric in-patients, 33 per cent of female psychiatric out-patients and 18 per cent of males across a range of psychiatric settings have experienced domestic abuse (Oram, Trevillion, Feder & Howard, 2013).

The most serious health consequence associated with domestic abuse is homicide. Difficulties arise when attempting to measure the extent of domestic abuse homicides, as official records may conceal deaths as accidental or attribute them to unknown causes (World Health Organization, 2002). Consequently, prevalence estimates are likely to underestimate the true extent of domestic abuse related homicides.

Legal remedies

The new criminal offence of coercive or controlling behaviour against an intimate partner or family member, which came into force on 29 December 2015, has a maximum penalty for someone found guilty of five years' imprisonment or a fine, or both (Section 76 Serious Crime Act 2015).

In March 2015, the Home Office published a fact sheet that summarises the legal position prior to the new offence stating that non-violent coercive behaviour, which is a long-term campaign of abuse, may fall outside common assault, which requires the victim to fear the immediate application of unlawful violence (Home Office, 2015b).

Stalking was made a specific criminal offence in England and Wales in November 2012, following amendments to the Protection from Harassment Act 1997. Some patterns of non-violent domestic abuse could be captured by legislation that covers stalking and harassment. However, the law on stalking and harassment does not explicitly apply to coercive and controlling behaviour in intimate relationships. It is not designed to capture the dynamic of sinister exploitation of an intimate relationship to control another, particularly where a relationship is ongoing. The element of control is not such a feature of stalking or harassment, which is generally intended to intimidate or cause fear.

Domestic abuse adds an extra layer to such intimidation, with perpetrators operating under the guise of a close relation or partner to conceal their abuse, safe in the presumption that the victim is likely to want to continue a relationship despite the abuse. For these reasons, domestic abuse may be said to be more subversive than stalking.

The fact sheet said it was important that the new offence did not impact on 'ordinary power dynamics in relationships': as such, the repeated or continuous nature of the behaviour and the ability of a reasonable person to appreciate that the behaviour will have a serious effect on its victim, are key elements of the new offence.

A defence is also included to provide a further safeguard against inappropriate use of the new offence. The defence will be available where the defendant can show that they believed they were acting in the victim's best interests and that their behaviour was objectively reasonable. This defence is intended to cover, for example, circumstances where someone was a caregiver for a mentally ill spouse, who by virtue of their medical condition, had to be kept in the home or compelled to take medication, for their own protection or in their own best interests. In this context, the spouse's behaviour might be considered controlling, but would be reasonable under the circumstances. The defence will not be available in cases where the defendant has caused the victim to fear violence.

There are also a number of other possible criminal offences for which perpetrators can be prosecuted in England and Wales. These can range from murder, rape and manslaughter through to assault and threatening behaviour.

In addition to the remedies provided by the criminal law of England and Wales, there are two important civil law remedies. These fall under the Family Law Act 1996 (as amended by Part 1 of the Domestic Violence, Crime and Victims Act 2004) and are known as 'occupation orders' and 'non-molestation orders'. An 'occupation order' is a court order which governs the occupation of a family home. It can be used to temporarily exclude an abuser from the home and surrounding area and give the victim the right to enter or remain. In certain circumstances, the court may attach a power of arrest to the occupation order.

A 'non-molestation order' is a court order which prohibits an abuser from molesting another person they are associated with. Molestation is not defined in the Act but has been interpreted to include violence, harassment and threatening behaviour. An order contains specific terms as to what conduct is prohibited and can last for however long is deemed appropriate by the court. Breach of a non-molestation order is a criminal offence.

Furthermore, the Protection from Harassment Act 1997 (as amended) provides civil and criminal remedies. These include non-harassment and restraining orders. The UK Government amended the Protection from Harassment Act 1997 in November 2012 to introduce two explicit offences of stalking. Domestic Violence Protection Orders (DVPOs) were rolled out across England and Wales from March 2014. Under the DVPO scheme, the police and magistrates can, in the immediate aftermath of a domestic abuse incident, ban a perpetrator from returning to their home and from having contact with the victim for up to 28 days. The scheme comprises an initial temporary notice (domestic violence protection notice, DVPN), authorised by a senior police officer and issued to the perpetrator by the police, followed by a DVPO that can last from 14 to 28 days, imposed at the magistrates' court. DVPOs are designed to help victims who may otherwise have had to flee their home, giving them the space and time to access support and consider their options (Home Office, 2015a).

DVPOs were piloted in three police force areas in 2011/2012. According to a Home Office evaluation, 'DVPOs were generally seen positively by practitioners and victim-survivors and were associated with a reduction in re-victimisation, particularly when used in "chronic" cases' (Home Office, 2013b). DVPOs were subsequently legislated in the Crime and Security Act 2010.

The Domestic Violence Disclosure Scheme (DVDS), commonly known in the UK as Clare's law, was rolled out across England and Wales from March 2014. The scheme allows anyone with concerns about a relationship to obtain information on previous violence committed by the partner and thus make informed choices about their options ('right to ask'). If police checks show that a person may be at risk of domestic abuse from their partner, the police will consider disclosing the information ('right to know'). There have already been 1,900 disclosures under the scheme (Home Office 2016). The Home Office are planning to publish an evaluation of the DVDS to promote its wider uptake.

The policy context

Government and local authority policies

Current UK government policy around domestic abuse builds on that of the previous Coalition Government (coalition of Conservative and Liberal Democrats: 2010–2015) and in March 2016 a new Violence Against Women and Girls Strategy was published (superseding the 2010 Violence Against Women and Girls Strategy). The new Strategy focuses on prevention of abuse, provision of services, partnership working and pursuing perpetrators. The new Strategy, although including other types of violence against women and girls, has a strong focus on domestic abuse. The new Strategy outlines the actions the UK Government proposes to take over the life of the government (2016–2020), which include work being undertaken by a range of Ministerial Departments including Home Office, Ministry of Justice, Department of Health, and Department for Communities and Local Government. These actions include committing central resources for specific projects and services focusing on domestic abuse, as well as supporting local commissioners to ensure that domestic abuse is embedded in local commissioning arrangements moving forward.

The provision of services for victims of domestic abuse is a matter for local authorities across England and Wales. Women's refuges receive funding from a mixture of sources, including rental income, charitable donations and local government. There has been concern in recent years about the funding of specialist refuges. A September 2014 report by one of the leading domestic abuse charities in the UK, Women's Aid, warned that these were at risk because of funding cuts and changing commissioning practices which did not 'value the specialist nature of services and the expertise of the sector' (Women's Aid, n.d.). In the July 2015 Budget, the Government announced via the Department for Communities and Local Government (DCLG) a £3.2 million fund to boost the provision of services, including refuges, for victims of domestic abuse. Local authorities were able to bid for a share of the fund from 24 August 2015. Details of the successful bidders were announced on 11 December 2015. Women's Aid issued a statement on the same date that welcomed the investment but called on the UK Government to commit to long-term refuge funding. In the November 2015 Spending Review and Autumn Statement the UK Government said it would provide '£40 million for services for victims of domestic abuse, tripling the dedicated funding provided compared to the previous four years and complementing the wider violence against women and girls' strategy'. In addition, until the UK Government negotiates an end to Value Added Tax (VAT) on sanitary products (imposed by the European Union and known as the 'Tampon Tax'), they have committed to provide £15 million a year to support a range of women's charities. Receipts from VAT on sanitary products have already been used to provide a £2 million donation to Women's Aid and Safelives, two national domestic abuse charities, to work with specialist organisations to improve early responses and ultimately help to save the lives of abused women and children.

The Convention on preventing and combating violence against women and domestic abuse (the 'Istanbul Convention') was adopted in April 2011. The Council of Europe website explains what the Convention means for state parties:

Governments that agree to be bound by the Convention will have to do the following:

- train professionals in close contact with victims;
- regularly run awareness-raising campaigns;

- take steps to include issues such as gender equality and non- violent conflict resolution in interpersonal relationships in teaching material;
- set up treatment programmes for perpetrators of domestic abuse and for sex offenders;
- work closely with NGOs; and
- involve the media and the private sector in eradicating gender stereo-types and promoting mutual respect.

Amnesty International has urged governments across Europe to ratify the Convention, and although 20 states have ratified the Convention so far, the UK has not. Although the UK signed the Convention in June 2012, it has been criticised for not subsequently ratifying it ('Istanbul Convention', 2015).

In a February 2016 parliamentary response, the UK Government said the following about ratification:

> this Government remains committed to ratifying it but have made it clear that we will not do so until we are absolutely satisfied that we fully comply with all articles but amendments to domestic law, to take extra-territorial jurisdiction over a range of offences (as required by Article 44), are necessary before the Convention can be ratified.
>
> (Parliamentary Question, 2016)

The Ministry of Justice is currently considering the approach to implementing the extra-territorial jurisdiction requirements in England and Wales and will seek to legislate when the approach is agreed and parliamentary time allows. The Ministry of Justice will be consulting Ministers in the devolved administrations formally about whether legislative changes on extra-territorial jurisdiction in England and Wales should extend to Scotland and Northern Ireland.

The Convention applies to the whole of the UK so any changes necessary to the criminal law in Scotland and Northern Ireland prior to ratification are matters for the devolved administrations.

Healthcare policies

In light of the increased risk of harm to women and infants, maternity services have been one of the foremost National Health Service (NHS) services to develop clear strategies to respond to domestic abuse. In 2000 the Royal College of Nursing (RCN) developed guidance on domestic abuse, which called for nurses to receive appropriate education and training on violence and abuse and to have a good working knowledge of sources of referral for women disclosing abuse (Royal College of Nursing, 2000). Then in 2003 the RCN established the Women's Mental Health Group, with the aim of promoting and supporting gender-sensitive mental-health nursing, and one of the group's key recommendations was that women receive support from staff who are competent in identifying signs of abuse and who have the ability to assess and prioritise patients' safety. Maternity services across England and Wales now implement routine enquiry about domestic abuse at antenatal booking appointments. All women registering their pregnancy with NHS maternity services are asked by midwives whether they have experienced domestic abuse.

To support NHS staff with routine enquiries, in 2005 the Department of Health developed clear guidelines on how to ask sensitively about domestic abuse (e.g. not asking women in the presence of others) and how to respond to disclosures (e.g. making referrals to domestic abuse services) (Department of Health, 2005). At present, however, many health professionals still do not routinely ask about domestic abuse as they are unsure of how to adequately support people who make a disclosure (Bailey, 2010; Rose et al., 2011). In response, the Department of Health commissioned an independent organisation – the National Institute for Health and Clinical Excellence (NICE) – to provide frontline agencies with detailed guidance on how to respond adequately to domestic abuse.

The National Institute for Health and Clinical Excellence (NICE) was established in 1999 by the UK Government and its aim is to determine which treatments should be available on the NHS. A separate body has been established to address the needs of NHS users in Wales – the All Wales Medicines Strategy Group – and this group generally follows the decisions of NICE. Scotland and Northern Ireland have separate organisations to make such decisions. The role of NICE is to assess new treatments as they become available and to provide evidence-based guidelines on how particular conditions should be treated and how health and social care services should best support people. It is a requirement of NHS Trusts to implement NICE decisions and the Trusts have to find the money to make the treatments available; it is not the role of NICE to provide financial support or commissioning strategies. In 2014 NICE developed detailed guidance on how local authority, health and social care services should identify and respond to domestic abuse. Following a review of the evidence base and current service responses, NICE developed the Domestic Violence and Abuse: Multi-Agency Working guidelines (National Institute for Health and Clinical Excellence, 2014). These guidelines ask NHS Trusts, social care services, commissioners and domestic abuse service providers in England to address domestic abuse in the following ways:

- For service providers to work with their strategic partners, and people who have experienced abuse, to develop a joint-strategy needs assessment in addressing domestic abuse, and to undertake a comprehensive mapping exercise to identify the extent of and any gaps in local area service provision.
- For commissioners to establish a commissioning strategy to ensure there are integrated care referral pathways and treatments for those who experience and perpetrate domestic abuse.
- For health and social care managers to create an environment that is conducive to disclosure of domestic abuse (e.g. through awareness-raising exercises, by creating private spaces for service users to disclose abuse, by

ensuring staff are knowledgeable about domestic abuse policies and procedures and are trained in identifying and referring cases of abuse).

- For service providers to deliver specialist advice and advocacy services to service users affected by domestic abuse – tailored to an individual's level of risk and need – and to improve access to services among people that find it difficult to use (e.g. people with disabilities, those from Black and minority ethnic groups, LGBT groups).
- For providers of services that support children and young people to identify and refer those who are affected by domestic abuse and to ensure specialist services are commissioned to support their needs.

During the development of the NICE guidelines, it was established that UK professionals in the health and social care sectors currently receive limited education and training on domestic abuse. Therefore, the NICE recommendations are that these professionals receive domestic abuse training on a rolling basis, which takes into account the turnover of staff and the need for top-up training to improve knowledge and competencies. The guidance calls for training on domestic abuse to also be incorporated within undergraduate or pre-qualifying criteria among health and social care professionals.

One of the key recommendations of the NICE guidance is that health and social care services develop clear care pathways for identifying, referring (whether internally or externally) and providing treatment to people experiencing and perpetrating abuse. These pathways should include robust mechanisms for the assessment of risk to those experiencing abuse and any children who may be affected. The care pathways should also include evidence-based treatments for people who have mental disorders, as they are a group at increased risk of harm. Commissioners of services are also encouraged to fund the evaluation of interventions for people who perpetrate abuse, as the current evidence base is sparse.

Criminal justice system responses

While it is clear that the responsibility to tackle domestic abuse in England and Wales does not rest solely with the police, it is clear that the police have an essential role to play in preventing, reducing and enforcing crime and, of course, keeping victims safe. In September 2013, the Home Secretary commissioned Her Majesty's Inspectorate of Constabularies (HMIC) to conduct a thorough inspection on the police response to domestic abuse.

HMIC were asked to:

- report on the effectiveness of the police approach to domestic abuse and abuse, focusing on the outcomes for victims and whether risks to victims of domestic abuse and abuse are adequately managed;
- identify lessons learned from how the police approach domestic abuse and abuse; and

- make recommendations in relation to these findings when considered along-side current practice.

To answer these questions, HMIC collected data and reviewed files from the 43 police forces across England and Wales. They spoke to 70 victims of domestic abuse who took part in focus groups throughout England and Wales (and a number of other victims in one-to-one interviews) and surveyed over 500 victims on-line. HMIC also surveyed nearly 200 professionals working with victims of domestic abuse.

HMIC inspected all police forces in England and Wales, interviewing senior and operational leads, and held focus groups with frontline staff and partners. They carried out visits to police stations (which were unannounced) to test the reality of the forces' approaches with frontline officers.

The report of HMIC's findings, 'Everyone's business: Improving the police response to domestic abuse' (Her Majesty's Inspectorate of Constabularies, 2014) found that, while most forces and police and crime commissioners have said that domestic abuse is a priority for their areas, this is not being translated into an operational reality. HMIC was concerned to find that, despite the progress made in this area over the last decade, not all police leaders are ensuring that domestic abuse is a priority in their forces – it is often a poor relation to other policing activity.

The main findings from the HMIC inspection found that,

> the overall police response to victims of domestic abuse is not good enough. This is despite considerable improvements in the service over the last decade, and the commitment and dedication of many able police officers and police staff. In too many forces there are weaknesses in the service provided to victims; some of these are serious and this means that victims are put at unnecessary risk. Many forces need to take action now. Domestic abuse is a priority on paper but, in the majority of forces, not in practice. Almost all police and crime commissioners have identified domestic abuse as a priority in their Police and Crime Plans. All forces told us that it is a priority for them. This stated intent is not translating into operational reality in most forces. Tackling domestic abuse too often remains a poor relation to acquisitive crime and serious organised crime.
>
> (Her Majesty's Inspectorate of Constabularies, 2014)

HMIC found that the factors that contribute to this in many forces are:

- a lack of visible leadership and clear direction set by senior officers;
- alarming and unacceptable weaknesses in some core policing activity, in particular the collection of evidence by officers at the scene of domestic abuse incidents;
- poor management and supervision that fails to reinforce the right behaviours, attitudes and actions of officers;

- failure to prioritise action that will tackle domestic abuse when setting the priorities for the day-to-day activity of frontline officers and assigning their work;
- officers lacking the skills and knowledge necessary to engage confidently and competently with victims of domestic abuse; and
- extremely limited systematic feedback from victims about their experience of the police response.

HMIC recommended that

> Police forces must take urgent action to improve the effectiveness of the service they offer to victims of domestic abuse; if they do this they will ensure that the risk to victims is better managed and, ultimately, they are made safer.
>
> (Her Majesty's Inspectorate of Constabularies, 2014)

Health service responses

Current practice responses

Clinicians are ideally placed to identify and respond to domestic abuse, as people experiencing domestic abuse report a greater willingness to disclose abuse to health professionals than the police (Yearnshire, 1997). However, UK health services have been criticised for failing to respond adequately to domestic abuse (Taket et al., 2003). Evidence suggests that clinicians rarely enquire about abuse and service users are reluctant to disclose such experiences in the absence of direct questioning (Howard et al., 2010; Rose et al., 2011). Barriers to enquiry among clinicians include a lack of confidence and expertise in dealing with domestic abuse, fears about offending patients and workload priorities (Rose et al., 2011; Trevillion et al., 2014). Barriers to disclosure of domestic abuse among service users include fear of further violence if the perpetrator becomes aware of the disclosure, shame and embarrassment, and fear that children may be removed from their care (Feder, Hutson, Ramsay & Taket, 2006; Rose et al., 2011).

Evidence-based treatments

There have been few high-quality evaluations of domestic abuse interventions in UK health settings to date. Early findings suggest that multi-faceted interventions, which include domestic abuse education for clinicians and clear care referral pathways for service users disclosing abuse, can improve health service responses to domestic abuse.

A recent UK cluster-randomised controlled trial of 48 general practices examined the effectiveness of a programme to increase identification of women experiencing domestic abuse and to improve referral to domestic abuse advocacy services (Feder et al., 2009). The 51 practices were randomised to either receive the programme ($n = 24$) or to a waiting list control group ($n = 24$) (i.e. to continue with their usual practice responses and to be offered the training once the trial is completed). The multi-component programme consisted of two 2-hour training sessions delivered by an advocate educator and a trained health professional on how to identify and support women disclosing abuse and how to refer them to advocacy services. This was followed by quarterly to half-yearly attendance by the advocate educator at practice meetings, the feeding back of anonymised clinical data about disclosure and referral to advocacy services and regular contact with practice staff to reinforce good practice guidance on domestic abuse. The 24 practices receiving the intervention were also asked to identify a study champion who would receive an additional 8 hours of training about domestic abuse, which they could integrate within the work of the practice. These teams were also provided with a prompt within electronic medical records to enquire about domestic abuse if patients presented with symptoms associated with abuse, and materials to raise awareness about domestic abuse within clinical areas. The primary outcome of this trial was the number of referrals to the domestic abuse advocacy services, measured from the 12 months preceding the intervention to the 12 months after the second training session was delivered. The trial found that there was a three-fold increase in clinicians' identification of domestic abuse and a six-fold increase in rates of referral to advocacy services among those practices that received the programme compared to those that were in the wait-list control (Feder et al., 2009).

Within mental healthcare settings, a recent study evaluated the effectiveness of a domestic abuse intervention involving reciprocal training between mental health and domestic abuse services, and a direct referral pathway to domestic abuse advocacy for psychiatric service users (Trevillion et al., 2014). This study was implemented with five community mental health teams, with three receiving the intervention and two continuing with usual care practice. The intervention consisted of:

- four hours of domestic abuse training for health professionals on how to identify and respond to domestic abuse experienced by women and men;
- six hours of mental health training for domestic abuse advisors (seconded to the study to provide support for mental health service users disclosing abuse in the intervention group);
- a domestic abuse manual for health professionals (incorporating good clinical practice and a list of domestic abuse support services);
- an information campaign on domestic abuse in clinical areas; and
- a direct referral pathway to the domestic abuse advocates for service users that disclosed abuse.

Among the teams receiving the intervention, mental health professionals reported improvements in their knowledge, attitudes and behaviours towards domestic abuse, and service users reported significant reductions in their experiences of abuse as well as significant improvements in their quality of life and social inclusion (Trevillion et al., 2014). These findings were not replicated among the teams that continued with usual care practice.

These initial findings from healthcare interventions suggest joint working practices between mental health and domestic abuse services can effectively support both the mental health and trauma needs of psychiatric service users experiencing victim. Further examples of inter-agency practices in England and Wales are outlined below.

Inter-agency responses

In England and Wales, it is now widely recognised that no single agency has the responsibility for tackling domestic abuse and that a multi-agency response is required. Therefore, over the last decade there has been a clear move towards working together and a clear acceptance that working in partnership is required to keep victims safe. Examples of joint-agency collaborations in the UK include Multi-Agency Risk Assessment Conferences (MARACs) and Independent Domestic Abuse Advisor (IDVA) services, as outlined below.

Multi-agency risk assessment conferences

Multi-Agency Risk Assessment Conferences (MARACs) were first introduced in England and Wales in April 2003. MARACs are meetings attended by a range of services including the police, Children and Family Social Services and health and housing representatives. There are approximately 250 MARACs currently operating in England and Wales, with the majority of meetings occurring at least monthly (Home Office Violent and Youth Crime Prevention Unit and Research and Analysis Unit, 2011). Between 2014 and 2015, 284 MARACs supported 80,151 cases in total. MARACs aim to improve the safety of people who are experiencing domestic abuse and are at high risk of harm, by developing coordinated action plans, between statutory and voluntary sector organisations (Pickles & Robinson, 2007). The aim of MARAC conferences is to:

- Increase the safety, health and well-being of victims and their children through inter-agency information sharing.
- Determine whether significant risks are posed by the perpetrator.
- Provide professional support to all those at risk and reduce repeat victimisation through development of coordinated safety plans.
- Offer specialist support to the victim which is independent of the criminal justice system through the Independent Domestic Violence Advisor role.
- Improve inter-agency accountability.

MARACs have been shown to improve outcomes for people experiencing domestic abuse, including increasing safety and reducing re-victimisation (Home Office Violent and Youth Crime Prevention Unit and Research and Analysis Unit,

2011; Howarth, Stimpson, Barran & Robinson, 2009; Robinson, 2004). These findings are particularly notable given the extensive histories of harm and repeated violence experienced among people referred to MARACs. In addition, MARACs are found to enhance multi-agency working partnerships and assist organisations in identifying and addressing knowledge gaps (Howarth et al., 2009).

A cost-benefit analysis of MARACs identified that for every £1 spent on MARACs, at least £6 of public money can be saved annually on direct costs to agencies such as the police and health services. This would save £740 million to the public purse (Co-ordinated Action Against Domestic Abuse (CAADA), 2010).

Independent Domestic Violence Advisors/Advocates

Increasing evidence on the effectiveness of advocacy services in improving outcomes for people experiencing domestic abuse (Wathen & MacMillan, 2003) has influenced the development of specialist Independent Domestic Violence Advisors (IDVAs) in England and Wales. IDVAs were introduced in the 2005 government Domestic Abuse National Action Plan, with a commitment to implement IDVAs in all specialist Domestic Abuse Courts (Home Office, 2005). Since 2006 the UK Government has invested over £14 million in the funding of IDVA posts and IDVA training (Home Office, 2009).

IDVAs are para-professionals that are trained to provide assistance and advice to people experiencing domestic abuse. They work closely with criminal justice and statutory agencies to coordinate a range of services to meet the needs of people experiencing abuse (Robinson, 2009). They are based in many different settings, including within third-sector domestic abuse agencies, health and criminal justice services. IDVAs provide support in relation to assessing risk and developing strategies to reduce further violence and harm; supporting criminal proceedings against abusers (if charges are made); housing and financial assistance; referral to relevant services; education on the dynamics of abuse and general emotional support. People experiencing domestic abuse may self-refer to receive support from IDVAs or they may be referred via health, social care or criminal justice system workers. A comprehensive evaluation of over 2,000 IDVA cases found that advocacy support is successful in reducing the frequency and severity of domestic abuse when intensive support and a number of interventions are available (Howarth et al., 2009). These findings highlight the value of inter-agency work; it is important, however, to note that the evaluation was not able to assess the outcomes of approximately 40 per cent of victims as they did not engage or dropped out.

References

Bailey, B.A. (2010). Partner violence during pregnancy: Prevalence, effects, screening, and management. *International Journal of Women's Health, 2*, 183–197.

Boyle, A., Robinson, S., & Atkinson, P. (2004). Domestic violence in emergency medicine patients. *Emergency Medicine Journal, 21*, 9–13.

Bundock, L., Howard, L.M., Trevillion, K., Malcolm, E., Feder, G., & Oram, S. (2013). Prevalence and risk of experiences of intimate partner violence among people with eating disorders: A systematic review. *Journal of Psychiatric Research, 47*, 1134–1142.

Co-ordinated Action Against Domestic Abuse. (CAADA). (2010). Retrieved 19 August 2016 from *www.endthefear.co.uk*

Crown Prosecution Service. (2015). *Violence against women and girls annual crime report 2014–2015*. HMSO, London.

Department of Health. (2005). Responding to domestic abuse: A hand book for health professionals. Retrieved 19 August 2016 from *http://domesticviolencelondon.nhs.uk*

Domestic Violence, Crime and Victims Act 2004. (2004). Retrieved 19 August 2016 from www.legislation.gov.uk/ukpga/2004/28/contents

Dutton, D.G. (2007). The abusive personality (2nd Ed.): Violence and control in intimate relationships. New York: The Guildford Press.

Fanslow, J.L., Norton, R.N., & Spinola, C.G. (1998). Indicators of assault-related injuries among women presenting to the emergency department. *Annals of Emergency Medicine, 32*, 341–348.

Feder, G.S., Hutson, M., Ramsay, J., & Taket, A.R. (2006). Women exposed to intimate partner violence. Expectations and experiences when they encounter health care professionals: A meta-analysis of qualitative studies. *Annals of Internal Medicine, 166*, 22–37.

Feder, G., Ramsay, J., Dunne, D., Rose, M., Arsene, C., Norman, R., Kuntze, S., Spencer, A., Bacchus, L., Hague, G., Warburton, A., & Taket, A. (2009). How far does screening women for domestic (partner) violence in different health-care settings meet criteria for a screening programme? Systematic reviews of nine UK, National Screening Committee criteria. *Health Technology Assessment, 13*, iii-113.

Golding, J.M. (1999). Intimate partner violence as a risk factor for mental disorders: A meta-analysis. *Journal of Family Violence, 14*, 99–132.

Her Majesty's Inspectorate of Constabularies. (2014). Retrieved 19 August 2016 from https://www.justiceinspectorates.gov.uk/hmic/wp-content/uploads/2014/04/improving-the-police-response-to-domestic-abuse.pdf

Home Office. (2003). *Safety and justice: The government's proposal on domestic violence*. London: Home Office.

Home Office. (2005). *Domestic violence: A national report*. London: Home Office.

Home Office. (2009). *Together we can end violence against women: A consultation paper*. London: Home Office.

Home Office. (2013a). *Domestic violence and abuse guidance*. London: Home Office. Retrieved 4 May 2016 from www.gov.uk/guidance/domestic-violence-and-abuse

Home Office. (2013b). Evaluation of the pilot of domestic violence protection orders. Retrieved 19 August 2016 from *www.gov.uk*

Home Office. (2015a). 2010 to 2015 government policy: Violence against women and girls. Retrieved 19 August 2016 from *http://www.gov.uk*

Home Office. (2015b). *Serious Crime Act 2015 Fact sheet: Domestic abuse offence*. Retrieved 4 May 2016 from https://www.gov.uk/government/uploads/system/uploads/attachment_data/file/416011/Fact_sheet_-_Domestic_Abuse_Offence_-_Act.pdf

Home Office. (2016). *Strategy to end violence against women and girls 2016–2020*. London: Home Office.

Home Office Violent and Youth Crime Prevention Unit and Research and Analysis Unit. (2011). *Research into Multi-Agency Risk Assessment Conferences (MARACs)* (pp. 1–109). London: Home Office.

Howard, L.M., Trevillion, K., & Agnew-Davies, R. (2010). Domestic violence and mental health. *International Review of Psychiatry, 22*, 525–534.

Howard, L.M., Feder, G., & Agnew-Davies, R. (Eds.). (2013a). *Domestic violence and mental health*. London: Royal College of Psychiatrists Publications.

Howard, L.M., Oram, S., Galley, H., Trevillion, K., & Feder G. (2013b). Domestic violence and perinatal mental disorders: A systematic review and meta-analysis. *PLoS Med 10*, e1001452.

Howarth, E., Stimpson, L., Barran, D., & Robinson, A. (2009). *Safety in numbers: A multi-site evaluation of independent domestic violence advocacy services*. London: The Henry Smith Charity.

Jaffe, P., & Burris, C.A. (1982). *An integrated response to wife assault: A community model*. Ottawa. Research Report of the Solicitor General.

Jonas, S., Khalifeh, H., Bebbington, P.E., McManus, S., Brugha, T., Meltzer, H., & Howard, L.M. (2014). Gender differences in intimate partner violence and psychiatric disorders in England: Results from the 2007 adult psychiatric morbidity survey. *Epidemiology and Psychiatric Sciences, 23*, 189–199.

Khalifeh, H., Howard, L.M., Osborn, D., Moran, P., & Johnson, S. (2013). Violence against people with disability in England and Wales: Findings from a national cross-sectional survey. *PLoS One 8*, e55952.

Khalifeh, H., Oram, S., Trevillion, K., Johnson, S., & Howard, L.M. (2015). Recent intimate partner violence among people with chronic mental illness: Findings from a national cross-sectional survey. *British Journal of Psychiatry, 207*, 207–212.

Kropp, P.R., Hart, S.D., & Belfrage, H. (2005) *The Brief Spousal Assault Form for the Evaluation of Risk (B-SAFER)*. Vancouver, Canada: Proactive Resolutions.

Lefly, M. (2015). 'Istanbul Convention: Britain drags its feet over women's rights'. *The Independent*. (2 August 2015). London.

MacMillan, H., Wathen, N., Jamieson, E., Boyle, M., McNutt, L., Worster, A., Lent, B. & Webb, M. (2006). Approaches to screening for intimate partner violence in health care settings: A randomized trial. *Journal of the American Medical Association*, 296(5), 530–536.

National Institute for Health and Clinical Excellence. (2014). *Domestic violence and abuse: Multi-agency working*. National Institute for Health and Care Excellence: London.

Office for National Statistics. (2015). *Violent crime and sexual offences. Chapter 2 –Homicide*. London: Office for National Statistics. Retrieved 14 May 2016 from www.ons.gov.uk/peoplepopulationandcommunity/crimeandjustice/compendium/focusonviolentcrimeandsexualoffences/2015-02-12/

Office for National Statistics. (2016). *Focus on violent crime and sexual offences*. London: Office for National Statistics. Retrieved 14 May 2016 from www.ons.gov.uk/peoplepopulationandcommunity/crimeandjustice/compendium/focusonviolentcrimeandsexualoffences/yearendingmarch2015

Oram, S., Trevillion, K., Feder, G., & Howard, L.M. (2013). Prevalence of experiences of domestic violence among psychiatric patients: Systematic review. *British Journal of Psychiatry, 202*, 94–99.

Parliamentary Question. (2016). *PQ 26764 [on implementing the Istanbul Convention], answered 22 February 2016*. Retrieved 14 May 2016 from www.parliament.gov.uk

Pickles, J., & Robinson, A. (2007). *Risk assessment and domestic violence: The multi-Agency MARAC Model of Intervention*. Community Care.

Protection from Harassment Act 1997. (1997). Retrieved 14 May 2016 from www.legislation.gov.uk/ukpga/1997/40/contents

Richardson, J.O., Coid, J., Petruckevitch, A., Chung, W.S., Moorey, S., & Feder, G. (2002). Identifying domestic violence: Cross sectional study in primary care. *British Medical Journal*, *324*, 274.

Robinson, A.L. (2004). *Domestic Violence MARACs for Very High-Risk Victims in Cardiff: A Process and Outcome Evaluation*. Cardiff: Cardiff University.

Robinson, A.L. (2009). *Independent Domestic Violence Advisors: A process evaluation*. Cardiff: Cardiff University.

Rose, D., Trevillion, K., Woodall, A., Morgan, C., Feder, G., & Howard, L.M. (2011). Barriers and facilitators of disclosures of domestic violence by mental health service users: A qualitative study. *British Journal of Psychiatry*, *198*, 189–194.

Royal College of Nursing. (2000). *Domestic violence: Guidance for nurses*. RCN, London.

Serious Crime Act 2015. (2015). Retrieved 14 May 2016 from www.legislation.gov.uk/ukpga/2015/9/contents/enacted

Smith, K., Osborne, S., Lau, I., & Britton, A. (2012). *Homicides, firearm offences and intimate violence 2010/11: Supplementary Volume 2 to crime in England and Wales 2010/11* London: Home Office.

Stanko, B. (2000). *The day to count: A snapshot of the impact of domestic abuse in the UK, London*. Royal Holloway, University of London.

Stark, E. (2007). *Coercive control: How men entrap women in personal life*. New York: Oxford University Press.

Stöckl, H., March, L., Pallitto, C., & Garcia-Moreno, C. (2014). Intimate partner violence among adolescents and young women: Prevalence and associated factors in nine countries: A cross-sectional study. *BMC Public Health*, *14*, 1.

Taket, A., Nurse, J., Smith, K., Watson, J., Shakespeare, J., Lavis, V., Cosgrove, K., Mulley, K., & Feder, G. (2003). Education and debate: Routinely asking women about domestic violence in health settings. *British Medical Journal*, *327*, 673–676.

Tjaden, P. (2000). Prevalence and consequences of male-to-female and female-to-male intimate partner violence. *Violence Against Women*, *6*, 142.

Trevillion, K., Hughes, B., Feder, G., Borschmann, R., Oram, S., & Howard, L.M. (2014). Disclosure of domestic violence in mental health settings: A qualitative meta-synthesis. *International Review of Psychiatry*, *26*, 430–444.

Trevillion, K., Oram, S., Feder, G., & Howard, L.M. (2012). Experiences of domestic violence and mental disorders: A systematic review and meta-analysis. *PloS One 7*, e51740.

Walby, S. (2009). *The cost of domestic violence: Up-date 2009*. Lancaster: Lancaster University.

Walby, S., & Allen, J. (2004) *Domestic violence, sexual assault and stalking: Findings from the British Crime Survey*. London: Home Office.

Wathen, C.N., & MacMillan, H.L. (2003). Interventions for violence against women: Scientific review. *Journal of American Medical Association*, *289*, 589–600.

Women's Aid. (n.d.). Domestic Abuse Services. Retrieved 19 August 2016 from *www.womansaid.org.uk*

Woodhouse, J., & Dempsey, N. (2016). *Domestic violence in England and Wales*. Briefing Paper (No. 6337). House of Commons: House of Commons Library.

World Health Organization. (2002). *World Report on Violence and Health*. Geneva: World Health Organization.

Yearnshire, S. (1997). Analysis of cohort. In S. Bewley, J. Friend, & G. Mezey, (Eds.), *Violence against women* (p. 45). London: RCOG Press.

4 Levels of prevention of intimate partner violence against women analysed from the multi-causal-ecological pyramidal model

The case of Spain

Victoria A. Ferrer-Pérez and Esperanza Bosch-Fiol

Violence against women (VAW) has been, and still is in many parts of the world, a hidden and invisible crime (UN, 2006; WHO, 2013). The consideration that women are objects of property of male family members and, by extension, of all males, and that they must submit to them, obey them, stay in their shadow, meet their needs, and satisfy their desires is one of the golden rules of patriarchy (Millet, 1969). If power is masculine, the ability to correct and punish also belongs to males (Alberdi & Matas, 2002). As a result, explicit violence, or the threat of resorting to this violence, is used as a form of control over the lives of millions of women, and this fear is transmitted from generation to generation.

Recourse to violence is present in many countries across the globe, although it is true that in the countries where women's rights are not formally promulgated the situation becomes truly desperate (UN, 2006; WHO, 2013). In general, the available data support the fact that VAW is a problem of epidemic proportions (Watts & Zimmerman, 2002; UN, 2006; WHO, 2013; FRA, 2014). In particular, intimate partner violence against women (IPVAW) is a serious social problem (Heise & García-Moreno, 2002; García-Moreno, Jansen, Ellsberg, Heise & Watts, 2006; Devries et al., 2013; Stöckl et al., 2013), and causes them and their children physical and psychological suffering (Campbell, 2002; Plichta, 2004; García-Moreno et al., 2006; WHO, 2013). While noting the extent and severity of this violence, the World Health Organization (2013) has highlighted the need and urgency for all sectors of society and all governments to commit to eliminating any tolerance for IPVAW and provide effective support to those who suffer.

In focusing on the case in Spain, it is important to remember that, after the dictatorship of General Franco (from 1939 to 1975), and during the process of transition towards democracy, the demands of different social movements began to infiltrate the political agenda. This led to, among many other things, the creation of institutions and organisations devoted to addressing the specific needs of women (Bonet, 2007). One of the greatest examples was the Women's Institute, created in December 1983 in compliance with and development of the principle of equality between women and men. This principle was enshrined in article 14 of the Spanish Constitution (passed in 1978) (Valiente, 2006; Women's Institute, 2008).

As Spanish society continued advancing and deepening its democratisation, other aspects contained in the Constitution of 1978 were developed. Among them, 17 autonomous communities or territories were created, depending on each case, with a greater or lesser degree of autonomy in their management (i.e. including their own parliaments, the ability to define the administrative bodies that they wished to equip themselves with, and the ability to design and implement their own laws) (Valiente, 2006; Biglia, Olivella & Jiménez, 2014). This differentiated administration resulted in each autonomous community designing their own equality bodies, the first of which were the Andalusian Institute for Women, the Catalan Institute for Women, and the Basque Institute for Women.

It is worth highlighting that owing to the drive of the Spanish feminist movement these equality bodies brought to light diverse questions and social issues that affected the lives of Spanish women. One of the most important of these issues was IPVAW, which has caused around 700 deaths and over 1,200,000 complaints since 2003 (GDGV, 2013). A notable consequence of the pressure of women's movements (De Miguel, 2008; Puleo, 2008) and the work carried out by the Women's Institute and its counterparts in the different autonomous communities, is passing in 2003 the Organic Law 1/2004 on Integral Protection Measures against Gender Violence. One of the most novel aspects of this law is that not only does it emphasise the need to intervene judicially in order to protect women subjected to IPVAW, but it also explicitly recognises the need to establish effective prevention systems at different levels within Spanish society (Puigvert, 2010).

In this chapter, we describe a multi-causal explanatory VAW and IPVAW model that we have developed called the Multi-causal-Ecological Pyramidal Model (MEP) (Bosch & Ferrer, 2013; Bosch, Ferrer, Ferreiro & Navarro, 2013). This model is comprised of five tiers (i.e. substrate patriarchal, differential socialisation, control expectations, triggers and outbreak of violence) as well as a filtering process. From this model, we detail a range of primary, secondary and tertiary preventive actions carried out in Spain and we will reflect about their results and their effects on IPVAW.

In this section, we will first present a brief conceptual approach to VAW and IPVAW and the background for the development of the MEP. To start with, the Convention on the Elimination of All Forms of Discrimination Against Women (CEDAW) was adopted in 1979 by the UN General Assembly. This is often described as an international bill of rights for women. The Convention defines discrimination against women as:

> ... any distinction, exclusion or restriction made on the basis of sex which has the effect or purpose of impairing or nullifying the recognition, enjoyment or exercise by women, irrespective of their marital status, on a basis of equality of men and women, of human rights and fundamental freedoms in the political, economic, social, cultural, civil or any other field.
>
> (CEDAW, 1979, Article 1, p. 2)

More specifically, the Declaration on the Elimination of Violence Against Women defines violence against women (UN, 1994) as follows:

> For the purposes of this Declaration, the term 'violence against women' means any act of gender-based violence that results in, or is likely to result in, physical, sexual or psychological harm or suffering to women, including threats of such acts, coercion or arbitrary deprivation of liberty, whether occurring in public or in private life.
>
> (UN, 1994, Article 1, p. 2)

As Noeleen Heyzer (2000) points out, this Declaration was a historic landmark for three basic reasons. First, it placed VAW within the framework of human rights by explicitly stating that all women have the right to enjoy fundamental rights and freedoms and that these rights should be protected. Moreover, the different forms of VAW are human rights violations and thus identified VAW as being a social problem and not a personal problem. Second, the Declaration broadened the VAW concept to include acts of physical, psychological and sexual violence and threats of violence within the family, community or state. Thus, VAW includes IPVAW, sexual harassment, female genital mutilation, honour crimes, etc. Third, because the Declaration highlighted that VAW is a form of gender-based violence, a prime risk factor for VAW is being a woman. Precisely because of this, many documents on the issue use the concepts of VAW (which describes the problem) and gender violence or gender-based violence (which incorporate the relationships of gender as a cause).

Stemming from this Declaration, VAW, and especially IPVAW, has become a key axis of action both for the United Nations and for its different agencies (WHO, OIT, etc.). An important landmark in this sense was the Fourth World Conference on Women, held in Beijing in 1995, which marked a turning point for the global agenda on gender equality. The Beijing Declaration and Platform for Action constitutes a programme of female empowerment. In addition, it established a series of strategic goals and measures to facilitate gender equality in 12 crucial spheres, one of which was VAW.

Since 2010, the UN has reorganised and re-founded the agencies and bodies devoted to promoting gender equality and empowering women. This led to the creation of the UN Women in July of 2010. One of the priority goals of this agency is to put an end to VAW and IPVAW.

Prevention as a weapon for the future

Prevention is a means of taking a tiered approach to minimise or warn someone of the possible risk of harm. Thus, prevention is largely directed at averting wrongdoing. Prevention, in the context of this chapter, refers to the steps taken to minimise the potential risk, or warning the likely victims to be alert by identifying the initial signs of a violent relationship.

When it comes to VAW prevention, efforts have mainly revolved around providing a protective response and attending to the needs of people affected by it. In this regard, it is posited that the best way to prevent VAW is to tackle its origins and structural causes (UN, 2006).

According to the UN Women and the different multi-causal models used to analyse VAW, their primary causes are sex discrimination, social norms, and sexual stereotypes (Heise, 1998; Bosch & Ferrer, 2002; Rodríguez-Menés & Safranoff, 2012). Hence, it is reasoned that VAW and IPVAW prevention must begin during the early stages of life and be focused on educating boys and girls on how to build relationships that are based on respect and sexual equality as the best way of ensuring swift, sustained headway in the prevention and eradication of gender-based violence.

Nonetheless, this is not the only possible way of working towards prevention. In the fields of individual and public healthcare the usual understanding is that prevention can be applied at three levels through primary, secondary and tertiary interventions. From a theoretical perspective these classifications are quite clear; however, the issue is much more complex. In fact, in many parts of the world, and also in Spain, VAW and IPVAW preventive campaigns are ongoing at different levels and have been for some time now. Nonetheless, the results are generally inconclusive. For instance, the available data do not show a significant decrease of VAW or IPVAW. In fact, if we take the serious economic crisis that began in 2008, with its negative repercussions on all countries (particularly those of southern Europe), the incidence of IPVAW has grown, while funding aimed at tackling the problem in general and working towards its prevention have been reduced (Beteta, 2013; Bosch, Aroca & Ferrer, 2014).

It might be hypothesised that one of the key underlying errors that has led to this situation is the naive belief that relatively simple preventive measures or programmes would suffice in tackling a complex patriarch-based issue. While this subject is too broad to be analysed in depth in this chapter, it is important to stress that the introduction of preventive VAW and IPVAW measures aimed at dealing with such a deep-rooted societal problem must comprise more than scattered preventive initiatives aimed at a single intervention level. It is also important to highlight the need for an underpinning conceptual framework, clearly articulated goals and a means of assessing the implementation of these programmes.

To this end, we propose that the MEP, which we have developed (Bosch & Ferrer, 2013; Bosch et al., 2013), is an adequate tool from which VAW and IPVAW preventive interventions can be framed, explained, and refined.

Explanatory models: Multi-causal-Ecological Pyramidal model (MEP)

Several reviews have pointed out that the first VAW explanatory models were uni-causal and considered that the origins of violence lay within the individual characteristics (e.g. personality, socio-economic situation, or stress) of women and men (Bosch & Ferrer, 2002). Though, now broader sociological (e.g. family conflict perspective or feminist perspective) and psychological (theory of social learning, of exchange, and of stress) explanations are beginning to be considered (Bosch & Ferrer, 2002).

The recognition of VAW as a violation of human rights, as mentioned above, establishes a different perspective of analysis. As pointed out by the in-depth study on all forms of violence against women (UN, 2006):

> The central premise of the analysis of violence against women within the human rights framework is that the specific causes of such violence and the factors that increase the risk of its occurrence are grounded in the broader context of systemic gender based discrimination against women and other forms of subordination. Such violence is a manifestation of the historically unequal power relations between women and men reflected in both public and private life.
>
> (UN, 2006, p. 27)

In the Spanish legal framework, specifically in the Preamble to the Organic Law 1/2004, it is made clear that:

> Gender violence is not a problem confined to the private sphere. On the contrary, it stands as the most brutal symbol of the inequality persisting in our society. It is violence directed against women for the mere fact of being women; considered, by their aggressors, as lacking the most basic rights of freedom, respect and power of decision.
>
> (Organic Law 1/2004, p. 41266)

Therefore, we have been working on a new explanatory model for VAW and IPVAW, the MEP. This model has been presented in some previous works (Bosch & Ferrer, 2013; Bosch et al., 2013) and it is made up of five tiers: (1) patriarchal substratum; (2) differential socialisation; (3) expectations of control; (4) trigger events; and (5) violence unleashed. It takes into account what we call a filtering process, that is, the decision-making process of the men who voluntarily abuse their gender-based privileges and therefore the use of violence. Each of the MEP's five tiers are outlined below.

The patriarchal substratum

To understand this first tier in the MEP it is important to remember the concept of patriarchy in the sense proposed by the North American feminist Kate Millett. In her book *Sexual Politics* (1969), she claims that patriarchy is made up of two basic components: a social structure which consists of a system of social organisation that creates and maintains a situation in which men have the power and privileges that women do not enjoy, and an ideology which represents a belief system that legitimises and maintains this power, and, in doing so gives authority to males.

That is to say, patriarchy is a system of dominance of males over women in different areas, common in all societies (although practised with more or less impunity depending on the democratic tradition and the laws in force in each country), and which feeds on misogynistic beliefs and sexist socio-cultural traditions (Lerner, 1986). However, the changes undergone by societies in the last few decades (most especially in the so-called 'first world') have produced significant transformations in the system of masculine dominance, with one of the most evident results of this being the increasingly blurred, masked nature of this power (Saltzman, 1990). We cannot ignore the fact that this dominance coexists in some democratic societies with laws that formally consecrate equality between men and women, therefore its tentacles are obliged to transit underground circuits that are often most elusive, but by no means less powerful (De Miguel, 1996).

It is worth pointing out the fact that this first tier in the MEP would bear significant similarities with the macro-system ecological models as Eva Gil and Inma Lloret (2007) summarised:

> Refer[ing] to the broadest environment which we call patriarchal society, ruled by a system of beliefs that defines the family roles of father as the head of the family and on a lower stratum the mother and children. Likewise, the man is associated to stereotypes of masculinity, strength and control, whereas the woman embodies the qualities of submission and obedience.
>
> (Gil & Lloret, 2007, p. 43)

The processes of differential socialisation or gender-based socialisation

The second tier in the MEP is made up of processes which determine how we learn to be boys, girls, men, and women, what models act as references, and what expectations are inferred.

For, according to the Theory of Differential Socialisation, all people acquire differentiated gender identities, and these identities have specific cognitive, attitudinal and behavioural styles, moral codes, and stereotypical norms of conduct assigned to each gender (Walker & Barton, 1983). In short, through the process of differential socialisation, men and women learn and take on sexual roles and gender-based stereotypes, clearly marking differences in all areas of life (emotional, behavioural, economic, etc.). In this regard, the Ending Violence Against Women and Girls: Programming Essentials (UNIFEM, 2010) points out: 'How men and women are socialized and the definitions and understandings of womanhood and manhood establish their positions of relative power and control at home and in society' (UNIFEM, 2010, p. 19).

Expectations of control

In psychology, the concept of expectations refers to the reasonable likelihood of carrying out or achieving something, when an event that is expected happens or when a certain eventuality takes place. In other words, an expectation is a more or less realistic and well-founded assumption (Bosch & Ferrer, 2013).

Within the MEP, it is understood that, once masculine superiority has been taken on board (derived from the patriarchal substratum and transmitted through socialisation processes), males will have interiorised their 'gender-based right' to control the lives of women, considering this a 'natural right', be it punitive, paternalist, or protectionist.

In order to grasp the weight of these expectations in the MEP and, ultimately, in the genesis of violence against women, it is important to point out the role of gender ideology (and particularly traditional gender ideology) – that is, the set of beliefs regarding roles and behaviours that are considered appropriate for men and women and concerning relationships between men and women (Moya, 2004). Thus, traditional gender ideology accepts patriarchal assumptions as regards to the differences between men and women and the social roles they must play, whereby it is taken for granted that men will take on the power and women will accept it submissively, legitimising the expectations of control of males over women. Within this context, it is therefore easy to imagine that when women attempt to devote their attention and their time to other activities or persons and, even more so, when in some way they question this power or its legitimacy (or when a trigger event happens), there is an escalation of violence.

Trigger events

An event is a relevant phenomenon or occurrence, whether it be individual or social, which takes place in a certain position or time. Within the MEP, a trigger event is a phenomena that may be interpreted by males with expectations of control (described above) as a sign that they may be losing this control, or that circumstances are arising that will exacerbate their need to control; and these may be personal (alcohol, drugs, marriage, birth of a child, separation, stress, etc.), social (economic crisis, change in social model, etc.) or political-religious (fundamentalism, ultra-conservative governments, etc.).

Thus, these trigger events would, for instance, include circumstances that increase stress and/or generate frustration, such as life changes, pregnancy, or the birth of a child which incorporate a new figure with whom to 'share' attention; and unpredictable situations such as unemployment, economic deprivation, an illness, and fights or arguments.

Further, the use or abuse of alcohol or other toxic substances has been repeatedly considered a possible trigger event of this violence, as it is considered to constitute an active disinhibitor that breaks or eliminates the moral restraints that usually stop violent behaviours from being put into practice, and/or to disturb the balance of certain neurotransmitters (Bosch et al., 2013). It has been observed that this consumption could be present in 30 to 50 per cent of the cases of gender-based violence worldwide (WHO, 2006), although some meta-analytical studies on the issue note that this association would vary substantially depending on the type of sample studied and the type of consumption the study refers to (Foran & O'Leary, 2008).

Violence unleashed

The fifth and final tier of the MEP is an unleashing of violence.

In addition to these five elements, the model also contemplates the existence of filtering processes. In other words, it is based on the consideration that males, in each of these tiers have the freedom to choose to reject the gender privileges of the patriarchal system and to reject the traditional model of masculinity. In fact, as Celia Amorós reminds us (2005), patriarchy is not an essence, but rather a metastable system of dominance exercised by individuals who, at the same time, are moulded by it. The fact that patriarchy is metastable means that its forms adapt to the different historical types of economic and social organisation, preserving to a greater or lesser extent; however, its nature as a system of exercising power and of distributing recognition between peers (Puleo, 2005). Thus, all of us as people form part of it and are forged by it, but this does not absolve us of the responsibility of attempting to distance ourselves critically from its structures and acting ethically and politically against its tenets and effects.

Hence, the use of violence can be said to be a choice, and only those who are most adherent to the traditional masculine role and misogyny, who do not at any time question the patriarchal mandates and their supposed gender privileges, will go through each and every one of the tiers described in the MEP, thereby adopting the patriarchal substratum with all its consequences and, eventually, ending up using violence against women.

Preventive levels according to the MEP

In the fields of individual and public healthcare three preventive levels are usually distinguished. In continuation, an analysis will be made of these levels, tying them in with the origins of this kind of violence and with the tiers of the MEP described above, commenting on possible intervention strategies in each case, and giving some examples of how they have been applied in Spain.

One initial level is primary prevention, aimed at stopping the problem from occurring and at exerting an influence on non-victims and/or on 'target populations'. In the case of violence to women, the objective is to put a halt to it before the problem occurs. For this purpose, this kind of initiative must be aimed at the whole of the population, although most intervention programmes will be directed at younger sectors of the population.

With the Primary Prevention Module as its basis (Guedes & Bott, 2009), the UN Women (2012) believe that this primary preventive level is the most strategic way of eradicating violence against women and girls, based on the following premises:

• Women and girls' human rights are upheld and a serious problem in the fields of public health, safety and justice is averted.
• It is always preferable to prevent problems rather than having to tackle them and deal with their devastating costs and consequences.

- In the long run, successful efforts in the field of primary prevention can improve women's situations in social, financial and healthcare terms, as well as society's broader wellbeing, through both the direct effects (an improved quality of life or health) and indirect ones (by avoiding violence, its consequences and the ensuing costs and squandered resources).

This type of prevention must be applied at different social levels in order to bring about institutional changes, while also launching intervention programmes for specific target groups and tackling the population as a whole on a more general, large-scale level. For an intervention strategy to work at this primary preventive level, the following goals must be achieved (Morrison, Hardison, Mathew & O'Neill, 2004), among others:

- To influence governmental policies and laws so that primary prevention is explicitly dealt with.
- To make changes to organisational practices so that the concept of sexual equality is incorporated and specific pro-active measures are established to ensure zero tolerance to violence.
- To foster networking.
- To mobilise communities, the education sector and social marketing.
- To improve individuals' awareness and their attitudes; to make sure that the message reaches young people; and to involve men and boys as allies.
- To empower women socially and financially.

In short, primary prevention is more effective when different methods are combined, such as mobilising the community, using the mass media, raising a greater awareness of the problem, working at school grassroots level, and bringing about changes to policies, at different levels of society. Efforts in the field of primary prevention are also more effective when they focus on:

- Changing individual and collective attitudes, beliefs and behaviours concerning gender rules and roles in a specific community.
- Putting into practice local and national strategies to empower women and eliminate gender differences.

Indeed, intervention programmes aimed at bringing about changes at an interpersonal, relational, community and social level or ones that mobilize the community against violence on a wider scale can have a big impact on changes in individual behaviour (Harvey, García-Moreno & Butchart, 2007). In the context of the MEP, and in terms of the origins of violence to women, this type of preventive strategy encompasses initiatives aimed at influencing or transforming the first tiers of the MEP, that is to say, patriarchal systems at base level and differential socialisation so that, through these influences, their structures are slowly broken down, patterns and beliefs are modified, and attitudes and behaviours are gradually changed. Some strategies that can be put into practice at this level, of a formal but no less necessary kind, include:

- The necessary legislative changes to 'clean up' any discriminatory articles in current legislation. The maximum expression of an intervention programme of this kind would be the approval of an Act like Spanish Organic Law 3/2007 on Effective Equality between Men and Women, which not only introduces measures to integrate the principle of equal opportunities for men and women in all walks of social, political and economic life, but reviews and amends other laws in which any element of discrimination might remain.

- The explicit introduction of a woman's right to a decent, non-violent life in the legislation in force. One example would be Organic Law 1/2004, above mentioned.

- A review of androcentric biases and greater visibility of the achievements of women throughout history in all branches of knowledge and walks of social and political life. One example would be the incorporation of gender studies in Spanish universities or the inclusion of gender as a crosscutting category in research and technology in Organic Law 14/2011 on Science, Technology and Innovation.

- A review and the elimination of symbolic violence that perpetuates traditional discriminatory roles and stereotypes in general and, more specifically, its review and elimination from cultural output (advertising, films, songs, television etc.), as established, for instance, in Organic Law 3/2007, above mentioned, in aspects like advertising.

- Educational initiatives and the incorporation of 'education in feelings' or a review of the myths of romantic love, both in formal and informal education and in cultural output, particularly when targeted at younger sectors of the population. These initiatives should include:

  - Promoting a greater awareness of the issue of gender in matters concerning equality. One example is the informative campaigns designed and carried out by the Women's Institute and by different bodies working in the field of equality.

  - Education in equality. There are many examples of educational materials on the subject (Urruzola, 2005; Laguna & Porcel, 2008; Aroca & Garrido, 2009; Ruiz, 2009; Biglia, Olivella & Jiménez, 2014) and also many websites (such as *EZ Isildu*, [Emakunde, 2011] or *Nahiko* [Emakunde, 2015]).

  - The inclusion of equal opportunities, equality and a respect for diversity in school curricula, and the elimination of traditional stereotypes. One example in Spain was the inclusion of a specific subject (Education for Citizenship) in primary and secondary education in order to tackle these issues. However, due to a change of government, this subject was taught in schools for only a short period of time and so it was not possible to assess its efficiency.

It is important to bear in mind that, at this primary preventive level, work must be focused on two different fronts: on the one hand, on women and girls, to help them in the empowerment process, and, on the other, on men and boys, to raise their awareness so that they come to question and reject male privilege that offers the appeal of dominance and control. Consequently, different strategies must be used in both cases. Two examples of primary preventive strategies directed specifically at men are the Gizonduz initiative by the Basque government, promoted by Emakunde (2008) and aimed at fostering a greater male awareness, involvement and participation in sexual equality and initiatives devised by Jerez City Council's (2016) 'Men for Equality'.

A second level of prevention is secondary prevention, directed at detecting this violence in its early stages and preventing it from progressing and/or escalating. In the case of violence against women, work at this level would include reducing the prevalence of this violence, early identification, and swift efficient intervention to put a stop to the violence as soon as possible with the fewest possible repercussions. Secondary intervention would take place within the education system, families, social environments, and the healthcare system. In the context of the MEP, this secondary preventive level entails working on the third and fourth tiers of the PM, the expectations of its control and on events that act as catalysts. More specifically, secondary prevention and the reduction of the prevalence of this violence would involve:

- Solid training for healthcare and educational professionals, providing them with the necessary know-how and strategies to detect risk situations and to arbitrate in finding ways of helping women at risk to become clearly aware of their situation and to seek safety. More specifically, training in equality must be included, aimed at:

    - healthcare professionals,
    - members of the legal profession, and
    - members of the security forces.

- Education for women and girls that allows them:

    - To identify possible myths and fallacies that might induce them to put up with situations where they are subject to violence.
    - To familiarise them with and help them take into account the legal resources and support at their disposal.
    - To identify the danger signals of violent outbursts that might endanger them, their sons and daughters, or other relatives.

A third level is tertiary prevention. This is aimed at helping the victims to recover from and prevent or alleviate possible trauma. In the case of violence against women, this level would include efforts to make female victims grasp their true situation so that they leave their partners, or participate in intervention programmes with the perpetrators in order to avert possible future cases. This level of prevention focuses on the last tier of the MEP, what are known as 'outbursts of violence', including further escalations of any kind, from low-intensity types (such as everyday male chauvinism) to the most brutal, devastating forms, with femicide as the maximum exponent.

Once again, proper prevention entails solid training for professionals from the fields of healthcare and the social services, equipping them with the necessary skills and strategies to offer psychological, social and healthcare support tailored to meet the needs of women and children who have survived this violence, keeping them safe and helping them to understand that they have not only been the victims of a cruel violent individual but also of a society that has encouraged this violence and induced these men into thinking that they are acting legitimately.

Tertiary initiatives must integrate the principles of therapeutic intervention, from a gender-related feminist perspective, as suggested by Mary Ann Dutton (2000) or Leonore Walker (2009), among others.

In activities directed at preventing violence against women or at repairing damage, women's empowerment as a preventive and/or reparative strategy is especially important (an objective contemplated in the two intervention models cited previously).

Marcela Lagarde (2007) defines empowerment as a process of change when each woman gradually or very swiftly relinquishes her role as a puppet in history, politics and culture or a pawn of others, takes command of her own life and becomes the protagonist of history, culture, politics and social life. It is a process of individual empowerment in which women become aware of their entitlement to certain rights, confident in their own ability to achieve their objectives. Given women's constant disempowerment and the problems they face in being valued, recognised and empowered, this process is fundamental. As Friedman pointed out (1992), empowerment is associated with access to and control over three types of powers:

1   *social* power, construed as access to the foundations of productive wealth;
2   *political* power, or an individual's access to decision-making processes, above all in matters concerning their own future; and
3   *psychological* power, construed as a sense of personal potency and individual autonomy.

Along these same lines, Rowlands (1997) pointed to the existence of three dimensions to empowerment:

1   a *personal* dimension: developing a sense of self-pride, self-confidence and individual autonomy;
2   empowerment within *close relations*: the capacity to negotiate and influence the nature of relations and decisions; and
3   a *collective* dimension: participation in political structures and collective cooperative action.

The tactics that are used to control and subjugate women change from one historical period to the next. Actions always spark a response, and so with each tier forward that is made in women's rights, a patriarchal response is also made to try and counteract this progress. There is one common denominator to all these tactics: the desire to crush women's self-esteem and to destroy their pride in themselves. What better way can there be to suppress an individual or a group than to encourage the belief that they are useless or inferior, given that an insecure person is more easily controllable. And what better way can there be to prevent this than to empower people, putting them in charge of their lives and their destinies.

Conclusion

This chapter tries to present, in a necessarily summarised form, the different levels of prevention tactics to address violence against women, using the MEP, in which the authors have be working for a long while. Faced with the gravity of this issue, its enormous prevalence worldwide (also in the specific case of Spain), and the flagrant attack against the human rights of millions of women all over the planet that it represents, it would seem logical to think that only in the prevention of this violence can we find the authentic route to its eradication, hopefully in the not too distant future. Thus, investment in both economic and human resources is essential. Nevertheless, for a programme along these lines to be able to be really effective, there must be a series of conditions and controls that will ensure its effectiveness and make full use of these resources. It is for this reason that, in our opinion, starting from consistent explanatory models facilitates this process, as does the use of rigorous assessment strategies that ensure that the effort carried out achieves, albeit in an elementary way, its aims. Ultimately, statistics ought to deliver the final verdict.

References

Alberdi, I., & Matas, N. (2002). *La violencia doméstica en España* [Domestic violence in Spain]. Barcelona: Fundación La Caixa.

Amorós, C. (2005). *La gran diferencia y sus pequeñas consecuencias … para las luchas de las mujeres* [The big difference and its small consequences … for the struggles of women]. Madrid: Cátedra.

Aroca, M., & Garrido, V. (2009). *Guía pedagógica para realizar un taller de prevención de la violencia de género basado en las obras "El infierno de Marta" y "La máscara del amor"* [Pedagogic guide for a workshop on the prevention of gender based violence in the works 'Hell Marta' and 'The Mask of Love']. Valencia: Algar.

Beteta, Y. (2013). La feminización de la crisis financiera global. La regresión del estado del bienestar en España y su impacto en las políticas de igualdad y de erradicación de la violencia contra las mujeres. Nuevos retos [The feminisation of the global financial crisis. The regression of the wlefare state in Spain and its impact on the equal opportunities policies and the campaigns to eradicate the violence against women. New challenges]. *Asparkía, 24*, 36–53.

Biglia, B., Olivella, M., & Jiménez, E. (2014). Legislative frameworks and educational practices on gender related violence and youth in Catalonia. *La Camera Blu, Revista di Studi di Genere, 10*(10), 1–20.

Bonet, J. (2007). Problematizar las políticas sociales frente a la(s) violencia(s) de género [Problematize social policy front (s) violence (s) gender]. In B. Biglia & C. San Martín (Eds.), *Estado de Wonderbra. Entretejiendo narraciones feministas sobre las violencias de género* (pp. 35–48). Barcelona: Virus.

Bosch, E., & Ferrer, V.A. (2002). *La voz de las invisibles. Las víctimas de un mal amor que mata* [The voice of the invisible. The victims of an evil love that kills]. Madrid: Cátedra.

Bosch, E., & Ferrer, V.A. (2013). Nuevo modelo explicativo para la violencia contra las mujeres en la pareja: el modelo piramidal y el proceso de filtraje [New explicanatory model for violence against women in couples: The pyramidal model and the filtering process]. *Asparkía, 24,* 54–67.

Bosch, E., Aroca, C., & Ferrer, V.A. (2014). The rearmament of aggressors: The economic crisis and its impact on intimate partner violence against women. *Procedia. Social and Behavior Sciences, 161*(19), 12–17.

Bosch, E., Ferrer, V.A., Ferreiro, V., & Navarro, C. (2013). *La violencia contra las mujeres: el amor como coartada* [Violence against women: Love as alibi]. Barcelona: Antrophos.

Campbell, J.C. (2002). Health consequences of intimate partner violence. *Lancet, 359,* 1331–1336.

CEDAW. (1979). Convention on the Elimination of All Forms of Discrimination against Women. UN General Assembly.

De Miguel, A. (1996). El conflicto de géneros en la tradición sociológica [Gender conflict in the sociological tradition]. *Sociológica: Revista de pensamiento social, 1,* 125–150.

De Miguel, A. (2008). La violencia contra las mujeres. Tres momentos en la construcción del marco feminista de interpretación [Violence against women. Three moments in the construction of feminist interpretation framework]. *Isegoría, 38,* 129–137.

Devries, K.M., Mak, J.Y.T., García-Moreno, C., Petzold, M., Child, J.C., Falder, G., Lim, S., Bacchus, L.J., Engell, R.E., Rosenfeld, L. Pallitto, C., Vos, T., Abrahams, N., & Watts, C.H. (2013). The global prevalence of intimate partner violence against women. *Science, 340,* 1527–1528.

Dutton, M.A. (2000). *Empowering and healing the battered woman: A model for assessment and intervention.* New York: Springer.

Emakunde. (2008). *Gizonduz.* Retrieved from www.berdingune.euskadi.eus/u89-congizon/es/contenidos/informacion/quees/es_gizonduz/quees.html

Emakunde. (2011). *EZ Isildu.* Retrieved from www.interior.ejgv.euskadi.eus/r42-4000/

Emakunde. (2015). *Nahiko.* Retrieved from www.emakunde.euskadi.eus/nahiko/-/informacion/nahiko/

Foran, H.M., & O'Leary, K.D. (2008). Alcohol and intimate partner violence: A meta-analytic review. *Clinical Psychology Review, 28,* 1222–1234.

FRA (European Union Agency for Fundamental Rights) (2014). *Violence against women: An EU-wide Surrey. Main results.* Luxembourg: Publications Office of the European Union. Retrieved from http://fra.europa.eu/sites/default/files/fra-2014-vaw-survey-main-results_en.pdf

Friedman, J. (1992). *Empowerment. The politics of alternative development.* Massachusetts: Blackwell Ed.

García-Moreno, C., Jansen, H.A., Ellsberg, M., Heise, L., & Watts, C.H. (2006). Prevalence of intimate partner violence: Findings from the WHO multi-country study on women's health and domestic violence. *Lancet, 368,* 1260–1269.

GDGV (Government Delegation for Gender Violence) (2013). *Fifth Annual Report of the National Observatory on Violence against Women.* Madrid: Ministry of Health, Social

Affairs, and Equality. Retrieved from http://msssi.gob.es/ssi/violenciaGenero/public aciones/colecciones/PDFS_COLECCION/Informe_Ejecutivo_V_Ingles.pdf

Gil, E., & Lloret, I. (2007). *La violencia de género* [Gender violence]. Barcelona: Universitat Oberta de Catalunya.

Guedes, P., & Bott, S. (2009). *Primary prevention module. End violence against women and girls.* Virtual Knowledge Centre. UN Women.

Harvey, A., Garcia-Moreno, C., & Butchart, A. (2007). *Primary prevention of intimate-partner violence and sexual violence.* Background paper for WHO expert meeting Geneva: WHO.

Heise, L.L. (1998). Violence against women: An integrated ecological framework. *Violence Against Women, 4,* 262–290.

Heise, L.L., & García-Moreno, C. (2002). Violence by intimate partners. In E.G. Krug, L.L. Dahlberg, K.A. Mercy, A.B. Zwi, & R. Lozano (Eds.), *World report on violence and health* (pp. 87–122). Geneva: World Health Organization.

Heyzer, N. (2000). Trabajando por un mundo libre de violencia contra la mujer [Working for a world free of violence against women]. *Carpeta de Documentos del Foro Mundical de Mujeres contra la Violencia* (pp. 13–24). Valencia: Centro Reina Sofía para el Estudio de la Violencia.

Jerez City Council. (2016). *Men for equality.* Retrieved from www.jerez.es/nc/webs_municipales/hombresxigualdad/

Lagarde, M. (2007). Claves para el empoderamiento de las mujeres [Keys to the empowerment of women]. *I Congreso Mujeres en el Mundo Liderando el Milenio.* Valencia: Palabras para la Igualdad.

Laguna, E., & Porcel. E. (2008). Edualter. Retrieved from www.edualter.org/material/actualitat/genere/castellano/index.htm

Lerner, G. (1986). *The creation of patriarchy.* New York: Oxford University Press.

Millet, K. (1969). *Sexual politics.* St. Albans, Herts: Granada Publishing.

Morrison, S., Hardison, J. Mathew, A., & O'Neill, J. (2004). An evidence-based review of sexual assault preventive intervention programs. Retrieved from https://www.ncjrs.gov/pdffiles1/nij/grants/207262.pdf

Moya, M.C. (2004). Actitudes sexistas y nuevas formas de sexismo [Sexist attitudes and new forms of sexism]. In E. Barberá & M.I. Martínez Benlloch (Eds.), *Psicología y género* (pp. 271–294). Madrid: Pearson.

Organic Law 1/2004 on Integral Protection Measures against Gender Violence. (2004). *Boletín Oficial del Estado núm. 313,* 42166–42197.

Organic Law 3/2007 on Effective Equality between Women and Men. (2007). *Boletín Oficial del Estado núm. 71,* 12611–12645.

Organic Law 14/2011 on Science, Technology and Innovation. (2011). *Boletín Oficial del Estado núm. 131,* 54387–54455.

Plichta, S.B. (2004). Intimate partner violence and physical health consequences: Policy and practice implications. *Journal of Interpersonal Violence, 19,* 1296–1323.

Puigvert, L. (Ed.). (2010). *Incidencia de la ley integral contra la violencia de género en la formación inicial del profesorado* [Incidence of comprehensive law against gender violence in the initial teacher]. Madrid: Instituto de la Mujer. Retrieved from www.inmujer.gob.es/areasTematicas/estudios/estudioslinea2012/docs/Incidencia_Ley_integral.pdf

Puleo, A. (2005). El patriarcado: ¿una organización social superada? [Patriarchy: A social organization overcome?]. *Temas para el debate, 133,* 39–42.

Puleo, A. (2008). La violencia de género y el género de la violencia [Gender violence and the gender of the violence]. In A. Puleo (Ed.), *El reto de la igualdad de género. Nuevas perspectivas en ética y filosofía política* (pp. 361–371). Madrid: Biblioteca Nueva.

Rodríguez-Menés, J., & Safranoff, A. (2012). Violence against women in intimate relations: A contrast of five theories. *European Journal of Criminology, 9*(6), 584–602.

Rowlands, J. (1997). *Questioning empowerment*. Oxford: Oxfam.

Ruiz, C. (2009). *Abre los ojos. El amor no es ciego* [Open your eyes. Love is not blind]. Sevilla: Instituto Andaluz de la Mujer. Retrieved from www.juntadeandalucia.es/institutodelajuventud/miraporlaigualdad/images/descargas/Abre%20los%20ojos.pdf

Saltzman, J. (1990). Gender equity: An integrated theory of stability and change. New York: SAGE.

Stöckl, H., Devries, K., Rotstein, A., Abrahams, N., Campbell, J., Watts, C., & García-Moreno, C. (2013). The global prevalence of intimate partner homicide: A systematic review. *The Lancet, 382*, 859–865.

UN (United Nations). (1994). *Declaration on the elimination of violence against women* (Res. A/R/48/104). Retrieved from www.un.org/documents/ga/res/48/a48r104.htm

UN (United Nations). (2006). *In-depth study on all forms of violence against women. Report of the Secretary-General* (A/61/122/Add.1). Retrieved from http://daccess-dds-ny.un.org/doc/UNDOC/GEN/N06/419/74/PDF/N0641974.pdf?OpenElement

UN Women. (2012). *Promoting primary prevention*. Retrieved from www.endvawnow.org/en/articles/318-promover-la-prevencion-primaria-.html

UNIFEM. (2010). *Ending violence against women and girls: Programming essentials*. Retrieved from www.endvawnow.org/uploads/modules/pdf/1360104854.pdf

Urruzola, M.J. (2005). *No te líes con los chicos malos* [Do not fall for the bad guys]. Retrieved from www.educandoenigualdad.com.

Valiente, C. (2006). *El feminismo de estado en España: El Instituto de la Mujer (1983–2003)* [State feminism in Spain: Women's Institute (1983–2003)]. Valencia: Institut d'Estudis Universitaris de la Dona.

Walker, L.E.A. (2009). *The battered woman syndrome*. New York: Springer. 3rd edition.

Walker, S., & Barton, L. (Eds.). (1983). *Gender, class and education*. Nueva York: The Falmer Press.

Watts, C., & Zimmerman, C. (2002). Violence against women: Global scope magnitude. *The Lancet, 359*, 1232–1237.

WHO (World Health Organization). (2006). *Interpersonal violence and alcohol*. Retrieved from www.who.int/violence_injury_prevention/violence/world_report/factsheets/pb_violencealcohol.pdf

WHO (World Health Organization). (2013). *Global and regional estimates of violence against women: Prevalence and health effects of intimate partner violence and non-partner sexual violence*. Geneva: Author. Retrieved from www.who.int/reproductive-health/publications/violence/9789241564625/en/index.html

Women's Institute. (2008). *La mujer en cifras (1983–2008)* [Women in numbers (1983–2008)]. Madrid, Spain: Author.

5 Domestic violence

An epidemic which demolishes the myth of the traditional Italian family

Bruno Meini

In the EU Member States, the term domestic violence is used variously, either to refer exclusively to intimate partner violence or also encompassing intergenerational violence such as violence against children as well as children's violence against their parents. The Istanbul Convention (Council of Europe, 2014b) specifies that, in the context of the Convention, domestic violence shall mean all acts of physical, sexual, psychological or economic violence that occur within the family or domestic unit, or between former or current spouses or partners, whether or not the perpetrator shares or has shared the same residence with the victim. Therefore, the definition in the Convention includes both intimate partner violence and intergenerational violence. But, the term domestic violence used in this chapter refers exclusively to intimate partner violence and excludes intergenerational violence (European Union Agency for Fundamental Rights, 2014).

Domestic violence is the most common form of violence against women. It affects women across the life span from sex-selective abortion of female fetuses to forced suicide and abuse, and is evident, to some degree, in every society in the world (Kaur & Garg, 2008). As previously seen, there lacks a generally accepted and clear definition of domestic violence, but its definition varies depending on the context in which the term is used. From a clinical or behavioral viewpoint domestic violence can be defined as "a pattern of assaultive and/or coercive behaviors, including physical, sexual, and psychological attacks, as well as economic coercion, that adults or adolescents use against their intimate partners" (Schechter & Edelson, 1999, pp. 122–123). Legal definitions across the nations generally describe specific conducts or acts which are subject to civil and criminal actions, and the specific language used may vary depending on whether the definition is found in the civil or criminal codes (Child Welfare Information Gateway, 2013).

Violence in intimate relationships is often cyclical. The domestic violence cycle can be described as a three-stage process articulated in distinct phases. The first is tension-building, where unresolved conflict and unexpressed anger collect. The victim at this time minimizes the tension. Explosion, the second phase, is when the abuser reacts to a sense of losing control by increasing the intensity of threats to the victim. The victim does not know how to reduce the tension or leave the environment. At this point the emotional, verbal, and/or physical abuse incident occurs. Last is the honeymoon period. Here the abuser seeks forgiveness in a contrite manner and promises never to let the abuse occur again. The victim is confused as she was just hurt yet she sees before her the potential of what the person could be if they did not display the controlling/ violent side of their actions. Obviously, the cycle begins again as tension rebuilds (Reiter, 2015, p. 118).

The combination of individual, relational, community and societal factors contribute to the risk of becoming a domestic violence victim or perpetrator (Sampson, 2006). Understanding these multilevel factors can help identify various opportunities for prevention. In general, literature around the prevention of domestic violence is centered on two main factors: risk and protective factors. Risk factors are primarily associated with detecting early warning factors that may contribute to domestic violence. On the other hand, protective factors aim to prevent domestic violence by focusing on interpersonal and quality of life domains by facilitating the learning of healthy relationship skills, personal development and respect (Wells, Abboud & Claussen, 2012). Risk factors can be identified as mental disorders (Humphreys & Thiara, 2003; Hegarty, 2011; Trevillion, Oram, Feder & Howard, 2012), partner's use of substances, especially heavy alcohol consumption (Sabia, 2004; Gebara et al., 2015), low socio-economic status (Chatha, Ahmed & Sheikh, 2014), young age (McCue, 2008, pp. 50–51), male dominance in the family, traditional gender norms (Pulerwitz et al., 2015), and social norms supportive of violence (World Health Organization, 2009), etc. Several studies have shown that women who were more highly educated (secondary schooling or higher) were 20–55 percent less likely to be victims of intimate partner violence compared to less-educated women. Likewise, men who were more highly educated were approximately 40 percent less likely to perpetrate intimate partner violence compared to less-educated men. Other factors that may decrease or protect against risk include: having benefited from healthy parenting as a child, having own supportive family, being part of an extended family and belonging to an association (World Health Organization & London School of Hygiene and Tropical Medicine, 2010, p. 31). Domestic violence is a critical public health problem with serious implications for the physical and psychological status of women across all societies and classes in the world (Alhabib, Nur & Jones, 2009).

This specific form of violence may lead to physical impairments, ranging from cuts and bruises to permanent disability and death, and is also often associated with specific mental and behavioral health problems such as depression and anxiety, phobias, panic disorder, post-traumatic stress disorder, suicidal behavior, self-harm, eating, and sleep disorders (Campbell, Laughon & Woods, 2006). In addition, women who are abused suffer an increased risk of unwanted pregnancy and induced abortion (Kaye, Mirembe, Bantebya, Johansson & Ekstrom, 2006) and sexually transmitted diseases, including HIV (MacQuarrie, Winter & Kishor, 2013). As trauma victims, they are also at an increased risk of misuse of psychoactive substances (Willson et al., 2000). A World Health Organization, London School of Hygiene and Tropical Medicine and South African Medical

Research Council multi-country study reported that the global prevalence of physical and/or sexual intimate partner violence among all ever-partnered women was estimated at 30 percent. The prevalence was highest in the African, Eastern Mediterranean and South-East Asian regions, where approximately 37 percent of ever-partnered women reported having experienced physical and/or sexual intimate partner violence at some point in their lives. Prevalence was lower in the high-income countries (23 percent) and in the European and the Western Pacific regions, where 25 percent of ever-partnered women reported lifetime intimate partner violence experience. The prevalence is already high among young women aged 15–19 years and rises to reach its peak in the age group of 40–44 years. The reported prevalence among women aged 50 years and older is lower but this estimate is rather approximate because it is based on data which come primarily from high-income countries. In addition, since most of the surveys are carried out by women aged 15 or 18 to 49 years, fewer data are available for the over-49 age group (World Health Organization, London School of Hygiene and Tropical Medicine and South African Medical Research Council, 2013).

The hidden epidemic

In most European Member States, until relatively recently, violence against women – particularly domestic violence – was considered a private matter in which the state played only a limited role. It is only since the 1990s that violence against women has emerged as a fundamental rights concern that deserves legal and political recognition at the highest level, and as an area where state parties, as those with a duty to protect, have an obligation to defend victims (European Union Agency for Fundamental Rights, 2014).

National criminal statistics in Italy on domestic violence are very limited. Data on the number of women murdered by intimate partners is available; however, there is no information on the gender of the perpetrator. Other data available are not disaggregated by relationship between victim and perpetrator; hence it is not possible to derive crimes committed in a domestic context (Stelmaszek & Fisher, 2013, p. 147).

In 2006, the Italian National Institute of Statistics conducted a survey of women over the entire national territory regarding being victims of sexual, physical, and psychological violence, a few years after an initial survey, conducted in 2002. The time period studied for victims' experiences of violence included lifetime experiences of violence and current experience (last 12 months) (Muratore, Barletta & Federici, 2008). For the 2002 survey, there were 60,000 women respondents, 22,759 of whom were aged 14–59 years. For the 2006 survey, the sample consisted of 25,000 women aged 16–70 years. Owing to the sensitivity of the issues, the telephone survey technique seemed best suited because it provided more anonymity and guarantee of protection. The data were gender disaggregated for the victim and the perpetrator. The survey showed that the phenomenon of violence against women was most commonly perpetrated by the partner or ex-partner, even in cases of homicide. A comparison of the Italian data with those of the U.S.A. for the period 2001–2006 showed a specificity of intimate partner violence in Italy that seemed to be related to cultural elements and psychological and psychopathologic factors (Carabellese, Tamma, La Tegola, Candelli & Catanes, 2014).

In 2007 the Italian Ministry of Home Affairs published a report that provided some data on homicides, sexual violence and stalking. This investigation reported on crime in Italy over almost four decades, 1968–2006, and included chapters on general crime, thefts, robberies, homicides, violence against women and organized crime (Ministero dell'Interno, 2007). Data on intimate partner homicides were available, although the data were not age disaggregated, neither for the victim nor the perpetrator, although data on gender of victims (not perpetrators) were available. Intimate partner murders were referred to as crimes of passion "Famiglia passioni amorose." This is a rather inopportune name for a crime of this magnitude.

Designating the taking of a life as a crime of passion removes not only the sense of the gravity of the crime and its irreversible nature, but also removes the responsibility from the perpetrator, as if the crime was not premeditated or intentional. From data provided in the report, in 2006, there were 192 murders committed by intimate partners in Italy. The highest number of murders committed was in 2002, with 211 persons killed by intimate partners. From the time period 2001–2006, victims were female in 63 percent of intimate partner homicides. This means that about 721 women were murdered by their intimate partners in a six-year period. These were the only police data available in the report regarding domestic violence. The information provided in the Violence against Women section of the report relayed findings of the aforementioned 2006 prevalence study and were not administrative data (Stelmaszek & Fisher, 2013, p. 147).

In January 2011 the United Nations Special Rapporteur on Violence against Women, Rashida Manjoo, visited Italy and explained the Italian situation. She spoke explicitly of domestic violence as of the most pervasive form of violence that continued to affect women across the country. Although statistics from the Rome Prosecutor's Office indicated a slight increase of reports on sexual offenses and domestic violence in 2010, 96 percent of women who were victims of violent acts by non-partners and 93 percent of victims of partner abuse did not report cases to the police. Moreover, 33.9 percent of women who had suffered violence at the hands of a partner and 24 percent by a non-partner had never talked about what happened to them. These data have not experienced significant changes. As a result, domestic violence in the private sphere remains largely an invisible and underreported crime (Manjoo, 2012). Italian service providers confirmed the analysis of the United Nations Special Rapporteur on Violence against Women and indicated a prevalence rate of up to 78 percent (Donne in rete contro la violenza, 2011).

Almost always, the violence continues over time and most of the cases are preceded by physical or psychological mistreatment and abuse, which shows the link between violence in the family and murder (femicide), including the feeling of pride hurt, jealousy, anger, desire for revenge and retribution against women, and the transgression of a behavioral model, a concept that involves cultural stereotypes linked to a patriarchal culture. Barbara Spinelli, Italian member of the European Parliament and legal expert in femicide, pointed out that the family kills more than the Italian mafia, more than foreign organized crime. She added that the home can be considered the most unsafe place for women. Maria Monteleone, Italian magistrate specialized in cases of violence against women, stated that in 90–95 percent of cases it is always the man who is the author of maltreatment, abuse and violence. Jealousy is an alibi which deserves a limited consideration. She added that a person who is not violent by nature should not kill their former spouse or partner (Revolting Europe, 2012).

Femicide is a term which was elaborated by Diana E.H. Russell and Jill Radford in a compilation of works published in 1992 with the following title: *Femicide, the Politics of Woman Killing*. In this compilation, it was defined by two authors as the misogynous killing of women by men (Russell & Radford, 1992) and it has its roots in the larger feminist discourse, emphasizing the patriarchal nature of society and the tendency to use violence as a tool of repression in the maintenance of male dominance. The term takes its form from the word-ending "cide," a derivative of the Latin word *ceadere* which means to kill, and *femina* which means woman or female. For the proponents of the term, this is simply more proof of the taboo nature of femicide and the silencing power of male structures within society, which prevent women from actively naming violence against them and resisting its multiple forms. The term, rather than indicating a new form of violence, is explanatory of a continuum of violence exerted against women which causes the death of the victim. More specifically, however, it is proposed as an alternative to the gender-neutral term of *homicide*. As such, it seeks to underscore the killing of women for being women, a phenomenon linked closely with sexual violence enacted to punish, blame and control the actions, emotions and behavior of women (Kaye, 2007).

Victims and perpetrators

The majority of female homicide victims are killed by male intimate partners (intimate-partner femicide) and are likely to be significantly underreported, even in areas with the most extensive and complete data collection. Death certificates in most countries do not include information on perpetrators of femicide. The majority of current research on intimate-partner femicide refers to the killing of a female by an intimate partner but there is little consistency in terminology used by researchers and service providers. The different frameworks, definitions, and classifications used for conceptualizing femicide make more difficult the collection of information from various sources, and lead to documentation that may not be comparable across communities or regions (Widyono, 2009, p. 8). In our analysis, however, femicide refers specifically to murders committed by current or former partners other than family members. That was a classification present in two studies carried out respectively in Chile (Rojas, Maturana & Maira, 2004) and in Costa Rica (Carcedo & Sagot, 2000). In other words, femicide is intended as intimate (or domestic) femicide (Dawson & Gartner, 1998).

The Center for Women Against Violence in Bologna, Italy, coordinated research on femicide for "Rapporto ombra" a report on the conditions of women produced for the Italian platform of "30 years of the Convention on the Elimination of all forms of Discrimination Against Women (CEDAW): work in progress" presented in July 2011 to the United Nations in New York City. This research emphasizes the centrality of mass media's role which often presents perpetrators of femicide as being on a rampage and killing sprees, generating among the public the false idea that femicide is mostly committed by men affected by a psychiatric illness. Instead, if we analyze the time interval between 2006 and 2010 less than 10 percent of the femicides were due to mental illness, and in less than 10 percent of the cases the motives were unemployment or economic difficulties. Most women resulted in becoming victims of femicide because of private matters such as separations or conflictual relationships. Between 2006 and 2009, 439 femicide victims were identified by researchers. Among these, in just 15 percent of the cases the perpetrator was unknown to the victim. In more than half of the cases, femicide occurred in intimate relationships and the perpetrator was the husband, lover, or ex-partner. The remaining cases resulted in the perpetrator being another relative of the victim or a man that she knew (acquaintance, colleague and neighbor). In addition, it deserves particular attention to the fact that femicides are named *crimes of passion* when perpetrator and victim are both Italian. If an offender and victim are migrants the femicide is called an *honor crime*. This different classification is discriminatory because it leads to the idea that these crimes as culturally related, and germane to foreign communities and their differing traditions. However, the same custom of clearing the family honor and justifying these practices invoked clauses resulting in a reduction in penalty, which was widespread in Italy until a few years ago (Spinelli & Italian NGO platform, 2011).

In 2014 the Italian helpline Telefono Rosa presented the annual report named *The Secret Voices of Violence*. According to the report, 128 women were killed by their husbands, male partners or former boyfriends in 2013, marking a slight increase compared to the 124 victims registered in 2012. The report also indicated that the majority of victims were women who belonged to the middle and upper classes. Specifically, at least 21 percent of victims had bachelor degrees and 53 percent of them were graduated in 2013. It also added that neither education nor professional emancipation seemed to be enough to protect women from domestic violence. The average age of the victims was also higher than before, with 28 percent of abused women aged between 45 and 54 and, for the first time since 2006, also 15 girls under the age of 15 were killed by male partners in 2013. In addition, according to the report, 64 percent among the male perpetrators had medium-high levels of education and socioeconomic status. Also, most of the offenders were men aged between 35 and 54 years, with only 15 percent of cases related to boys and men under 35. In conclusion, we can observe that cultural or economic background is not directly connected to gender-based violence in the country, meaning that both men and women belonging to the middle and upper classes are often respectively authors and victims of abuse as well (Ralli, 2014).

In June 2015 the second edition of the multipurpose survey "Women's Safety" was funded by the Department for Equal Opportunities of the Italian Presidency of the Council of Ministers and prepared by the Italian National Institute of Statistics. This survey estimated that 6,788,000 women experienced some form of violence at least once in their lifetime. According to this survey 31.5 percent of women between the ages of 16 and 70 have faced physical or sexual violence during their lifetime: specifically, 20.2 percent of them had suffered physical violence (4,353,000), 21 percent sexual violence (4,520,000), 5.4 percent the most severe forms of sexual abuse such as rape (652,000) and attempted rape (746,000). Women also faced many threats (12.3 percent). Just over 11 percent reported being victims of shoving and jostling (11.5 percent), or slaps, kicks, punches, and bites (7.3 percent). Other times they had been hit with objects which could have hurt them (6.1 percent). In addition, 13.6 percent of them had faced at least one episode of physical or sexual violence by their current or former partner (Istat, 2015).

Legal framework

As of the end of 2014, about one in seven Italian women had suffered physical or sexual violence at the hands of a partner or former partner in the course of her lifetime. In some regions, the figure is closer to one in five. This is reported by a study conducted by the Italian National Institute of Statistics, which surveyed 21,000 women across the country's 20 regions. Nearly one-third of them suffered some form of physical or sexual violence in their lifetime. The data is alarming, especially considering there are clear indications that violence was underreported in some regions. For example, in Calabria the rate of partner violence was the lowest in all of Italy at 8.4 percent. But the female homicide rate in the region, an alternative measure of violence, is among Italy's highest with a 2013 body count of 10 in every million women. In addition, in some regions the situation seems to be out of control. In Abruzzo, for example, rates of violence against women have been climbing higher above the national average for the past 10 years (Bouvier, 2015).

Table 5.1 shows the data regarding women who have experienced violence in their romantic relationships with their current partner or ex-partner over time. These data are taken from the two editions of the multipurpose survey "Women's Safety" which were compiled by the Italian National Institute of Statistics and published respectively in 2008 and 2015. This comparison considers the data of the last five years of both surveys in order to understand the changes of the phenomenon of violence against women over time.

The 2015 survey reports that the number of women who have suffered at least one form of physical or sexual violence amounted to 2,435,000 cases over the last 5 years; that is 11.3 percent of women between the ages of 16 and 70. Over a

Table 5.1 Comparison of women aged between 16 and 70 years who are victims of physical or sexual violence perpetrated by a current partner or former partner in the last five years: 2006 and 2014

Types of violence	Current partner[a]		Ex-partner[b]		Partner or ex-partner[c]	
	2006	2014	2006	2014	2006	2014
Physical or sexual violence	4.4	3.0	6.0	5.0	6.6	4.9
Physical violence	3.3	2.3	4.6	4.1	5.1	4.0
Sexual violence	1.6	1.1	2.9	2.1	2.8	2.0
Rape or attempted rape	0.2	0.2	1.0	0.8	0.7	0.6

Source: Istat, 2015.

Notes
a per 100 women who have a current partner.
b per 100 women who have an ex-partner.
c per 100 women with current or ex-partner.

million and a half suffered physical violence, that is, 1,517,000 (7 percent), There were 1,369,000 victims of sexual violence (6.4 percent); 246,000 women suffered rapes or attempted rape (1.2 percent). The 2014 survey adds that 1,1900,000 women have suffered violence in multiple relationships, over the last five years, (4.9 percent), specifically 496,000 women with their current partner (3 percent) and 538,000 women with a former partner (5 percent). But, rate of violence between these couples rises to 12.5 percent if we consider only those women who have interrupted a coupled relationship in the last five years for another relationship. In addition, if we make a comparison between the data of the last five years of the two surveys we can notice the following significant improvement: a reduction of the episodes of physical and sexual violence committed by former or current partners (see Figure 5.1). Therefore, violence in its most violent forms (rape and attempted rape) remains almost unvaried (Istat, 2015, p. 8).

In the second report the youngest women and the most educated women are indicated to be the two groups of women who have suffered more violence from ex-partners, whereas separated and divorced women are those most at risk. There is also a significant difference between immigrant and Italian women regarding the level of relationship violence in the last five years: 4.9 percent of immigrant women versus 2.8 percent of Italian women. Fifteen percent of married immigrant women had also had violent partners who did not live with them because of work or studies being far from home, which means that at least some husbands have remained in the country of origin of their wives. Over the past five years, the categories of immigrant women most at risk of violence are Moroccan and Romanian with 13.5 percent and 13.7 percent respectively. Moroccan women's primary risk for victimization was 11 percent with 7.8 percent suffering from sexual violence and 7 percent suffering from physical violence.

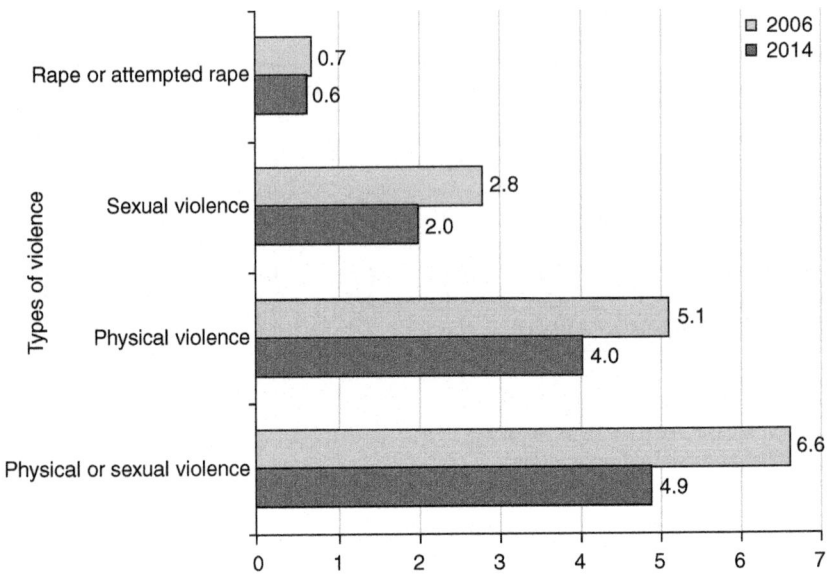

Figure 5.1 Types of violence committed by partner or ex-partner in the last five years: 2006 and 2014.

Source: Istat, 2015.

Female students in Italy have seen the level of violence with an ex- or current partner reduce significantly when compared to 2006 data from 17 percent to 11.9 percent with ex-partners, and from 5.3 percent to 2.4 percent for current partners (Istat, 2015).

Psychological abuse often precedes, occurs with, and/or follows physical or sexual abuse in relationships. The psychological aspect deserves special attention because victims who lose their independence, self-esteem, and dignity tend to remain in abusive situations. The abuse is perpetrated by a domestic partner to maintain power and control in the relationship. To assert control, the abuser uses "brainwashing tactics" similar to those used on prisoners of war, hostages, or members of cults. Common features of brainwashing include isolation, humiliation, accusation, and unpredictable attacks. The abusive environment produces real and anticipated fear, which contributes to the battered woman's belief that her situation is hopeless and that she must depend on her abuser (Mega, Mega, Mega & Harris, 2000).

In 2014 Italian women victims of psychological violence perpetrated by a current partner amounted to about 4,400,000 cases, that is, 26.4 percent of the women who had relationship as a couple. This percentage decreases only slightly to 22.4 percent when one considers only women who suffered psychological violence namely without being accompanied by acts of physical or sexual violence. In both situations, this was a significant drop compared to 2006, as in that year the percentage of women who suffered psychological violence accompanied by acts of physical or sexual violence amounted to 42.3 percent whereas that percentage decreased to 35.9 percent for women who suffered psychological violence only (Istat, 2015, p. 12).

As shown in Table 5.2, from 2004 to 2013, there were 1,632 cases of femicide, of which 1,151 occurred at home (70.5 percent). In 2013, domestic femicides represented 68.2 percent of the total femicides.

Italian domestic femicides show regularity over the time as they are always about two-thirds of the total of femicides (see Figure 5.2). Therefore, such killings are only a relatively small proportion of total homicides. In about 80 percent of the cases, the victims and assailants knew each other before the assassination, and in a significant portion of the cases, they were members of the same family. In approximately 60 percent of cases, spouses, partners, and ex-partners were the guilty parties (Iezzi, 2013, pp. 54–55). This form of violence calls for implementation of a broader plan of action, involving the police, and raising people's awareness on this pressing social issue (Polizia di Stato, 2013).

Domestic violence in Italy is indirectly covered in the criminal code under different articles not specific to domestic violence. The articles include: article 572 (maltreatment within the family), article 575 (homicide), article 582 (injuries with healing time above 20 days), article 605 (kidnapping), article 609 (sexual acts with minor), article 610 (private violence), article 612 (severe threatening). Stalking is a separate offense that was introduced into the criminal code in 2009 (Stelmaszek & Fisher, 2013, p. 147).

In the first half of 2013, 81 women were killed in Italy, 75 percent of them by someone close to them (Nadeau, 2013). This statistic pushed Prime Minister, Enrico Letta, to intervene urgently with the approval of the Decree-Law No. 93 of

Table 5.2 Femicide trends in Italy: 2004–2013

Year	Total homicides	Total femicides		Domestic femicides	
	Count	*Count*	*Rate*	*Count*	*Rate*
2004	705	184	26.1	126	68.5
2005	597	138	23.1	98	71.0
2006	618	181	29.3	134	74.0
2007	630	145	23.0	98	67.6
2008	610	147	24.1	105	71.4
2009	590	173	29.3	132	76.3
2010	530	158	29.8	111	70.3
2011	551	170	30.9	120	70.6
2012	524	157	30.0	105	66.9
2013	502	179	35.7	122	68.2
Total	5,857	1,632	27.9	1,151	70.5

Source: EURES, 2014.

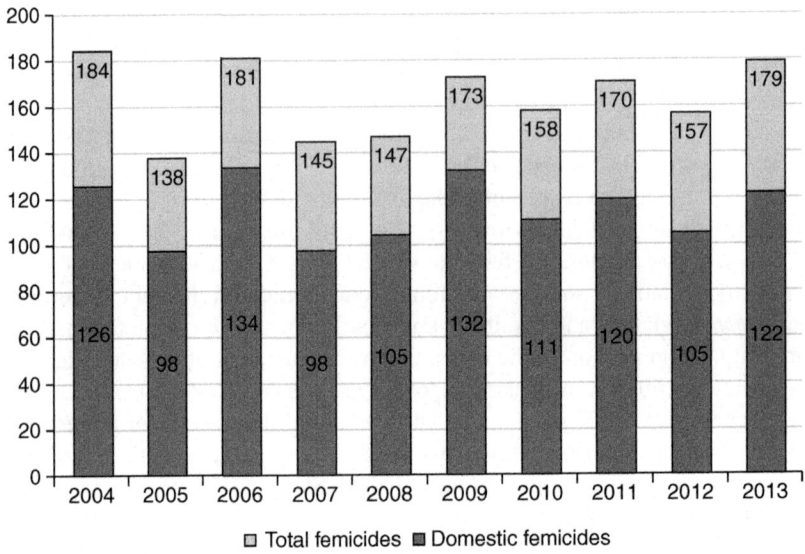

Figure 5.2 The share of domestic femicides on the total number of femicides: 2004–2013.

Source: EURES, 2014.

August 14, 2013 which contained new harsher measures against femicide. The decree was converted into law on October 15, 2013, and established "Urgent provisions on safety and for the fight against gender-based violence, as well as on civil protection and compulsory administration of provinces" (Council of Europe, 2014a, p. 58). That was a significant step forward in tackling gender-based violence and stalking, although its efficacy risks being strongly weakened due to a lengthy criminal trial process (Council of Europe, 2014a). The new law builds upon the progress made in May 2013, when Italy's lower Chamber of Deputies ratified the Council of Europe Convention on preventing and combating violence against women and domestic violence (Istanbul Convention). The Council of Europe treaty (Council of Europe, 2014b), is intended to create a framework to prevent, prosecute and eliminate violence against women in European countries (McRobie, 2013). As for prevention, the law strengthens the so-called "warning" (*ammonimento*), namely the already in force administrative measure which can be requested by the victim to the *Questore*, the officer in charge of the police force, public order and related administrative services, by providing for the mandatory removal of the violent man from the family house, as well as a gun ban, driving disqualification, and the ability to use electronic surveillance tools to monitor perpetrators (e.g., electronic tagging). The Italian government also adopted a special preventive measure, namely the implementation of an Extraordinary Action Plan against

Sexual and Gender-based Violence by the Italian Minister in charge of Equal Opportunities (article 5 of the Decree-Law No. 93 of 2013), with the contribution of civil society. This public body is responsible for the implementation of the Plan; an inter-ministerial task force on violence against women was established on July 22, 2013 by the Presidency of the Council of Ministers. A task force, or the development of a technical panel, was organized into seven sub-groups reflecting the Plan's aims in order to better identify institutional strategies and concrete measures to combat gender-based violence. This plan is also in line with the Conclusions on Combating Violence against Women, and the Provision of Support Services for Victims of Domestic Violence, adopted by the Council of the European Union on December 6, 2012 (Council of Europe, 2014a, pp. 58–60). In this document, the Council adopted a few measures to tackle the problem. First, the Council makes clear that custom, tradition, culture, privacy, religion, and so-called honor can never justify violence. These factors also give no reason for avoiding the obligations of Member States in their efforts to prevent and eliminate violence and prosecute perpetrators. The Council of Ministers calls for coordinated policies at a local, national, and international level to combat and eliminate all forms of violence against women. Second, strong emphasis has been placed on collecting data on victims and perpetrators as information concerning violence against women is often hidden, and as a result it limits understanding of the real extent of the problem and its consequences. It also impedes further development of policies, strategies and actions. Third, the ministers called on the Member States and the European Commission to develop and implement action plans, including programs or strategies to combat all forms of violence against women and girls, involving all relevant legislative and non-legislative measures. The Council also calls for more appropriate training of relevant professionals in the area. Fourth, the Council recommends a European helpline to assist victims of violence against women to be established by Member States and the European Commission. Fifth, the European Parliament, and the European Commission, as well as Member States, are invited to contribute actively to this issue. For example, they could consider signing, ratifying and implementing the Council of Europe Convention on Preventing and Combating Violence and taking more primary prevention measures to combat violence against women. Lastly, the Council invited the European Parliament, European Commission and Member States to ensure appropriate and sustainable funding (Council of the European Union, 2012).

Regarding the punishment of offenders, the law introduced new aggravating circumstances. In particular, penalties are increased if children under 18 years of age witness violence, and if the victim is in a particularly vulnerable situation (i.e., pregnant). Moreover, the idea of femicide is further strengthened by the introduction of the particularly close relationship between the victim and the perpetrator as an aggravating circumstance (i.e., if the perpetrator is the victim's spouse or partner, or non-cohabiting partner). In line with the guiding principles established by the Istanbul Convention, the Italian law is aimed at ensuring greater protection for victims both in relation to hearings (which will work to protect vulnerable persons) and through a system guaranteeing transparency during ongoing investigations and legal proceedings and envisaging the obligation to inform victims about support services existing at the local level. The special social implications of this crime explain the granting of legal aid for victims whose income exceeds the income limits fixed by the national legislation. Furthermore, in compliance with the Istanbul Convention, protection is extended to foreign victims, for whom the law provides for the possibility of obtaining a humanitarian residence permit. This measure was established by Legislative Decree No. 286/1998 consolidating the provisions regulating immigration and the rules relating to the status of foreign nationals, which can be converted into work permits with no time-limit (Council of Europe, 2014a, pp. 58–59). However, these lawful measures should be accompanied by long-term gender-sensitive, comprehensive education and training programs (Mammone, Parini & Veltri, 2015, p. 65).

Conclusion

Domestic violence produces significant consequences both at personal and public level in Italy. The loss of human security, personal safety, and the risk of serious harm or death is met with costs that must be absorbed by the public sector such as health, justice, education and social services. The effects of domestic violence are broad. Impacts to the individual can be experienced as a loss of personal well-being, reduced social participation, absenteeism from the workplace, deleterious health outcomes, and substance abuse. The impact on children who witness domestic violence is also concerning as they are exposed to emotional trauma, depression, injury and other physical, emotional and behavioral problems (Montecchi, 2011; Wells et al., 2012).

Italian women's rights advocates say the problem is not a lack of laws against domestic violence, but rather a lack of charges against, and arrests and prosecutions of the mostly male offenders. In addition, there is a lack of resources to help women who are stuck in violent relationships to get out and stay out of these dangerous relationships. This situation warrants attention for several reasons. First, Italy has one of the lowest fertility rates in the world: an average of 1.4 children per woman as of 2012 (the replacement rate is at least 2.0). The reason for that is Italy also possesses a huge concentration of educated women. At one point in the past decade, it sported the highest rate of female PhDs in the world. An educated female population is not as subject to high rates of domestic abuse as an uneducated one. When a woman is economically independent, she is less likely to be trapped in an abusive relationship. She has more options available which can allow her to leave her partner more readily (Erbe, 2013).

It is of primary importance to address people's behavior and attitudes toward violence, however, it will require long-term commitments. Community healthcare providers can implement awareness and behavior change programs in the community in order to create a community-based response to violence by educating community members about the costs and consequences of abuse, and advocating for nonviolent relationships. Exposing violence and enabling vulnerable and marginalized people to receive necessary services will help break the life cycle of violence and promote the rights of women and girls (Shane & Ellsberg, 2002, p. 8).

References

Alhabib, S., Nur, U., & Jones, R. (2010). Domestic violence against women: Systematic review of prevalence studies. *Journal of Family Violence*, *25*(4), 369–382.

Bouvier, S. (2015, November 25). The hardship of women trying to escape domestic violence in Italy. *La Stampa*. Retrieved from www.lastampa.it/2015/11/25/esteri/lastampa-in-english/the-hardship-of-women-trying-to-escape-domestic-violence-in-italy-yuSvH TsBudNuk9ViNWKy9O/pagina.html

Campbell, J., Laughon, K., & Woods, A. (2006). Impact of intimate partner abuse on physical and mental health: How does it present in clinical practice? In G. Roberts, K. Hegarty & G. Feder (Eds.), *Intimate partner abuse and health professionals: New approaches to domestic violence* (pp. 43–60). San Diego, CA: Elsevier.

Carabellese, F., Tamma, M., La Tegola, D., Candelli, C., & Catanes, R. (2014). Women victims of violent partners: The Italian situation amid culture and psychopathology. *Journal of Forensic Sciences*, *59*(2), 533–539.

Carcedo, C., & Sagot, A.M. (2000). *Femicide in Costa Rica 1990–1999*. Washington, DC: Pan American Health Organization.

Chatha, S.A., Ahmed, K., & Sheikh, K.S. (2014). Socio-economic status and domestic violence: A study on married women in urban Lahore, Pakistan. *South Asian Studies: A Research Journal of South Asian Studies*, *29*(1), 229–237.

Child Welfare Information Gateway. (2013). *Definitions of domestic violence*. Washington, DC: U.S. Department of Health and Human Services, Children's Bureau.

Council of Europe. (2014a). *Compilation of contributions from member states on key challenges and good practices on access to justice for women victims of violence at national level*. Strasbourg: Council of Europe.

Council of Europe. (2014b). *The Council of Europe Convention on Preventing and Combating Violence against Women and Domestic Violence*. Strasbourg: Council of Europe – Amnesty International.

Council of the European Union. (2012, December 6). *Council conclusions on combating violence against women, and the provision of support services for victims of domestic violence – 3206th ESPCO Council meeting*. Brussels: Council of the European Union.

Dawson, M., & Gartner, R. (1998). Differences in the characteristics of intimate femicides: The role of relationship state and relationship status. *Homicide Studies: An Interdisciplinary & International Journal*, *2*(4), 378–399.

Donne in rete contro la violenza. (2011). *13th Wave conference, October 11–13, 2011, Rome – Research and survey group D.I.RE association: "Statistics for 2010: 3rd national survey."* Retrieved from www.direcontrolaviolenza.it/wcontent/uploads/2014/03/e.waves-tatistic.pdf

Erbe, B. (2013, August 23). Domestic violence: A plague in US and Italy. *The Korea Times*. Retrieved from www.koreatimes.co.kr/www/news/opinon/2013/08/197_141630.html

EURES. (2014). *Secondo rapporto sul femminicidio in Italia: caratteristiche e tendenze del 2013*. Roma: EURES.

European Union Agency for Fundamental Rights. (2014). *Violence against women: An UE-wide survey – main results*. Vienna: European Union Agency for Fundamental Rights.

Gebara, C.F.P., Ferri, C.P., Lourenço, L.M., Vieira, M.T., Bhona, F.M.C., & Noto, A.R. (2015). Patterns of domestic violence and alcohol consumption among women and the effectiveness of a brief intervention in a household setting: A protocol study. *BMC Women's Health, 15*(78), 1–8. DOI: 10.1186/s12905–015–0236–8

Hegarty, K. (2011). Domestic violence: The hidden epidemic associated with mental illness. *British Journal of Psychiatry, 198*(3), 169–170.

Humphreys, C., & Thiara, R. (2003). Mental health and domestic violence: "I call it symptoms of abuse." *British Journal of Social Work, 33*, 209–226.

Iezzi, F.D. (2013). Italian women in the new millennium: Emancipated or violated? An analysis of webmining of fatal domestic violence. *Rivista Italiana di Economia, Demografia e Statistica, 67*(2), 47–65.

Istat (2015). *La violenza contro le donne dentro e fuori la famiglia- Anno 2014.* Roma: Istat. Retrieved from www.west-info.eu/the-map-of-violence-against-women-in-italy/dipartimento-per-le-pari-opportunita-e-istat-la-violenza-contro-le-donne-dentro-e-fuori-la-famiglia-anno-2014

Kaur, R., & Garg, S. (2008). Addressing domestic violence against women: An unfinished agenda. *Indian Journal of Community Medicine : Official Publication of Indian Association of Preventive & Social Medicine, 33*(2), 73–76.

Kaye, D.K., Mirembe, F.M., Bantebya, G., Johansson, A., & Ekstrom, A.M. (2006). Domestic violence as risk factor for unwanted pregnancy and induced abortion in Mulago Hospital, Kampala, Uganda. *Tropical Medicine & International Health, 11*(1), 90–101.

Kaye, J. (2007). Femicide. In *Online encyclopedia of mass violence*. Retrieved from www.massviolence.org/Femicide

MacQuarrie, K.L.D., Winter, R., & Kishor, S. (2013). *Spousal violence and HIV: Exploring the linkages in five sub-saharan African countries.* Calverton, MD: ICF International.

Mammone, A., Parini, E.G., & Veltri, G.A. (2015). *The Routledge handbook of contemporary Italy: History, politics, society.* Abingdon, Oxon; New York, NY: Routledge.

Manjoo, R. (2012). *Report of the Special Rapporteur on violence against women, its causes and consequences, Rashida Manjoo – Addendum Mission to Italy.* Geneva: United Nations Human Rights Council.

McCue, M.L. (2008). *Domestic violence: A reference handbook.* Santa Barbara, CA: ABC-CLIO.

McRobie, H. (2013, August 13). The unsafe house of Italy: Violence against women does not break for summer. Retrieved from https://www.opendemocracy.net/5050/heather-mcrobie/unsafe-house-of-italy-violence-against-women-does-not-break-for-summer

Mega, L.T., Mega, J.L., Mega, B.T., & Harris, B.M. (2000). Brainwashing and battering fatigue. Psychological abuse in domestic violence. *North Carolina Medical Journal, 61*(5), 260–265.

Ministero dell'Interno. (2007). *Rapporto sulla criminalità in Italia. Analisi, Prevenzione, Contrasto.* Roma: Ministero dell'Interno.

Montecchi, F. (2011). *Dal bambino minaccioso al bambino minacciato. Gli abusi e la violenza in famiglia: prevenzione, rilevamento e trattamento* (2nd ed.). Milano: Franco Angeli.

Muratore, M.G., Barletta, R., & Federici, A. (Eds.). (2008). *La violenza contro le donne. Indagine multiscopo sulle famiglie "sicurezza delle donne." Anno 2006.* Roma: Istituto Nazionale di Statistica.

Nadeau, B. (2013, August 9). Italy passes new anti-domestic violence measures. *The Daily Beast*. Retrieved from www.thedailybeast.com/witw/articles/2013/08/09/italy-passes-new-anti-domestic-violence-laws-to-combat-femicide-epidemic.html

Polizia di Stato. (2013, December 2). International Day to Stop Violence Against Women. Retrieved from www.poliziadistato.it/articolo/view/31099/

Pulerwitz, J., Hughes, L., Mehta, M., Kidanu, A., Verani, F. & Tewolde, S. (2015). Changing gender norms and reducing intimate partner violence: Results from a quasi-experimental intervention study with young men in Ethiopia. *American Journal of Public Health, 105*(1), 132–137.

Ralli, E. (2014). *More women from medium and upper classes are victims of domestic abuse*. Retrieved from http://neurope.eu/article/persistent-high-level-violence-against-women-italy

Reiter, M.D. (2015). *Substance abuse and the family*. New York and London: Routledge.

Revolting Europe. (2012, March 8). Domestic violence claims more victims than the mafia. Retrieved from http://revolting-europe.com/2012/03/08/domestic-violence-claims-more-victims-than-the-mafia/

Rojas, S., Maturana, C., & Maira, G. (2004). *Femicidio en Chile*. Santiago, Chile: Corporación La Morada.

Russell, D.E.H., & Radford, J. (1992). *Femicide, the politics of woman killing*. Buckingham, UK: Open University Press.

Sabia, J.J. (2004). Alcohol consumption and domestic violence against new mothers. *Journal of Mental Health Policy and Economics, 7*(4), 191–205.

Sampson, R. (2006). *Domestic violence*. Problem-Specific Guide, No. 45. Washington, DC: Office of Community-Oriented Policing.

Schechter, S., & Edelson, J. (1999). *Effective intervention in domestic violence and child maltreatment cases: Guidelines for policy and practice*. Reno, NV: National Council of Juvenile and Family Court Judges.

Shane, B., & Ellsberg, M. (2002). Violence against women: Effects on reproductive health. *Outlook, 20*(1), 1–8. Retrieved from www.path.org/publications/files/EOL20_1.pdf

Spinelli, B., & Italian NGO platform "30 years CEDAW: Work in progress." (2011). *Shadow report with reference to the 6th periodic report on the implementation of the CEDAW*. Convention submitted by the Italian Government in 2009. Italy, June, 2011. Retrieved from http://www2.ohchr.org/english/bodies/cedaw/docs/ngos/Lavori_in_Corsa_for_the_session_Italy_CEDAW49.pdf

Stelmaszek, B., & Fisher, H. (2013). *Wavecountry report 2012: Reality check on data collection and European services for women and children survivors of violence. A right for protection and support?* Vienna: WAVE-office/Austrian Women's Shelter Network.

Trevillion K., Oram, S., Feder, G., & Howard, L.M. (2012). Experiences of domestic violence and mental disorders: A systematic review and meta-analysis. *PLoS ONE, 7* (12), e51740. DOI: 10.1371/journal.pone.0051740

Wells, L., Abboud, R., & Claussen, C. (2012). *Domestic violence in ethno-cultural communities: Risk and protective factors*. Calgary, AB: University of Calgary, Shift: The Project to End Domestic Violence.

Widyono, M. (2009). Conceptualizing femicide. In PATH, South African Medical Research Council, World Health Organization & InterCambios (Eds.), *Strengthening understanding of femicide: Using research to galvanize action and accountability*. Retrieved from www.path.org/publications/files/GVR_femicide_rpt.pdf

Willson, P., McFarlane, J., Malecha, A., Watson, K., Lemmey, D., Schultz, P., Gist, J., & Fredland, N. (2000). Severity of violence against women by intimate partners and associated use of alcohol and/or illicit drugs by the perpetrator. *Journal of Interpersonal Violence, 15*(9), 996–1008.

World Health Organization. (2009). *Changing cultural and social norms supportive of violent behaviour*. Geneva: World Health Organization.

World Health Organization & London School of Hygiene and Tropical Medicine. (2010). *Preventing intimate partner and sexual violence against women: Taking action and generating evidence*. Geneva: World Health Organization.

World Health Organization, London School of Hygiene and Tropical Medicine and South African Medical Research Council. (2013). *Global and regional estimates of violence against women: Prevalence and health effects of intimate partner violence and non-partner sexual violence*. Geneva: World Health Organization.

6   Domestic violence in Austria

Maximillian Edelbacher and Josef Hörl

Introduction

Definitions and risk factors of domestic violence

Domestic violence (also called family violence) is a global and serious phenomenon. Just to mention the extreme case, the fact is that one is more likely to be murdered by a family member than by anyone else. Yet, much controversy exists about how to define domestic or family violence and its components. Violence may be narrowly defined as "an act carried out with the intention of, or perceived as having the intention of, physically hurting another person" (Gelles & Straus, 1979, p. 554). Of course, "physical hurt" can range from a slight slap to murder. Similarly, the "intent to hurt" can include many forms and degrees of hostility, even the death of the other may be desired. One argument in favor of restricting the definition to patterns that clearly are harmful and not to be tolerated under any circumstances, is that it would ensure that these serious problems are not underemphasized. On the other hand, it has been argued that focusing narrowly on physical violence that clearly causes serious harm is too restricted as a conception because it does not include negative and abusive behaviors like sexual annoyance, isolating and confining the partner from any social relationships, persecution, privation, humiliation, neglect, and psychological and verbal abuse, which may be as threatening as physical violence. The psychological abuse often does not occur clearly and it may have longitudinal and disruptive effects on victims.

There are different conceptions and moral codes regarding the degree to which the use of violence in a given situation is legitimized by social norms. The use of physical force may be approved or required by the norms of the society, for example, we should note that the traditional European legal system countenanced wife battering. Until the late twentieth century, domestic violence was not consistently prosecuted because of patriarchal presuppositions. Being assaulted by one's own husband was considered (and in some degree still is considered) a private matter and not on a par with crime committed by strangers. In fact, a British study finds that domestic violence offenders are less likely than those convicted of crimes outside of domestic contexts to be sentenced to prison.

Further, of those imprisoned, domestic violence offenders receive significantly shorter sentence terms (Bond & Jeffries, 2014).

Most feminist authors argue that patriarchy and resulting patterns of male power, domination, and control are the primary or even ultimate causes of violence toward wives (Dobash & Dobash, 1979). Apart from the patriarchy argument, scientists have developed an abundance of biological, psychological and social theories striving to explain the ubiquitous existence of domestic violence, ranging from evolutionary processes, to mental illness, to social learning of aggression or poverty issues. In any case, we are confronted with the paradox that harm is purposely inflicted by those who are supposed to care for or depend on one another. In this context Gelles and Straus (1979) argue that we have to consider that the family is high on both intimacy and privacy. Family interactions cover a vast range of activities. This means that there are more "events" over which a dispute or a failure to meet expectations can occur. The huge emotional investment which is typical of family relationships carries with it an implicit right to influence the behavior of others. Consequently, the dissatisfactions over undesirable activities of others are further exacerbated by attempts to change the behavior of the other. Thus, the family is likely to be the venue of more and more serious stress compared to other groups (e.g., at the workplace). Furthermore, we have to consider the fact that the family is usually composed of people of different genders and age. Coupled with the existence of generational and gender differences in culture and outlook on life, this makes the family an arena of culture conflict.

In identifying concrete risk factors it is useful to follow the suggestion by Tolan, Gorman-Smith and Henry (2006) in differentiating individual characteristics and relationship factors. Research to identify individual characteristics as risk factors for violence has largely focused on male perpetrators. Across studies (Capaldi & Gorman-Smith, 2003), the strongest predictors of domestic violence perpetration are a history of prior aggression. Psychopathology, low impulse control and low self-esteem have also been related to domestic violence perpetration. The forms of mental illness varied and included anxiety disorders, depression, antisocial personality disorder, and alcohol and drug dependence. Individuals who grew up in families characterized by unskilled parenting and poor family functioning also have higher rates of domestic violence. Obviously, single factor explanations as those mentioned have their drawbacks.

The emphasis in research on men as perpetrators and women as victims is remarkable. One of the reasons for this emphasis on perpetrators is increased sensitivity about "blaming the victim," that is to say the victim is made responsible because of her provocative or otherwise unacceptable behavior. If relationship issues are raised in the context of domestic violence, suspicion is that the hidden agenda is to downplay the male partner's responsibility for his violent behavior. Domestic violence advocacy groups in particular assert that victims should under no circumstances be made to believe that they have even partly caused their own troubles and "got what they deserve." Advocacy groups are insisting that perpetrators must realize that it was not the female partner who provoked the violent acts they had committed but that they themselves had intentionally and deliberately used violence. Consequently, anti-violence training programs for male perpetrators concentrate their efforts at building and enhancing empathy and understanding with regard to the consequences that violence has for the victims (Ille & Kraus, 2008).

While individuals need to be held responsible for harmful behavior it cannot be easily denied that much of family violence has multiple determinants. Beyond the individual, characteristics of the relationship and social context have consistently been found to contribute to risk. Nevertheless, up to now there has been only limited attention to relationship factors in explaining domestic violence, despite evidence from studies of such factors that qualities of the relationship provide independent explanation (Capaldi & Gorman-Smith, 2003). It seems that partner violence is related to low relationship skills or difficulty in maintaining quality relationships. Similarly, men who were violent in their marriage reported having felt more stress during marital interactions than did nonviolent men. Further, domestic violence is at least partly dependent on constraints and similar shared histories that lead to partnering with individuals with greater aggressive tendencies. Assortative partnering by antisocial behavior has been demonstrated with several samples (Krueger, Moffitt, Capsi, Bleske & Silva, 1998). These findings suggest that relationship factors can be an important component in explaining and addressing domestic violence, particularly in light of findings that suggest much bidirectional violence among couples.

Contextual and situation factors also play an important role (Mears, Carlson, Holden & Harris, 2003). Women living in poverty, struggling with money in their own relationships or living in disadvantaged neighborhoods are disproportionately affected by domestic violence. Alcohol use by either partner is related to increased levels of domestic violence, with the likelihood elevated further when both partners use alcohol. In this case, alcohol use may act as a situation factor, increasing the likelihood of violence by reducing inhibitions and impairing an individual's ability to interpret cues.

Finally, there is evidence that the presence of one form of family violence across the life span is a risk factor for the presence of another form (Graham-Bermann & Edleson, 2001). Childhood abuse is one of the best predictors of domestic violence. Inter-generational transmission means that violence between parents may be observed and directly modeled in later relationships with partners. This violence between parents legitimizes later violence against intimate partners. Further, physical abuse toward a child may teach that child that aggression is a tactic to use in family relationships.

Prevalence of domestic violence

Victims of domestic violence can either be male or female. As far as incidence is concerned, depending on which study is used, the ratio of women being victimized in domestic violence is between 90 percent and 95 percent (Watkins, 2005). Even though domestic violence has also become a concern for men, it must be noted that the outcome of domestic violence in terms of physical and psychological injuries tends to be considerably more negative for females then for males. Victims of domestic violence are predominantly thought of as a spouse to the perpetrator. However, the relationship of the victim to the perpetrator may include the categories of spouse, parent, sibling, child, grandparent, grandchild, in-law, step-parent, step-child, step-sibling, and other family member relationships. Traditionally, acts of domestic violence have been thought of as occurring within heterosexual relationships. With the increase in the number of open homosexual and lesbian relationships, law enforcement officials and prosecutors must recognize and deal with same-sex domestic violence within their communities. The victims of domestic violence not only can be identified by relationship, but there is also the victim factor of age. The age of the perpetrator is important to the understanding of domestic violence because it explains when, during a person's life, they are more likely to become a victim and why. We must consider the ethnicity of the victim (and the perpetrator) as well because women in immigrant families in many cases are completely dependent on the perpetrator socially and economically.

The most recent prevalence of violence survey carried out in Austria is the Violence in the Family and in Close Social Spheres: Austrian Prevalence Study on Violence against Women and Men (Kapella, Baierl, Rille-Pfeiffer, Geserick & Schmidt, 2011). The study is a national prevalence survey of violence against both women and men. The data was collected employing face-to-face interviews and in an online survey of 1,292 women and 1,042 men, aged 16–60 years. The study examines experiences of domestic violence in three stages of life: childhood violence (up to the age of 16), adult lifetime from the age of 16, and the last three years. Data is gender disaggregated for victims and perpetrators, and the relationship between victim and perpetrator is also given for rates of violence. The forms of violence measured were psychological and physical violence, sexual harassment and sexual violence. According to the findings roughly 86 percent of women experience psychological violence at some point in their lifetime since the age of 16, whether in private of public spheres. Furthermore, 57 percent of women experience physical violence, 74 percent of women experience sexual harassment and 29.5 percent of women experience sexual violence. The findings show that physical violence, sexual violence, sexual harassment and psychological violence are mostly committed by men against women.

It should be noted that domestic violence results not only in pain and distress, but also in costs for the victims and society as a whole. In research conducted by Haller and Dawid (2006) the public costs of domestic violence were estimated. The following types of cost were taken into account: police authorities; court authorities; labor cost (incapacity for work); welfare assistance; healthcare; support centers for victims. The annual overall cost of domestic violence amounted to more than 78 million euro (2004/2005) in Austria.

Legal and social measures against domestic violence in Austria

Legal provisions constitute an important type of intervention. Legislators and courts can affect the concrete life environments of victims and perpetrators to a considerable extent. However, it was not until the 1970s that persistent indifference toward domestic violence eventually was shattered by the new women's movements and the idea gained ground that domestic violence is not a private affair but of public concern and must be considered a serious crime. However, it took more than another 25 years before initiatives succeeded in their efforts to demand and promote legal protection for persons affected by domestic violence as a criminal act. At last, the Austrian Federal Act on Protection against Domestic Violence entered into force on May 1, 1997. Corresponding provisions were laid down in the Security Police Act.

Knowledge of the legal measures in the general population has grown, but is still limited. A majority of 58 percent (up from 38 percent in 1999) of the Austrian population knows (or at least assumes) that there are special laws in place governing domestic violence against women (Eurobarometer, 2010). The fundamental idea of the legislation is that it is a responsibility of the state to enable law enforcement agencies, notably the police, to assure victims of domestic violence that they shall receive comprehensive and complete protection against violence as well as extensive support, and furthermore they shall have the possibility to stay in their own home. In particular, the bill consists of three elements which were developed in combination and are tuned to each other: (1) eviction and barring orders by the police for a duration of two weeks or – under certain preconditions – four weeks; (2) longer-term protection by means of a protective temporary injunction under civil law (3 months and more); (3) support for the victims, violence prevention measures and coordination of the interventions by establishing institutions labeled either "intervention centers" or "violent protection centers" (Logar, 2005). According to the statistics of the Federal Ministry of the Interior, the data shown in Table 6.1 on the implementation of the Protection against Violence Bill were collected.

As can be seen, the number of evictions and barring orders has risen considerably. This is probably less due to growing violence than to the fact that the new legal measures are increasingly adopted by the police and are a tool that is used in practice. It should be mentioned, however, that the growing number of evictions has been registered mainly in urban areas; in rural regions the number of evictions is markedly lower. The number of infringements of expulsion orders is

Table 6.1 Austrian Federal Ministry of the Interior, data on the implementation of the Protection against Violence Bill

Year	Eviction/barring orders
1998	2,673
2000	3,354
2005	5,618
2011	7,993
2012	8,063
2013	8,307
2014	7,587

surprisingly small (about 12 percent). It would appear that perpetrators take this measure seriously, not least because an infringement entails further punitive sanctions, even police detention. Thus, expulsion orders by the police seem to be an effective measure (Haller, 2005).

The law does not exclusively protect women or female spouses. For example, there are quite a number of cases where teenagers who were evicted from home because they were threatening their parents. Nevertheless, it is clear that the vast majority of victim cases concerns women, most of them spouses or partners of younger or middle age. It is important to note that the number of elderly (female but also male) victims is growing. Elderly victims provide a special challenge for law enforcement because elderly couples may exhibit violent behavior but at the same time not so few couples are involved in a long-standing and mutual helping or caregiving relationship as well. An eviction order leads then to a gap in necessary caregiving tasks.

The aim of comprehensive protection implies not only measures of intervention but also of prevention. Despite the fact that women's shelters are still a necessary institution the new shift of paradigm is that not the victim (and her children) but the perpetrator should be removed from the home and its immediate surroundings. It is up to the victim to determine – ideally after counseling by an intervention center (see below) – whether the eviction will provide sufficient protection or whether she should rather move to a safe place, such as a woman's shelter, at least for a few days. The police are entitled to impose eviction and barring orders on perpetrators for a certain period of time; as already mentioned, re-entering is barred for two or four weeks. It is completely up to the perpetrator to find an accommodation on his own, be it a friend's or a relative's home, a hotel room or a shelter for the homeless. Usually, the search for an alternative accommodation is much easier in larger cities than in rural areas. The barring order can be extended if the person at risk applies to the family court for an interim injunction. This extension is often approved in cases when for example, a divorce suit is pending. In a recent (2013) addition to the law, the off limits area can be extended to the workplace of the victim or her children's kindergarten.

As mentioned, the idea of banning the perpetrator from the home, even if he is the owner, proved to be quite effective. Obviously, the Domestic Violence Act features highly extended police power. In particular, for a barring order it is not required that the person at risk has experienced a previous violent attack by the perpetrator; it is sufficient that the police officer gains the impression that a dangerous attack on life, health or freedom is imminent. The perpetrator has to hand over keys to the police and is only allowed to take some of his personal belongings with him. There is a checkup by the police and if the perpetrator is found at home during the validity of the barring order he is fined for this offense or even arrested under Administrative Criminal Law, especially when he refuses to leave the home. It is important to note that the victim cannot influence the imposition of a barring order nor its revocation and can be fined too if they allow the perpetrator to re-enter the home.

Unfortunately, there is a lack of serious consequences for violation of protective orders. Perpetrators against whom restraining orders have been issued face no confinement even if they repeatedly violate the order. There have been several cases of women murdered by their barred husbands (Logar, 2005). In most cases, the courts rule against a detention despite perpetrators' threats referring to the law's provision that detention would constitute a violation of the perpetrators' rights.

Another major development is a second Protection Against Domestic Violence Act which entered into force in 2009. The aim was to enhance the duration and effectiveness of the existing protection measures and to introduce additional provisions regarding domestic violence. In particular, persistent perpetration of violence is now covered as a new criminal offense with the intention to cope more effectively with maybe less dangerous but unrelenting aggressive maltreatment.

All these massive measures are not an infringement of the private sphere of family life pursuant to Article 8 of the European Convention on Human Rights because the right to physical integrity of an individual is regarded as weightier (Das & Unterlercher, 2014). As mentioned before, family systems are characterized by the existence of massive emotional investment and often ambivalent and changing feelings of affection and hate. It is a common experience that perpetrators engage in fault-finding, regarding the victim guilty because she behaved in such a way as to provoke or deserve violence. Rejecting such excuses and firmly insisting on the responsibility of the perpetrator are absolute musts which have to start with the police intervention. Accordingly, police intervention must not create the impression that the behavior of the woman played any role. It does not matter whether the person exposed to violence wants the police to intervene, and, as already mentioned, to obtain an eviction order or not. Intervening police officers must resolutely face the perpetrator and draw his attention to his responsibility for the violent act and its consequences. Law enforcement officers must, therefore, refrain from making any statements that could be interpreted by the perpetrator as condoning his violent behavior.

Notwithstanding that the Protection Against Domestic Violence Act is in force, the traditional instrument of "dispute settlement" is still available to police; officers talk to the conflicting parties, seeking to appease them and to mediate between victim and perpetrator. Dispute settlements have decreased continuously since the 1990s but are still frequently utilized. This method is applied especially by police officers in rural areas. Obviously, they are reacting in this way because of their reluctance to interfere in family conflicts (Haller, 2008).

In other cases, the intervening police officer on the spot, who is confronted with an apparently ambiguous conflict situation, may be inclined to use the barring order as a less severe measure when an arrest would have been more appropriate. Possibly the increased employment of female police officers will prove favorable in developing more empathy toward victims.

Of course, the success of any anti-violence laws depends on further awareness-raising that domestic violence is an unacceptable violation of the rights of women and the willingness of the victims themselves or their family members or friends and neighbors to report cases of violence and severe mal-treatment. However, the reluctance to report a case of unacceptable behavior is still common and, consequently, the dark figure probably is high.

Social intervention measures

Parallel to and in close cooperation with law enforcement agencies, practical intervention and counseling work for victims of domestic violence is provided by non-governmental organizations. In all of Austria's nine provinces they run "intervention centers" (in some places called "violence protections centers"), funded in equal parts by the federal Ministry of the Interior and the Ministry of Women's Affairs. Regularly, police officers intervening in cases of domestic violence are obliged to refer the victims to the services of these centers for further help and support; it is, however, up to the victims to decide whether they want to accept the help offered to them. The staff of the intervention centers sup-ports the victims and their children in all matters concerning their protection and the securing of their rights, in civil as well as in criminal lawsuits. The interven-tion centers use a two-fold approach. On the one hand they provide help for victims contacting them and on the other hand they make phone calls, home visi-tations and other assiduous efforts to offer help. This proactive approach is necessary because victims of domestic violence are all too often afraid or too intimidated to seek help by themselves. One of the core tasks of the intervention centers is to assess the danger inherent in the situation and to plan safety meas-ures together with the victim. The support for those affected and the preventive measures against violence should not end too soon. As far as possible follow-up procedures are employed; the person affected by domestic violence is contacted again after a certain time-span.

There is a national women's helpline in Austria. In 2014, the helpline assisted 8,020 callers including 6,937 cases of practical counseling for women. The hel-pline is run by the non-governmental organization Austrian Women's Shelter Network. It operates 24/7, is free of charge and provides assistance to women survivors of all forms of violence against women. Multilingual assistance is pro-vided in eight foreign languages. There is also online counseling provided (VAÖ, 2014).

There are 30 women's shelters in each of the nine Austrian provinces with 759 shelter places available. The first women's shelter was opened in 1978 in Vienna. All 30 shelters are run by independent women's organizations. The shel-ters accept women survivors of violence and their children. In 2014, a total of 1,645 women and 1,603 children were accommodated. Currently, Austria meets the Council of Europe Task Force Recommendations for women's helpline pro-vision, but with 9 percent of women's shelter places missing, it does not yet meet the recommendations for women's shelter provision. In 2013, a shelter accommodating women and girl survivors of forced marriage was opened in Vienna. In five of the shelters, the women can be accommodated for a period of four to six months, while in the remaining shelters women can stay up to 12 months. As yet, the supply of places in women's shelters is insufficient, so that sometimes women and children seeking help cannot be admitted right away. The shelters are predominantly funded by the state while other subsidies and private donors make only comparatively little contributions. The problem of financing is permanent: most women's shelters have to struggle for their financial means every year; if the administration pursues a policy of cutting expenses, this often has an impact on women's organizations (WAVE, 2014; www.frauenhaeuser-zoef.at).

In rural regions the nearest women's shelter or counseling center are often out of reach of the women concerned. Services for immigrant women, refugees, and other groups with special needs are often lacking. In particular, the admission of elderly women to shelters meets special obstacles and thus continues to be rather the exception than the rule today. Shelters have either not yet or barely been adjusted to clients whose capacity has declined to perform activities of everyday living or to manage their household independently; staff mostly lacks specific training in interactions with older people and even less so when they are in need of care. Relying on the support of external, mobile services is often considered problematic. Shelters are conceived as temporary solutions and the reintegration of frail older women into a private housing environment appears difficult. There is also the problem that many older women who are abused by their partners wish to keep contact with their adult children and/or grandchildren; since the addresses of women's shelters to which victims are admitted have to be kept secret, visits appear problematic as this secrecy cannot be guaranteed in such cases.

Awareness of domestic violence against women in Austria and the European Union

The following data are taken from the most recent Eurobarometer (2010) survey dealing with this topic. Generally, it can be said that (compared to an earlier survey in 1999) awareness of the issue has grown, tolerance of domestic violence has fallen, and support for strong measures against perpetrators has risen. The survey also shows that more and more people hear about domestic violence in the media, which may be a sign that this issue is now less of a taboo topic. Overall awareness is higher among women than among men. Younger people are systematically more informed and more sensitive to the issue. This seems to point to a change in people's mentality. The younger generation is more likely than older generations to consider each type of domestic violence as serious.

The vast majority of EU citizens (98 percent) have heard of domestic violence against women, with 92 percent (in Austria only 86 percent) of respondents saying that they have heard it being discussed on television. Magazines and newspapers are the next most common media by which people hear about the subject (59 percent), while 41 percent say they have heard about domestic violence against women on the radio and 29 percent have heard about it through friends. Other places where this topic is raised include the family circle

(17 percent), books (16 percent), the Internet (15 percent), the workplace (15 percent), the cinema (13 percent), at school (9 percent), or elsewhere (3 percent). Only 2 percent (down from 4 percent in a similar survey in 1999) of EU respondents say they have not heard anything about domestic violence against women.

Across the EU, 25 percent (in Austria 20 percent) of respondents say that they know a woman within their circle of friends or family who has been a victim of domestic violence. Twenty one percent (in Austria 18 percent) of respondents say they know a woman in their immediate area or neighborhood who has suffered this sort of violence, while 11 percent (in Austria also 11 percent) say they know of a case where they work or study.

The results show a general rise in the number of people saying that they know of a victim of domestic violence. For example, 25 percent (in Austria 20 percent) now say they know of someone in their friend or family circle, up from 19 percent (in Austria from 14 percent) in the 1999 survey. From the data available it cannot be concluded whether this demonstrates that levels of domestic violence have risen, or whether instead awareness and willingness to talk about these issues have grown.

Analysis of gender differences reveals that women in the EU tend to be more aware of victims of domestic violence than men. More women (29 percent) than men (21 percent) say they know a victim of domestic violence among their friends or family circle. The pattern is repeated for the other criteria, with 23 percent of female respondents saying they know a victim in their immediate area or neighborhood, as opposed to 18 percent of men, and 13 percent of female respondents saying they know a victim where they work or study, compared with 9 percent of men. Detailed gender analysis for Austria is not available.

At the EU level, 21 percent (in Austria 18 percent) of people say they know of somebody in their circle of friends and family who subjects a woman to violence. Eighteen percent (16 percent in Austria) know of somebody in their immediate area or neighborhood who does this, while 8 percent (in Austria also 8 percent) of people know of someone where they work or study.

The trend among the EU15 shows an overall increase in the number of respondents who reported knowing someone who subjects a woman to domestic violence. Twenty one percent (in Austria 18 percent) of EU15 respondents say they know of somebody within their circle of friends and family, up from 17 percent (in Austria up from 13 percent) in the previous survey.

A majority of people (78 percent, in Austria 63 percent) across the European Union believe that domestic violence against women is "very common" or "fairly common" in their countries. Only a small cross-section of European society thinks that domestic violence is either "not very common" (17 percent) or "not at all common" (1 percent), with 4 percent saying they do not know. Since 1999 the perception of domestic violence has increased significantly in most countries.

An overwhelming majority (84 percent, in Austria 79 percent) of EU respondents says that violence against women is unacceptable and should always be punishable by law. Women are generally more likely to advocate punishment for those who commit violence than men. A noticeable minority (12 percent, in Austria 16 percent) believe that this kind of violence is unacceptable, but should not always be punishable by law, while a very small fringe thinks that domestic violence is acceptable in certain circumstances (2 percent, in Austria 3 percent) or in all circumstances (1 percent, in Austria also 1 percent). More people in all Member States think that domestic violence against women is unacceptable and should always be punishable by law than 10 years earlier.

Among the many possible causes for domestic violence against women it is especially noteworthy that – comparing the recent data from the EU15 countries with the results of the earlier survey – many more people now see religious beliefs as a cause than in 1999. Two-thirds (in Austria 62 percent) of respondents now see this as a cause, up from 47 percent (in Austria up from 46 percent) who said the same in 1999. Presumably, this result should be seen in connection with the influx of Islamic migrants with strong beliefs in Islamic faith now settling in Europe.

Police experiences in Austria

After the end of the Second World War society in Austria started to change. Women became independent from men, staying home as housewives was not usual any more, they had to work in their own jobs and lived more and more on their own income. Their growing independence reduced their acceptance of violent men. One of the co-authors of this chapter has 40 years' service as a police employee and this experience can be contributed here. In the 1970s, at the start of a police career, it still was rather rare that domestic violence cases were reported to the police. Of course domestic violence always happened and happens today, too. But from the 1950s to the 1970s a great change took place in how such cases were handled in families and by society in Austria. Even in the 1970s only a small number of such cases were reported and police had to intervene rather seldom. Violence against women and children mainly were reported if neighbors witnessed such violence and called police to ask for help. In this period of time, awareness of reporting domestic violence against women and children was underdeveloped. Men could act rather rudely and had nothing to fear from their partner, wife or children calling the police. But this kind of behavior changed dramatically when women became independent, based on having their own income and after starting awareness campaigns pushing women's human rights. Between the 1950s and the 1970s, the whole society experienced an enormous change, because women became involved more and more in an intensive working process, their independence increased and violent men were not tolerated. Women were no longer afraid of being divorced and losing their economic basis because they provided their own income.

Is domestic violence a class phenomenon?

Seen from the point of view as a practitioner, an issue of discussion is the question: Where does domestic violence happen? In the literature domestic violence is seen in all social classes. Domestic violence happens in the classes of the rich people as well as in the classes of the poor people. Working in the outside districts of Vienna – the city has 23 districts and some districts represent more or less the wealthier parts of the city – it was very clear, from a practical work understanding, that police are confronted with more domestic violence in poorer areas of cities.

In the "old days" when police were confronted with a domestic violence claim, experienced elder police officers intervened by speaking with the couple, especially the violent man, telling him that if they had to show up again he would be arrested and taken to prison. The police officers did not need the order of a prosecutor or a judge. The competence of these elder officers and their appearance was, in most of the cases, enough to stop domestic violence. Only a short comment was written in the report book, nothing else. This method has changed. Today, mainly young officers have to intervene, acting officially and correctly. Based on the new laws against domestic violence, every step has to be documented by writing and saving files in a computer, which is registered in a database.

Sometimes elder and young police officers discuss the best way of addressing the situation. Seen from a citizens-oriented point of view, these elder methods of community policing seemed to be very effective and efficient. Today, when police are confronted with crimes of juveniles, every police action, every step of policing is written down and has to be documented in a file. Very often the elder police officers have the impression that these changes restrict the personal freedom of each of us. These procedures diminish our personal freedom of deciding and acting in accordance with basic common sense.

The daily police reality is the experience that poor people need much more support from the police than rich ones. There still exists this difference between the academic stand-point and the practical experience. Of course, domestic violence can happen everywhere, but the reality is that conflicts appear much more often in the poorer areas. Working with the police force for nearly 40 years, the following examples from practical experience suggest that poorer people are much more often victims of violence than the wealthy.

Examples of domestic violence in Austria from a police perspective

Acting for more than 20 years as police chief of a homicide squad, the Major Crime Bureau, and finally, the chief of the Criminal Investigation Department South in Vienna, I was primarily confronted with murder crimes or other major crime cases. These following examples of domestic violence – that can happen everywhere in the world – show that the most dangerous area is the home.

In lower classes a different language is spoken. The largest district of Vienna is called Favoriten. In Vienna there live about 1.8 million people. Out of them more than 180,000 live in Favoriten. The district started to grow in the end of the nineteenth century when Vienna became the sixth largest city of the world.

The wall around Vienna was torn down in 1860s and a boom of new representative buildings was built in the 1870s. The Ringstrasse became the symbol of power of the Austria-Hungarian Monarchy. Because of these activities many people came from all parts of the Monarchy to Vienna. These young men and women came full of hope for a better life. Many settled down in Favoriten, where they had to stay under very bad living conditions. Today nearly the same situation happens. Many foreigners, migrants from the Balkan area or from Turkey, choose Favoriten as their first destination when coming to Vienna. Because of their living conditions and their origin, the language that is spoken there is a very clear and basic one. If there is a quarrel, a verbal fight between parties, very often they threaten each other by saying: "I hack di um" ("I kill you"). Because of the different use of language, even the courts do not interpret these words as a classic threat of killing – very often the judges interpret such sayings as "regional limited discrimination." The language in Favoriten has a simpler and more basic meaning than in other districts of Vienna.

Case of murder due to jealousy – August 1955: Conflict between partners is very often based on jealousy. The following example represents this very clearly. There are many motives to hurt or kill someone, but in conflicts between partners, jealousy plays a main role. It happens independently of time, age or location. Jealousy is such a strong emotion that the outcome of such conflict can end very dramatically. In August 1955 a butcher living with his wife in Favoriten under rather simple living conditions learned that his wife was having an affair with a neighbor. He found a note written that his wife and the neighbor could not meet together as they planned. The conflict with his wife ended because she left him and flew to her sister telling him that she wanted a divorce. He became so fed up, disappointed and angry that he took his butcher-knife, followed her to her sister's flat, and stabbed her like an animal. The sister called the police, the butcher tried to commit suicide, but failed. He was sentenced to 15 years in prison.

Jealous wife knifes her husband – May 1974: My first so-called murder case dealt with the tragedy of a young couple. They lived under rather poor conditions in a small flat and had a small income. The newly married husband liked to go out in the evenings. He mainly visited a nearby pub (in Austria it is called a Gasthaus) drinking some beers and flirting with the female servants. His wife became jealous and on May 24, 1974 she searched for him and found him in the pub flirting with a female server. She ran home to get her husband's gun and wanted to come back to the pub. Meanwhile, her husband followed her home and they met together at the entrance of the house. She was angry, threatened him with the weapon and unfortunately shot him. Her husband died immediately. Because she had not planned to kill him, she was only sentenced to prison for 10 months.

An artist painter and his model – December 1981: An Austrian artist, a painter, lived with a beautiful young lady named Tina who worked as a photo-model. They had differences and wanted to settle them. The artist's brother should have helped to calm down the conflict, but when he came to the artist's flat he found the model, Tina, severely wounded by a knife. The model died. Her friend was sentenced to 18 years in prison. When he was in prison, he fell in love with a social worker who was employed in the prison. He escaped from the prison, but returned because of his new love. He was a very emotional man; maybe in the future he will become a famous painter, too.

Alcohol and sex – a dangerous partnership – October 2000: A young Polish couple lived in Favoriten and had a decadent partnership based on alcohol and sex. As long as both partners found their satisfaction the partnership functioned. But by the excessive use of alcohol the man started to have sexual problems. His girlfriend teased him because of his "impotence" – he became angry, lost control completely and knocked her down with a hammer. She died. He stabbed her vagina brutally with a knife and pushed her dead body into the shower where he left her for two weeks, sleeping next to the dead body. He was later arrested and sentenced to life in prison.

Uncontrolled jealous man killed his girlfriend – September 2001: In the end of September 2001 a 24-year-old woman, Sandra, reported to the police that her former boyfriend had threatened and hit her several times while they lived together for about four years. She left him and he threatened her by saying: "If I cannot have you any longer, nobody shall be your friend in the future." Her boyfriend was a boxer and police knew he was dangerous. The prosecutor was informed, but no arrest warrant was issued. When police were called again, they found Sandra in her home, dead. The offender had stabbed her neck killing her. It was proved that her former boyfriend killed her. He was sentenced for a long period of time.

Afghanistan citizen shows a different understanding – 2001: Society in Austria has changed dramatically in the last 20 years. Nearly one-fifth of the 8.6 million population have a foreign background. Not only are people from the neighboring countries like Czech Republic, Hungary, the Balkan area or Turkey coming to Austria and Vienna; there is also much immigration from Asia and Africa. Very often these immigrants bring with them a very different culture, understanding of violence, and habits about how to treat girlfriends, women and children. Based on my experience, it seems that motives of crimes are similar in all continents and cultures. One of the strongest motives for acting aggressively is jealousy. A young man from Afghanistan was arrested by the Taliban fighters and escaped after some years. Meanwhile, his girlfriend flew to Austria, Vienna. The young man had to learn that she had a new boyfriend. This was the starting point for a terrible murder. He killed his former girlfriend and her new partner by using a knife and stabbing them terribly. Both died, and the offender was arrested and sentenced to many years in prison.

Very often such fights do not end as murder cases. In the majority of cases the victim is just hurt, wounded or threatened. Police have to handle such cases of violence between people who generally know each other. Very often violence is the last way to "solve" such conflicts.

References

Bond, C.E.W., & Jeffries, S. (2014). Similar punishment? Comparing sentencing outcomes in domestic and non-domestic violence cases. *British Journal of Criminology*, *54*, 849–872.

Capaldi, D.M., & Gorman-Smith, D. (2003). The Development of Aggression in Young Male/Female Couples. In P. Florsheim (Ed.), *Adolescent romantic relations and sexual behavior: Theory, research, and practical implications* (pp. 243–278). Mahwah: Erlbaum.

Das, J., & Unterlercher, B. (2014). Developing Programmes for Victims of Domestic Abuse. In M.A. McFarlaine & R. Canton (Eds.), *Policy transfer in criminal justice. crossing cultures, breaking barriers* (pp. 233–249). Houndmills, Basingstroke: Palgrave Macmillan.

Dobash, R.E., & Dobash, R. (1979). *Violence against wives: A case against the patriarchy*. New York: Free Press.

Eurobarometer. (2010). Special Eurobarometer 344/Wave 73.2 – Conducted by TNS Opinion & Social at the request of Directorate-General for Justice, Freedom and Security. Brussels: European Commission.

Gelles, R.J., & Straus, M.A. (1979). Determinants of violence in the family: Toward a theoretical integration. In W.R. Burr, R. Hill, F.I. Nye, & I.L. Reiss (Eds.), *Contemporary theories about the family* (pp. 549–581). New York: Free Press.

Graham-Bermann, S.A., & Edleson, J.L. (2001). *Domestic violence in the lives of children*. Washington, DC: American Psychological Association.

Haller, B. (2005). Gewalt in der Familie: Evaluierungen des Österreichischen Gewaltschutzgesetzes. In A. Dearing, B. Haller (Eds.), *Schutz vor Gewalt in der Familie. Das österreichische Gewaltschutzgesetz* (pp. 269–388). Vienna: Verlag Österreich.

Haller, B. (2008). Different effects of domestic violence in urban and rural areas. In M.K. Krenn, R. Weiss, & R. Logar (Eds.), *Ten years of Austrian anti-violence legislation* (pp. 27–31). Vienna: Federal Chancellery – Federal Minister for Women and Civil Service.

Haller, B., & Dawid, E. (2006). *Kosten häuslicher Gewalt in Österreich*. Vienna: Institut für Konfliktforschung.

Ille, B., & Kraus, H. (2008). The Vienna training programme for violent men. In M. Krenn, K. Weiss, & R. Logar (Eds.), *Ten years of Austrian anti-violence legislation* (pp. 250–259). Vienna: Federal Chancellery – Federal Minister for Women and Civil Service.

Interventionsstelle gegen Gewalt in der Familie. (2015). Vienna. In *Taetigkeitsbericht 2014* (p. 68). Retrieved from www.interventionsstelle-wien.at/taetigkeitsbericht-2014

Kapella, O., Baierl, A., Rille-Pfeiffer, C., Geserick, C., & Schmidt, E.M. (2011). *Gewalt in der Familie und im nahen sozialen Umfeld: Österreichische Prävalenzstudie zur Gewalt an Frauen und Männer*. Vienna: Österreichisches Institut für Familienforschung.

Krueger, R.F., Moffitt, T.E., Capsi, A., Bleske, A., & Silva, P.A. (1998). Assortative mating for antisocial behavior: Developmental and methodological implications. *Behavior Genetics*, *28*, 173–186.

Logar, R. (2005). The Austrian model of intervention in cases of domestic violence. Expert paper presented at the UN Expert Group Meeting: Violence against Women: Good Practice in Combating and Eliminating Violence against Women, May 17–20, 2005, Vienna.

Mears, D.P., Carlson, M.J., Holden, G.W., & Harris, S.D. (2003). Reducing domestic violence revictimization: The effects of individual and contextual factors and type of legal intervention. *Journal of Interpersonal Violence*, *16*, 1260–1283.

Tolan, P., Gorman-Smith, D., & Henry, D. (2006). Family violence. *Annual Review of Psychology, 57*, 557–583.

VAÖ. (2014). *Jahresbericht 2014*. Vienna: Verein autonome Österreichische Frauen-häuser/Frauenhelpline gegen Gewalt.

Watkins, P. (2005). Police perspective: Discovering hidden truths in domestic violence intervention. *Journal of Family Violence, 20*, 47–54.

WAVE. (2014). Austria. In *Country Report 2013. Reality Check on European Services for Women and Children*. Vienna: WAVE Network & European I.

7 Domestic violence in Turkey

Unreported cases and civic/state response

Özgür Solakoğlu, M. Tugba Erdem,
Suheyl Gurbuz, and Eray Karlidag

Introduction

The Department of Economic and Social Affairs of the United Nations Secretariat (2010) reported that the lifetime prevalence of intimate partner violence (IPV) among the ever-partnered or ever-married women in China and Hong Kong SAR and Canada is 6 percent and 7 percent respectively. This percentage is above 10 percent in Italy, above 20 percent in Mexico, around 40 percent in Turkey, and over 48 percent in Zambia (The Department of Economic and Social Affairs of the United Nations Secretariat, 2010). These numbers clearly indicate that domestic violence is one of the most important social problems all over the world.

Turkey is among the countries where domestic violence remains high. According to Bianet (2016), which gathers data from media sources such as newspapers, websites, and news reports, 217 women were murdered in 2010, 257 women in 2011, 165 in 2012, 214 women in 2013, 281 in 2014, and 278 in 2015. Husbands, partners, ex-husbands, and ex-partners mostly account for approximately 50 percent of the murders. The former minister of justice, during a speech to respond to a parliamentary question, provided a shocking statistic for violence against women that showed a 1400 percent increase in women murdered in the five years between 2002 and 2007 (Cetin, 2015).

Other than murders, physical and sexual abuse which result in injuries also remain as a significant social problem in Turkey over those years. Ilkkaracan (1998) found that nearly 58 percent of women who live in the eastern part of Turkey reported that they suffered from physical violence and approximately 52 percent of them reported that they suffered sexual violence from their husbands. Altinay and Arat (2007), in their national survey, found that 34 percent of women had been subjected to physical violence at least once. Yüksel-Kaptanoğlu and Çavlin (2015) found that the proportion of women who have reported lifetime physical violence is 36 percent in 2014. The percentage of sexual violence is 12 percent and 38 percent of women have experienced at least one of these two forms of violence (Yüksel-Kaptanoğlu & Çavlin, 2015). This result indicated that physical violence is accompanied by sexual violence in most cases (Yüksel-Kaptanoğlu & Çavlin, 2015). Korkut-Owen and Owen (2008) state that domestic violence against women ranges between 25 percent and 30 percent in Turkey.

Studies of domestic violence in Turkey also considered these variables while analyzing the problem. However, there are some other variables that can be correlated with domestic violence in Turkey. Patriarchal family structures and traditional norms and values are significant factors affecting the role of women in Turkey (Şahin et al., 2010). Even though they are prohibited and acknowledged as a violation of human rights, early and arranged marriages, a second wife (kuma) and preplanned marriages that involve exchanging girls between families (berdel) are still among the encountered practices in Turkey (Şahin et al., 2010). Şahin et al. (2010) found that early marriage and arranged marriage are significantly correlated with domestic violence. Furthermore, killing in the name of honor, or honor killing, is one of the reasons of femicide as a form of domestic violence that is faced in several countries including, but not limited to, Bangladesh, Egypt, Jordan, Lebanon, Pakistan, and Turkey (UNICEF Innocenti Research Centre, 2000). Any reason, such as alleged adultery, premarital relationship (with or without sexual relations), rape, falling in love with a person of whom the family disapproves, can be enough for a male member of the family to murder the woman (UNICEF Innocenti Research Centre, 2000). Official reports indicate that 1091 women have been murdered in honor and custom killings between 2000 and 2005. Cetin (2015) provided that, in addition to honor killing, demand for separation/divorce, jealousy, refusal of a man's will, psychological crises and unemployment, rejection, drug addiction, a woman's decision about her own life, and sexual attack are among the reasons for femicides committed between 2008 and 2013 in Turkey. While the studies on domestic violence, some of which discussed above, have been on the rise in Turkey, unreported cases are an issue that has to be examined along with underlying reasons. Therefore, the following section will discuss this important topic.

Unreported cases of domestic violence in Turkey

In Turkey, studies have shown that around 50 percent of the women experience domestic violence (Arikan, 1993; Amnesty International, 2005; Kocacik & Dogan, 2006), and this rate seems to be increasing (Toktaş & Diner, 2015). Despite its high prevalence, domestic violence incidents are underreported in Turkey (Izmirli, Sonmez & Sezik, 2014). This chapter examines the reasons for the low rate of domestic violence reporting in Turkey. These reasons can be categorized into three main groups: cultural factors, socio-demographic factors, and institutional factors. Cultural factors consist of the society's level of patriarchy and masculine gender norms, brides-money, the rate of early marriages, family confidentiality issues, and lack of familial support. Socio-demographic factors, on the other hand, involve poverty, illiteracy and low education levels, rural residence, living in large household sizes, and feelings of powerlessness. Finally, institutional factors are related to the welfare state system, experiences in police stations, and guesthouse/shelter conditions.

Cultural factors

The high prevalence of domestic violence incidents and low rates of reporting are generally explained by the characteristics of Turkish culture (Kara, Ekici & Inankul, 2014). It acknowledges that men establishing dominance over their wives have higher adherence to traditional roles of masculinity (Glick, Sakalli-Ugurlu, Ferreira & Aguiar de Souza, 2002; Izmirli et al., 2014). Also, as patriarchal authority is respected culturally (Hortacsu, Kalaycioglu & Rittersberger-Tilic, 2003), Turkish women are expected to obey their husbands. Another factor contributing to the high prevalence of domestic violence and its justification by both men and women is the concept of "brides-money," which is paid for by the woman's father at the beginning of the marriage. Despite its recent decline in the country, the practice of brides-money is highly correlated with domestic violence and its toleration (Erkan, 2003; Kocacik & Dogan, 2006).

The practice of early marriage is mainly observed in the eastern and rural parts of Turkey as a part of the culture. These places also have low education levels and high rates of poverty. Women who were married early tend to abstain from reporting domestic violence to institutions (Marshall & Furr, 2010; Izmirli et al., 2014). In these areas of the country, some girls are married at as young as 11 years old. Around 15 percent of the marriages in Turkey include brides younger than 18 (UNICEF, 2015). These young girls are often forced to get married to a man against their will. Since they are too young and they generally have little or no education, they lack the power to resist their fathers and husbands. This prevents them from seeking institutional help when they are exposed to domestic violence (Cakmak, 2009; Gokler, Arslantas & Unsal, 2014). Also, they are almost always economically dependent on their husbands. This dependency forces them to suffer silently from maltreatment at home (Kocacik & Dogan, 2006).

Akadlı-Ergöçmen, Türkyılmaz and Abasoğlu-Özgören (2015) highlighted that most women experiencing domestic violence are raised with the idea that "what happens within the family should stay in the family." This perspective prevents victims from even considering institutional application as an option to fight against domestic violence. Therefore, women experiencing domestic violence are hesitant to receive institutional support. Even after they make the application, they often continue to question whether they made the right choice. According to Akadlı-Ergöçmen (2015), women who face violence usually do not consider institutional support as an option until they cannot bear it anymore. Interviews conducted with women experiencing violence indicate that they often prefer trying to endure it for a while. This period of enduring physical or sexual violence can last many years. In some cases, it can take 30–35 years for a woman to seek institutional support against violence. One important reason that women apply to institutions is the extension of violence to their children. Although women try to endure domestic violence perpetuated on themselves for quite a long time, the enduring period is often shorter when their children are in danger (Sallan Gül, 2011a).

Another important determinant of institutional application related to domestic violence is the support of a woman's own family, especially her mother. Although quantitative studies indicate that the level of help received from families is very low in cases of domestic violence, women's own mothers play an important role in helping the victim get institutional support in Turkey. Men's families, on the other hand, often do not provide any support for the women to prevent violence (Akadlı-Ergöçmen, 2015).

Socio-demographic factors

Poverty is among the most important socio-demographic factors related to unreported cases of domestic violence in Turkey. With increased wealth, individuals are less likely to hold traditional attitudes toward femininity and masculinity (Marshall & Furr, 2010; Gokler et al., 2014). In Turkey, the majority of women are homemakers with little economic independence. This decreases the rate of domestic violence reports in the country (Izmirli et al., 2014). Combined with the patriarchal mindset in the country, poverty has been a significant contributor both to domestic violence and its underreporting in Turkey (Erder, 2005, pp. 118–119).

Illiteracy and low education levels also contribute to the low rates of domestic violence reporting in Turkey. The eastern part of the country and the rural areas host the highest rates of female illiteracy in the country. Since literacy and education facilitate self-esteem, self-consciousness, and cognitive capacity, these factors help women to feel empowered to stand against domestic violence (Sallan Gül, 2013). Furthermore, literate individuals can better understand the content of news in the media (Kagitcibasi, Goksen & Gulgoz, 2005). Therefore, these women are more likely to appeal to authorized institutions than illiterate women and women with lower education when they face violence at home (Nassbaum, 2000). Also, literacy can help women to question and object to the patriarchal attitude of their society (Marshall & Furr, 2010; Gokler et al., 2014).

From a geographical perspective, women living in rural residences are less likely to report violence they experience at home (Gokler et al., 2014; Izmirli et al., 2014). The eastern part of Turkey has a higher rural residency ratio compared to other parts of the country. This area is also more traditional and a strict moral code is implemented rigorously. Also, other factors that are likely to increase the number of unreported cases of domestic violence, such as poverty, illiteracy, patriarchy, brides-money, and early marriages, are observed more often in this part of the country (Sallan Gül, 2011b).

Furthermore, living in a large household is another factor that prevents Turkish women from seeking help from related institutions (Kocacik & Dogan, 2006). Some Turkish women experience violence from their fathers and elder brothers before they get married. Since they naturalize violence from childhood, they tend to justify the domestic violence they are exposed to from their husbands (Kocacik & Dogan, 2006). Also, the new generations in such conditions are likely to become insensitive in terms of domestic violence. They simply justify it and consider violence and gender inequality as social norms (Sallan Gül, 2013).

The final prominent socio-demographic reason of unreported domestic violence incidents is feelings of powerlessness. Although some women experiencing domestic violence are aware that there are institutions that can help them escape their situation, they do not think that they are able to do it (Palermo, Bleck & Peterman, 2014). These women feel that they are powerless. They learn about such institutions, but they lack the courage needed to do what is necessary (Icon Institute, 2009; Palermo, Bleck & Peterman, 2014). Also, women who consider applying to institutions generally do not have a comprehensive knowledge about their rights (Kara et al., 2014).

Institutional factors

In addition to female socio-demographic factors, macro-level institutional factors also play a role in domestic violence underreporting. Many scholars argue that male hegemony and patriarchy are reinforced in welfare states as they provide more socioeconomic advantages for men than women (Walby & Mayhill, 2004; Sallan Gül, 2013). In particular, the welfare state approach acknowledges women as responsible for taking care of children and the elderly, whereas men are considered the breadwinners. This results in employers who privilege male workers over females (Dedeoglu, 2010, p. 260). Also, women who are out of the labor market do not have much social protection provided by the state. Although the welfare system in Turkey provides relatively better protection compared to most countries, it is still far from the desired level (Bugra & Keyder, 2008).

Another barrier Turkish women face in seeking institutional help is an unwelcoming experience in police stations. Police stations are generally the first place that women approach when they are looking for institutional help. However, interviews with women experiencing domestic violence indicate that law enforcement personnel often do not evaluate the situation from a gender equality perspective. Instead, they attempt to reconcile the man and the woman. Also, many times, police officers do not want to interfere with the family (Kara et al., 2014). This attitude emanates from Turkish culture which prohibits coming between the personal business of a husband and wife. These factors contribute to women's hesitancy to take the domestic violence issue to the institutional level (Sallan Gül, 2013). Furthermore, interviews with police officers suggest that the majority feel that domestic violence is not within law enforcement's responsibility. In addition, some officers do not have the necessary training or personal qualities, such as empathy, to handle these situations and establish good communication with the female victims (Kara et al., 2014).

Although some women report domestic violence cases to the police, they complain that they are not directed to a shelter immediately. The lack of cooperation between police and shelters seem to be the root of this problem. When police officers cannot place a victim in a safe place, they try to convince the victim to withdraw her complaint and go back to her home where she is likely to experience more violence (Kara et al., 2014).

Akadlı-Ergöçmen et al. (2015) state that women experiencing domestic violence generally have positive opinions about guesthouses and shelters. However, there are also some negative feelings reported by the victims. Most complaints mention the oppressive environment they experience in the shelters. Often, they complain of being treated like prisoners, and feel that shelters are sometimes worse than their oppressive homes. Yet, they generally do not express these complaints to the officials out of fear of being expelled from the shelter. Toktaş and Diner (2015) argue that guesthouses and shelters are unable to host domestic violence victims for long periods of time. Most shelters require victims to leave after one to three months. The necessity to return home is a general deterrent for most women considering the idea of applying to such institutions. Therefore, Vaugh and Stamp (2003) recommend that shelters and guesthouses should allow victims to stay until they become able to make a fresh start in life, rather than restricting them to a certain time period. Most commonly, these shelters impose time restrictions due to insufficient funds and local authority preferences (Toktaş & Diner, 2015). Furthermore, these institutions would be even more beneficial if they offered seminars to domestic violence victims that boosted self-confidence and domestic violence awareness as well as vocational training for career opportunities (Haaken & Yragui, 2003).

In conclusion, victims of domestic violence often face a multitude of barriers in reporting their experiences and seeking help. According to numerous studies, increasing reporting of such incidents to related institutions and officials is the best possible solution for domestic violence against women (Akadlı-Ergöçmen et al., 2015). Therefore, it is necessary to provide adequate legal infrastructure and appropriate sources of help for women in Turkey. In addition to providing such opportunities, women should be empowered and enabled to use them. Without pathways to avoid these aforementioned barriers, these institutions may become idle. Increasing employment and social security protection for women, increasing female education levels, and improving conditions in police stations and shelters are just a few of the most effective ways to increase domestic violence report rates.

Reponses to domestic violence in Turkey

Legal developments

Considering domestic violence in Turkey, notably, awareness of the issue of violence against women was created after the 1980s' women's movement which was a result of political consciousness and awareness invigorated with public protests (Yüksel-Kaptanoğlu & Tarım, 2014; Yıldız, Bal & Binbir, 2015). Thereby, the struggle against gender-based violence became more institutionalized in accordance with the women's movement in Turkey. The very first protest against violence against women occurred in 1987 as Women's Solidarity March against Beating calling for a change in public approach to violence (Yıldız, Bal & Binbir, 2015). Various campaigns, activities and scientific research in the field of violence were triggered and efforts for preventing and combatting violence were made. As a result, unprecedented organizations and counseling centers and shelters for women like The Purple Roof Women's Shelter Foundation and Women's Solidarity Foundation were established in the early 1990s (Yüksel-Kaptanoğlu & Tarım, 2015).

The major change in the policies concerning women has been in the legal field. New laws were enacted by the Parliament, for example, in 2005, Municipal Law 5393 was enacted which allows municipalities to open shelters for women and children. Accordingly, municipalities with a population of 50,000 and over can choose to open, however, municipalities with a population of 100,000 and over are required to open protective shelters for women and children. The Law 4320 on the Protection of Family in 1998 was the first important amendment regarding legislation enclosing the aim of preventing domestic violence which was adopted in 2007. The law gave the state the duty of the protection of women who were exposed to violence and the provision of social services (Sallan Gül, 2013). In 2012, this law was reregulated by Law 6284 on the Protection of Family and Prevention of Violence against Women as a result of studies led within the Ministry of Family and Social Policies. This latest law involves provisions on financial and health aid to the women exposed to violence (Sallan Gül, 2013).

A prime ministerial circular published in 2006, number 17, gave rise to studies for the combatting of violence against women. Moreover, the National Action Plan for Combatting Violence against Women 2007–2010 was published to support the implementation of the precautions involved in a 2006/2007 circular by designating the institutions in charge of goals, priorities and activities. With this way, it is aimed to constitute a manual in the combat of violence against women. Further the National Action Plan for 2012–2015 was prepared in coordination with the General Directorate on the Status of Women. Four main goals of the plan are given as follows: to eliminate legal regulations about gender equality, violence against women and domestic violence; to encourage social awareness and mentality transformation about gender equality etc.; to regulate healthcare facilities for battered women and their children; and lastly, to enforce cooperation between institutions and organizations for executing better services for battered women and their children.

Civic developments

In Turkey, three types of shelters provide services for battered women. Women who escape from domestic violence in Turkey can go to the police or apply to a civil organization for women's shelters, municipality counseling or state-led centers. There are non-governmental organizations (NGOs), centers run by the municipalities and the General Directorate on the Status of Women (KSGM) as a unit of the Ministry of Family and Social Services. According to the KSGM, in 2008 there were 49 shelter houses (25 Social Services and Child Protection Agency (SHÇEK) centers included) for survivors of domestic violence (KSGM,

2009). In 2012, the numbers increased to 83 in total consisting of 55 SHÇEK, 25 municipality centers and three civil-run organizations (Erbaydar-Paksoy, 2012). One year after, in 2013, the number was raised to 120 shelters in 73 cities of Turkey due to the information provided by the Ministry; and, 87 of them are led by the state and 32 by the municipalities, whereas only one is run by a civil organization (Milliyet, 2013). Based on statistics of the Ministry, no shelters exist in eight cities with a population of 100,000 and over, even though it was obliged by the aforementioned law. Therefore, insufficiency of the quantity of shelters and guesthouses for domestic violence and the lack of sensitivity is discussed in the media (Milliyet, 2013).

The oldest NGO is the Purple Roof Foundation for Women's Shelters founded in 1990, followed by Women's Solidarity Foundation, Solidarity with Women Foundation and Women's Center Foundation. Municipality-led centers for women's shelters are opened with the Protection of Family Law issued in 1998 as mentioned above. For example, Bakırköy and Şişli municipalities in Istanbul were the first ones to initiate women's shelters in 1990 and 1992 (Toktaş & Diner, 2015). The centers under KSGM are named the General Directorate of Social Services and the Protection of Children (SHÇEK) which serves orphaned children as well as battered women (Toktaş & Diner, 2015). All three types of shelters that women can apply to in case of violence will be elaborated on in the following sections. Then, what services these shelters provide to which women will be discussed. There are very limited studies about the women's shelters in Turkey; thus, Toktaş and Diner's (2015) latest research will be referenced in this section.

The Purple Roof Women's Shelter Foundation (2015) launched its first shelter in 1995; however, it was closed due to financial difficulties. However, since 2005 with changes in administration and financial supports, the Foundation has been running women's shelters (Toktaş & Diner, 2015). Legal procedures are rather flexible in civil organizations like the Purple Roof Women's Shelter Foundation, for example there is no strict time limit compared to SHÇEK women's shelters. According to the 2015 Activity Report of the Foundation, in the first six months of the year 2015, 370 women with their children applied to the women's shelter. Most women applying to the Foundation resided in Istanbul (73 percent) and were aged between 25–34 (36 percent).Marriage status is crucial in terms of applications to an official women's shelter, in particular; however, in the percentages of the Foundation, legally married women constitute the majority, although unmarried and religiously married women are also included. The main forms of domestic violence women reported being exposed to when applying to the Foundation were respectively, psychological (45 percent), physical (25 percent), sexual (14 percent), economic (14 percent), and digital violence and stalking (1 percent). Moreover, due to the Report, most women were exposed to violence from their husbands and ex-husbands or another male of the family, for example, their father. They applied for mainly social assistance, legal support and other reasons, for example, psychological consultation or abortion. If in the first six months only 49 women were provided help in the shelter, approximately 1 percent of the total, it can be argued that capacity problems are present.

Centers run by municipalities are under Law 4320, allowing municipalities with a population of over 50,000 and obliging municipalities with a population over 100,000 to open shelters for women. After the first shelters opened in Istanbul, in 1993 the first shelter of Ankara was initiated in Altındağ municipality (Toktaş & Diner, 2015). Research in one women's shelter in Turkey found that only six out of 39 municipalities in Istanbul were running shelters and two were planning to open shelters in 2010 (Toktaş & Diner, 2015). One of the main problems in opening a shelter was denoted as providing security, according to the research. Although many municipalities are required to open shelters, because of the insignificance of the issue in regard to local elections and voting campaigns for mayors, municipalities do not give the issue much attention (Toktaş & Diner, 2015).

In fact, survivors of domestic violence apply first to "intermediary stations" and then are located to an official shelter (Toktaş & Diner, 2015). Complaints about the scarcity of these stations and limited capacity are discussed in terms of inefficiency in providing protection to women exposed to violence, which may lead to force women to turn back to the violent environment, furthermore inducing their death. State-led "women's guesthouses," abbreviated as SHÇEK shelters, can accommodate up to 50 women within a maximum 24- month period (Toktaş & Diner, 2015). This time period varies from three to six months for women staying with their children, however, a special permission is required for such extensions, for example in the case of honor killings. This does not demonstrate the sole problem with SHÇEK shelters.

Another problem concerns the secrecy of residing in an official shelter. First, women who apply for SHÇEK shelters or municipality counseling centers are required to apply with their official identity cards, which is usually problematic because their leaving of the house is a contingent matter so concern for the identity card may not arise (Toktaş & Diner, 2015). Second, an official certificate of residence is required which requires registration at an administrative office in the neighborhood of the SHÇEK. The secrecy of the address is critical for women and children exposed to domestic violence (Toktaş & Diner, 2015). Third, confidentiality of all kinds of private information is essential (Karataş, Şener & Otaran, 2008).

As a matter of fact, few women after being exposed to violence apply to official or non-official institutions. The results of research are that only 11 percent seek institutional help in case of violence, even though 85 percent of battered women are informed about women's shelters and 56 percent of women in general have been subject to either physical or sexual violence (Akadlı-Ergöçmen et al., 2015). Surprisingly, no regional differences were observed in their study about the proportion of women applying to shelters. Neither education nor wealth levels of women affected the percentage significantly. One of the reasons for such a low application rate may be based on the legal procedures for registration at any shelter as mentioned above. Another interesting reason may be that women may think that they deserved domestic violence. It is underlined that in studies conducted in Turkey, the results denote that women think that they may have acted in ways in which to deserve violence (Harcar, Çakir, Sürgevil & Budak, 2008). The Turkish Population and Health Care Research (2004) found that reasons for women believing they were deserving of violence included burning the meal, answering back to the husband, spending too much money, neglecting nurture of the children, and rejecting sexual intercourse. The percentage of women agreeing with deserving violence was found to be 26.8 percent in only Istanbul (Harcar et al., 2008). This may stem from two facts; first, the representations of social institutions focusing on the right and intrinsic nature of violence; and second, children growing up in the environment of violence experiencing being beaten and witnessing physical violence may cause tendencies toward and acceptance of violence (Harcar et al., 2008). One study found that out of 147 women 63.7 percent were beaten in their childhood and 40.4 percent of women were beaten by their partners (Hıdıroğlu, et al., 2006). A more significant finding of this study is furthermore, 78.1 percent of participant women express that they agreed that they were deserving violence due to certain reasons begetting violence (Hıdıroğlu, Topuzoğlu & Karavuş, 2006).

Other alternatives aside, official and non-official shelters consist of the police ALO 155 hotline, gendarmerie (police with official military status), or ALO 156 hotline, ALO 183 Women and Children's Social Support Line, Violence Prevention and Monitoring Centers (ŞÖNİM), family courts, prosecutor's offices, governor's district offices, the bar association, the Provincial Directorate of the Ministry of Family and Social Policies, and hospitals and health institutions (Akadlı-Ergöçmen et al., 2015). For example, police in rural areas gendarmerie, police with a military status, are one of the prevalent institutions that violence-exposed women apply to. The police constitute a primary place for assistance before applying to a center or organization for domestic violence. Particularly, the police's role becomes critical in the case of honor killings. Afterwards, police are obliged to refer women exposed to domestic violence to either a shelter or counseling centers (Akadlı-Ergöçmen et al., 2015). The percentage of women referred by police to formal and civil women's shelters for domestic violence is 40 percent, according to the Research on Domestic Violence in Turkey (Palermo, Bleck & Peterman, 2014). Problems may also occur during this process where police often attempt to reconcile the man and send the woman back to her home, although the directive of the Ministry of Interior is very clear about referring women to shelters instead of sending them back home, which cannot be considered as a preventive intervention for domestic violence (Toktaş & Diner, 2015). Due to the results of the Report, the percentage of reconciliation of husbands with their wives is 27 percent and issuing cautionary decisions is 23 percent (Akadlı-Ergöçmen et al., 2015). At times, physical violence is perceived to be a reason for reconciliation whereby the percentage of referral to formal and civil women's shelters for domestic violence decreased to just 9.6 percent (Akadlı-Ergöçmen et al., 2015).

Violence Prevention and Monitoring Centers (ŞÖNİM) were established in 2012 by the decree of Law 6284 on the Protection of the Family and the Prevention of Violence against Women. ŞÖNİM has been operating in 14 pilot cities of Turkey since 2012. ŞÖNİM is a means by which to fight against domestic violence, consisting of support and monitoring services for the prevention of violence and effective use of precautions. Major aims are rapid and effective services for victims of domestic violence. These centers operate 24 hours a day, 7 days a week in coordination with open-streetscape surveillance cameras and "security buttons." "Security buttons" are given to women exposed to domestic violence which have telecommunicating and messaging attributes in case of domestic violence. A woman retaining these buttons may communicate with the police if she thinks her life is in danger. Police then locate her or the location of the perpetrator of violence using surveillance cameras, and direct the nearest police force to respond to the crisis (Sabah, 2012).

Conclusion

As discussed in the introduction, the level of domestic violence in Turkey is higher than in Western countries. In addition, unreported cases make the problem worse. The awareness of domestic violence has been on the rise, and state/civic response to domestic violence has been becoming more effective over the last 20 years. However, it is too early to say whether these precautions are enough to prevent domestic violence in Turkey.

References

Akadlı-Ergöçmen, B. (2015). *Institutional application process regarding violence against women*. Research on Domestic Violence against Women in Turkey. Ankara: Elma Teknik Basim Matbaacılık.

Akadlı-Ergöçmen, B., Türkyılmaz, A.S., & Abasoğlu-Özgören, A. (2015). *Coping strategies for violence against women*. Research on Domestic Violence against Women in Turkey. Ankara: Elma Teknik Basim Matbaacılık.

Altinay, A.G., & Arat, Y. (2007). *Violence against women in Turkey: A nationwide survey*. Istanbul: Punto.

Amnesty International. (2005). Ask Amnesty: Women's Human Rights Defender Canan Arin. Retrieved January 27, 2010 from www.amnestyusa.org/askamnesty/live/display. php?topic=46

Arikan, C. (1993). Kadin ve siddet [Women and violence]. T.C. Devlet Bakanligi Kadinin Statusu ve Sorunlari Genel Mudurlugu Yayinlari [Turkish State Ministry Directorate General for Status and Problems of Women], *8*, 21–23.

Bianet (2016). Erkek siddeti cetelesi. Retrieved from http://bianet.org/kadin/bianet/133354-bianet-siddet-taciz-tecavuz-cetelesi-tutuyor

Bugra, A., & Keyder, C. (2008). Kent Nüfusunun En Yoksul Kesiminin İstihdam Yapisi ve Gecinme Yöntemleri, Bogazici Universitesi Sosyal Politika Forumu Arastirma. Raporu, Istanbul (in Turkish).

Cakmak, D. (2009). Türkiye'de Çocuk Gelinler. Retrieved June 7, 2009 from www.umut. org.tr/ (in Turkish).

Cetin, I. (2015). Defining recent femicide in modern Turkey: Revolt killing. *Journal of International Women's Studies*, *16*(2), 346–360.

Dedeoglu, S. (2010). "Endüstriyel Üretimde Kadin ve Göcmen Emegi: Atarerkillik ve Enformel Emek." In Saniye Dedeoglu ve Melda & Yaman Oztürk (Eds.), *Kapitalizm, Ataerkillik ve Kadin Emegi Türkiye Ornegi*. Sosyal Arastırmalar Vakfı, Istanbul (in Turkish).

The Department of Economic and Social Affairs of the United Nations Secretariat. (2010). Violence against women. In S. Mrkić, T. Johnson, & M. Rose (Eds.), *The World's Women: Trends and Statistics*. New York: United Nations.

Erbaydar-Paksoy, N. (2012). Kadın Sığınmaevleri. Retrieved February 12, 2016 from www.huksam.hacettepe.edu.tr/Turkce/.../siginmaevi_aylikyazi.doc

Erder, S. (2005). "Urban migration and reconstruction of the kinship networks: The case of Istanbul." In R. Liljeström & E, Özdalga (Eds.), *Autonomy and dependence in the family: Turkey and Sweden in critical perspective*, Swedish Research Institute in Istanbul Transactions, *11*, 117–138.

Erkan, R. (2003). A small trail out of patriarchy: A progressive NGO & abused women in Southeastern Turkey. *Women's Health & Urban Life: An International and Interdisciplinary Journal*, *2*, 61–76.

Glick, P., Sakalli-Ugurlu, N., Ferreira, M.C., & Aguiar de Souza, M. (2002). Ambivalent sexism and attitudes toward wife abuse in Turkey and Brazil. *Psychology of Women Quarterly*, *26*, 292–297.

Gokler, M.E., Arslantas, D., & Unsal, A. (2014). Prevalence of domestic violence and associated factors among married women in a semi-rural area of Western Turkey. *Pakistan Journal of Medical Sciences*, *30*(5), 1088.

Haaken, J., & Yragui, N. (2003). Going underground: Conflicting perspectives on domestic violence shelter practices. *Feminism & Psychology*, *13*, 49–71.

Harcar, T., Çakir, Ö., Sürgevil, O., & Budak, G. (2008). Kadına yönelik şiddet ve Türkiye'de kadına yönelik şiddetin durumu. Toplum ve Demokrasi. *2*(4), 51–70.

Hıdıroğlu, S., Topuzoğlu, A., Ay, P., & Karavuş, M. (2006). The assessment of the factors influencing physical violence against women and children: A primary health care center based study in Istanbul. In *Yeni Symposium: Psikiyatri, Nöroloji ve Davraniş Bilimleri Dergisi* (Vol. 44, No. 4, pp. 196–202). Cerrahpasa Medical Faculty.

Hortacsu, N., Kalaycioglu, S., & Rittersberger-Tilic, H. (2003). Intrafamily aggression in Turkey: Frequency, instigation, and acceptance. *The Journal of Social Psychology*, *143*, 163–184.

Icon Institute, Hacettepe University Institute of Population Sciences, BNB Consulting. National Research on Domestic Violence against Women in Turkey. Retrieved from www.kadininstatusu.gov.tr/upload/kadininstatusu.gov.tr/mce/eski_site/tdvaw/doc/Main_report.pdf. 2009

Ilkkaracan, P. (1998). Exploring the context of women's sexuality in Eastern Turkey. *Reproductive Health Matters*, *6*(12), 66–75.

Izmirli, G.O., Sonmez, Y., & Sezik, M. (2014). Prediction of domestic violence against married women in Southwestern Turkey. *International Journal of Gynecology & Obstetrics*, *127*(3), 288–292.

Kagitcibasi, C., Goksen, F., & Gulgoz, S. (2005). Functional adult literacy and empowerment of women: Impact of a functional literacy program in Turkey. *Journal of Adolescent & Adult Literacy*, *48*, 472–489.

Kara, H., Ekici, A., & Inankul, H. (2014). The role of police in preventing and combating domestic violence in Turkey. *European Scientific Journal*, *10*(20), 1–21.

Karataş, S., Şener, Ü., & Otaran, N. (2014). Kadın Sığınmaevleri Kılavuzu. Ankara: T.C. Başbakanlık Kadının Statüsü Genel Müdürlüğü. Retrieved February 12, 2016 from http://kadininstatusu.aile.gov.tr/data/542a8e0b369dc31550b3ac30/Kadin%20Siginmaevleri%20Kilavuzu.pdf

Kocacik, F., & Dogan, O. (2006). Domestic violence against women in Sivas, Turkey: Survey Study. *Croatian Medical Journal*, *47*(5), 742–749.

Korkut-Owen, F., & Owen, D.W. (2008). *Kadına Yönelik Aile İçi Şiddet*. T.C. Kadının Statüsü Genel Müdürlüğü.

KSGM (2009). Türkiye'de Kadına Yönelik Aile İçi Şiddet Araştırması 2008. Retrieved February 12, 2016 from www.hips.hacettepe.edu.tr/TKAA2008-AnaRapor.pdf

Marshall, G.A., & Furr, L.A. (2010). Factors that affect women's attitudes toward domestic violence in Turkey. *Violence and victims, 25*(2), 265–277.

Milliyet (2013, August 25). Women's shelters cannot keep up with victims. *Turkish-Daily*.

Nassbaum, M.C. (2000). *Women and human development: The capabilities approach.* Cambridge, MA: Harvard University Press.

Palermo, T., Bleck, J., & Peterman, A. (2014). Tip of the iceberg: Reporting and gender-based violence in developing countries. *American Journal of Epidemiology, 2*, 95. Research on Domestic Violence in Turkey. Hacettepe Üniversitesi, Nüfus Etütleri Enstitüsü, 2004: Ankara, Turkey.

Sabah. (2012, October 18). Minister Şahin pushed the "violence button." *Turkish-Daily*.

Şahin, N., Timur, S., Ergin, A., Taşpinar, A., Balkaya, N., & Çubukçu, S. (2010). Childhood trauma, type of marriage and self- esteem as correlates of domestic violence in married women in Turkey. *Journal of Family Violence, 25*(7), 661–668. DOI:10.1007/s10896–010–9325–5

Sallan Gül, S. (2011a). *Türkiye'de Kadin Siginmaevleri: Erkek Siddetinden Uzak Yasama Acilan kapilar mi?* Baglam Yayinlarii, Istanbul.

Sallan Gül, S. (2011b). Türkiye Kadın Dernekleri Sanliurfa Ilinde Kadın Intiharları Arastirmasi. July 25, (in Turkish). Retrieved February 2, 2011 from www.tkdf.org.tr/sanliurfaporu.pdf" www.tkdf.org.tr/sanliurfaporu.pdf

Sallan Gül, S. (2013). The role of the state in protecting women against domestic violence and women's shelters in Turkey. *Women's Studies International Forum, 38,*107–116. DOI:10.1016/j.wsif.2013.01.018

Toktaş, Ş., & Diner, C. (2015). Shelters for women survivors of domestic violence: A view from Turkey. *Women's Studies, 44*(5), 611–634. doi:10.1080/00497878.2015.1036158

Turkish Population and Health Care Research. (2004). Hacettepe Üniversitesi, Nüfus Etütleri Enstitüsü: Ankara, Turkey.

UNICEF Innocenti Research Centre. (2000). *Domestic violence against women and girls.* Florance.

UNICEF. (2015). Unicef Data Website for Child Marriage. Retrieved February 12, 2016, from http://data.unicef.org/child-protection/child-marriage

Vaughn, M., & Stamp, G.H. (2013). The empowerment dilemma: The dialectic of emancipation and control in staff/client interaction at shelters for battered Women, *Communication Studies, 54*, 154–168.

Walby, S., & Myhill, J. (2004). Domestic violence, sexual assault and stalking: Findings from the British Crime Survey, Home Office Research Study, 276, London.

Yıldız, Bal & Binbir, (2015). Kadına şiddetin adı. *Uşak Üniversitesi Sosyal Bilimler Dergisi, 8*(1), 139–161.

Yüksel-Kaptanoğlu, I., & Çavlin, A. (2015). *Prevalence of violence against women.* Research on Domestic Violence against Women in Turkey. Ankara: Elma Teknik Basim Matbaacılık.

Yüksel-Kaptanoğlu, I., & Tarım, S.A. (2015). *Introduction.* Research on Domestic Violence against Women in Turkey. Ankara: Elma Teknik Basim Matbaacılık.

8 Status of victims of spousal violence and the future tasks

The case of Japan

Susumu Nagai

Prior to passage of the Act on the Prevention of Spousal Violence and the Protection of Victims (Gender Equality Bureau Cabinet Office (GEBCO), 2001), the National Coalition Against Domestic Violence (NCADV) in the U.S. had defined the term domestic violence (DV) as, 'the wilful intimidation, physical assault, battery, sexual assault, and/or other abusive behaviour' as part of 'a systematic pattern of dominance and control' perpetrated by one intimate partner against another' (NCADV, 2016b, p. 1). Physical, sexual, psychological violence, and emotional abuse are included in it. Domestic violence is found 'in every community, irrespective of age, economic status, sexual orientation, gender, race, religion, or nationality' around the globe (NCADV, 2016a). The abuser constantly tries to maintain dominance and control over the abused, whose relationships may end in 'physical injury, severe psychological trauma, and in severe cases, even death. The influence of this victimization can cross generations and last a lifetime' (NCADV, 2016a).

As the Ministry of Justice points out, the philosophy of gender equality is stipulated in the Japanese Constitution and the principle of gender equality has been legislatively established by the Equal Employment Opportunity Law and other laws (Ministry of Justice, 2016). But, in reality, fixed ideas on gender roles such as that the man should work outside and the woman should remain at home are prevalent and deep-rooted in society even today and cause various kinds of gender discrimination in homes and workplaces (Ministry of Justice, 2016). It was only after the long and winding road which the stakeholders in domestic violence, namely, battered women and victim advocates, kept walking while they continued to make a history of milestones and achievements so as to prevent intimate partner violence, that the United Nations recognized domestic violence as an international human rights issue and issued a Declaration on the Elimination of Violence Against Women (1993). In 1995, at the Fourth World Conference on Women held in China, Beijing a Declaration was made, which included that all nations must, 'Prevent and eliminate all forms of violence against women and girls' (United Nations, 1995).

The Tokyo Metropolitan Government set up a Tokyo Women's Consultation Center after the International Women's Year of 1975. This Center focused on domestic violence and opened the first public shelter for victims (Yunomae,

2001). In 1992, the investigation committee on Violence from Husbands and/ or Intimate Partners conducted a national survey on victimization of DV. In 1997, the Tokyo Metropolitan Government then conducted their own survey on violence against women. Over half of respondents reported being 'victimized for one or two times' or 'frequently' from psychological violence, one-third (33.0 per cent) reported physical violence, and just over 20 per cent (20.9 per cent) were victims of sexual violence. This survey showed us that these women had undergone serious violence (Tokyo Metropolitan Government, 1998; Kojima, 2002).

Non Governmental Organizations (NGOs) developed empowerment activities such as setting up a national network of women's shelters. In 1998, the Committee on Cohesive Society came into being in the House of Councillors, and in 2000, the Project Team on Violence against Women was officially inaugurated mainly by female lawmakers. Finally, on 6 April, in 2001, Japan's Act on the Prevention of Spousal Violence and the Protection of Victims Act No. 31 of 2001 came into existence. This bill was sponsored by a cross-party group of lawmakers. The Act went into effect on 13 October 2001 (Kainou, 2001).

The Japanese Gender Equality Bureau Cabinet Office, recognizes that spousal violence constitutes a serious challenge to human rights, that the majority of victims of spousal abuse are women, and that when women find it difficult to achieve economic self-reliance they are subject to violence from their spouses. This adversely affects the dignity of individuals impeding the realization of genuine equality between women and men.

Supplementary Provisions of the Act (GEBCO, 2001), are stated as follows:

In consideration of respect for individuals and equality under the law expressly stipulated in the Constitution, progress has been made in Japan through efforts toward the protection of human rights and the realization of genuine equality between women and men. Nevertheless, even though spousal violence constitutes a serious violation of human rights, as well as being a crime, efforts to relieve victims have not always been adequate in all instances. In addition, the majority of victims of spousal violence are women. When women who find it difficult to achieve economic self-reliance are subject to violence from their spouses, it adversely affects the dignity of individuals and impedes the realization of genuine equality between women and men. In order to improve these conditions and to achieve the protection of human rights and the realization of genuine equality between women and men, we must establish measures to prevent spousal violence and protect victims. Such action will be in line with the efforts taken by the international community to eradicate violence against women.

(GEBCO, 2001, p. 2)

This Act was intended to prevent spousal violence and protect victims through the establishment of a system to deal with spousal violence, providing for notification, counselling, protection and support for self-reliance. The Act has so far been revised three times in order to further strengthen its provisions. It is applicable to all foreign residents who live in Japan as well as Japanese citizens.

We realize that males may be victims of domestic violence and are thus protected under the Act, as are victims in de facto states of marriage, or unmarried, partners or former spouses, and in cases where violence is inflicted both before and after a separation. The Act also recognizes that violence includes not merely bodily harm, but also psychological and sexual violence. However, protection orders apply only to bodily harm and/or life-threatening intimidation (GEBCO, 2001). The Act also states in Article 23 that officials shall, in the performance of their duties, take into consideration the psychological and physical conditions of the victims and their environment, respect their human rights, and give due consideration to ensuring their safety and protecting their privacy (GEBCO, 2001).

Spousal Violence Counselling and Support Centers

Spousal Violence Counselling and Support Centers (SVCSC) are strongholds, set up in each prefecture, which offer consultation, counselling, and temporary protection for victims and accompanying family members, and provide various kinds of information including:

1   consultation and introductions to organizations that provide counselling;
2   counselling;
3   assurance of safety in an emergency and temporary protection of victims and accompanying family members;
4   provision of information and other forms of support that will promote the self-reliance of victims;
5   provision of information pertaining to the use of the protection order system; and
6   provision of information pertaining to the use of facilities where victims may live and receive protection, and other forms of support (GEBCO, 2001).

Temporary protection

Coupled with providing counselling services, the Women's Consulting Offices in each prefecture offer temporary protection for domestic violence victims where victims can stay in safety for a short period of time with their children. From time to time Women's Consulting Offices provide victims with temporary protection consigning them to private shelters and other organizations. Private shelters are run by private-sector organizations where victims can seek and find emergency or provisional refuge. These shelters provide support for victims, such as accommodations, meals, and clothing, as well as various forms of counselling (GEBCO, 2008).

Welfare systems

Depending on the status of residence, income and other conditions, victims may be able to use the welfare system components suitable to them including medical insurance, child benefits, and public assistance (GEBCO, 2008).

Punishment of abusers

It is prohibited in Japan for a person to inflict physical harm or bodily injury upon another person, even between spouses. A victim of spousal violence should not hesitate to notify or report it to the police (GEBCO, 2008).

Protection Orders

In cases where a victim is subjected to bodily harm or life-threatening intimidation by a spouse or they are highly likely to receive serious harm to life or body from continuous spousal violence, Protection Orders shall be issued to the abuser by a district court, subject to a written petition to the court. Protection Orders consist of the following:

1   Order Prohibiting Approach to the Victim: This order forbids the abuser from approaching the victim, or loitering in the vicinity of the victim's domicile (except for the domicile that the victim shares as the main home with the abuser), workplace, or other places for six months.
2   Order Prohibiting Phone Calls or Other Behaviour: This order prohibits the abuser from committing the following acts with regard to the victim for the period specified in Order 1 above:

    a   requesting a meeting;
    b   telling matters that suggest that the spouse is monitoring the victim's behaviours;
    c   extremely rude or violent words and deeds;
    d   phone calls without saying anything, or repeated phone calls, facsimile transmissions or e-mail messages (except in cases of urgent necessity);
    e   phone calls, facsimile transmissions or e-mail messages at night (between 10 p.m. and 6 a.m.) (except in cases of urgent necessity);
    f   sending filthy materials, animal carcasses or other extremely disgusting or repulsive materials, etc.;
    g   revealing matters that harm the victim's dignity, etc.; and
    h   revealing sexually insulting materials, or sending documents, pictures or other sexually insulting materials (GEBCO, 2008).

3   Order Prohibiting Approach to the Victim's Child or Relatives: This is an order that, when deemed necessary in order to prevent the victim from being obliged to meet the abuser with regard to the child or relative, etc., prohibits the abuser from approaching the victim's child (minor living with the

victim) or relative (relative of the victim, or another person who has a close relationship with the victim in his/her social life), and from loitering in the vicinity of the victim's residence, workplace, etc. for the period specified in Order 1 above.

4   Order to Vacate: This order obliges the abuser to vacate the residence shared as the main home with the victim, and not to loiter in the vicinity of the victim's residence for a period of two months.

Violation of a protection order by the abuser is punishable by imprisonment with work for a maximum term of one year or a fine with a maximum of one million yen (GEBCO, 2008).

Petitions for Protection Orders must include the description of the specific circumstances and sufficient evidence to prove serious and imminent victimization, and the content of the victim's contact with or without a consultation with a police officer or a Spousal Violence Counselling and Support Center. For those who cannot afford the costs of (translation or interpretation when) preparing the documents necessary for filing a petition, there is a system of legal aid whereby the costs are advanced and then repaid in instalments (GEBCO, 2008). For foreign residents, there is additional information on the renewal of their period of stay, change in status of residence, staying in Japan without a valid visa, and the handling of alien registration cards (GEBCO, 2008).

Legal amendment of the Act

In Japan it is not easy to arrest offenders with assault and/or injury charges because of the difficulty of identifying the date and time of the offences and of collecting evidence, and these cases are time consuming to investigate. Therefore, with a view to protecting victims' safety in an expeditious way, protective orders were improved and expanded.

Under the Act on the Prevention of Spousal Violence and the Protection of Victims, violence between men and women in legal marriages or common-law marriages that had been exposed to previous violence, protection and support for the victims was made a government duty, and various measures were stipulated such as establishment of Spousal Violence Counselling and Support Centers and creation of a system of protective orders. In addition, in line with the Basic Policy concerning Measures for the Prevention of Spousal Violence and the Protection of Victims that was based on the Act and the Third Basic Plan for Gender Equality, efforts were made to improve measures to prevent spousal violence and protect victims and support their self-sufficiency.

The Act was revised in 2004 for the first time. There were two essential points in the amendment. One of them was that the definition of spousal violence was broadened to include psychological violence with words and/or attitudes as well as physical violence. In addition, protection orders were to be given to separated spouses as well (GEBCO, 2008). In 2006, the Gender Equality Bureau of the Cabinet Office published a summary of various surveys concerning spousal violence. According to the summarization, approximately one-third of women and 17.4 per cent of men who participated in the survey either experienced physical assault and/or threats, or had been coerced into sexual acts, with more than 10 per cent of women being assaulted repeatedly. In the majority of these cases, violence first took place after marriage; however, 13.5 per cent of women and 5.2 per cent of men reported dating violence. The majority of victims were women in their twenties and thirties. Also, it was not uncommon for live-in unmarried men or women, and same-sex couples to be involved in violence and abuse (GEBCO, 2006).

The Act was revised again in 2007. In the second revision, protective orders were expanded to include threats to a person's life or body as well as physical violence, and orders to prohibit phone calls, as well as orders to prohibit being in the vicinity of a victim's family members, were newly added. Support systems of municipalities were also strengthened and specified by stipulation of duties to formulate basic municipal plans and make efforts to establish Spousal Violence Counselling and Support Centers closer to victims' residences. Moreover, the Act was amended once again for the third time in 2013. Under the third revision, the definition of victims of spousal violence was broadened to include those cohabitating with abusive partners.

Data on spousal violence

In 2014, the Cabinet Office conducted a random sample questionnaire on victimization of spousal violence. The questionnaire was distributed to the total number of targets of 5,000 individuals over 20 years of age. The number of valid responses was 3,544, and the ratio of valid responses was 70.9 per cent. They were asked whether they were at least once subject to any kind of the following spousal violence: bodily harm, psychological assault, financial pressure and/or sexual coercion. Nearly one-quarter (23.7 per cent) of the 1,401 females reported being subject to spousal violence ('once or twice' 14.0 per cent and 'frequently' 9.7 per cent) while 72.1 per cent of them answered 'never' and 4.2 per cent gave no answer. On the other hand, those males (the total of 1,272) who reported being subject to spousal violence amounted to 16.6 per cent ('once or twice' 13.1 per cent and 'frequently' 3.5 per cent) whereas 80.5 per cent of them answered 'never' and 2.9 per cent did not reply.

Based on the data gathered by the Gender Equality Bureau (2015), Spousal Violence Counselling and Support Centers (247 in total across the nation, and 74 Centers set up by municipalities in each prefecture) received 35,943 actual cases. This is quite an increase from the 11,035 persons seeking assistance in 2002. In addition, in 2014 there were 31,855 visitors; those who did not follow through after the initial contact (GEBCO, 2015).

The total number of spousal violence victims recognized by the National Police Agency (NPA) in 2002 was 3,608, which grew to 59,072 in 2014 (GEBCO, 2015). Temporary protection given by the Women's Consultation Centers (WCC) in each prefecture in 2002 was 10,903. By 2009 that number had risen to 12,160, with just over one-half being family members, declining to 11,082 in 2014 with a small fluctuation range. Fifteen to twenty per cent of those presenting at the shelter were homeless or victims of human trafficking.

The total number of protection orders administered by the courts was 1,398 in 2002, which increased to 3,125 in 2014; 14–17 per cent of those petitioners dropped their requests (GEBCO, 2015).

Based on the data provided by the NPA (2014), the total number of victims of domestic violence whose victimizers were arrested was 59,072; of those victims 175 victims (92 females and 65 males) were murdered, 2,953 victims (2,775 females and 178 males) had been physically assaulted, and 2,697 victims (2,550 females and 147 males) suffered injuries.

The Basic Act on Crime Victims and victim measures in Japan

Before the establishment of the Basic Act on Crime Victims, they were forgotten people in the criminal justice system. However, academics, criminal justice professionals, bureaucrats, and journalists began to pay substantial attention to victims of crime. The Basic Act on Crime Victims, a Japanese version of the 1984 Victims of Crime Act of the U.S. was established in 2004 (Cabinet Office, 2004; National Police Association (NPA), 2016).

Mr. and Mrs. Asaichi Ichinose are known as the trailblazers of the victim movement in Japan (Sato, 1978; 10th session of the Diet, Committee on Judicial Affairs No. 29, 2 July 1975). Their beloved only son was stabbed to death by a teen assailant in 1966. They visited other surviving families all over Japan, and 257 individuals held a meeting in Yokohama in 1972 to form a national association of homicide survivors. The media covered the harsh reality of the homicide survivors. In 1975, although a few young scholars helped them give unsworn testimony in the Lower House Judicial Affairs Committee to create a compensation system for crime victims, their appeal was in vain. Mr. Ichinose lost his sight and passed away two years later.

Mr. Isao Okamura, a lawyer, became a homicide survivor in October 1997 when his wife was murdered at the entrance of their home by an evil man with unjustifiable resentment towards the lawyer due to a business transaction. He took this occasion to become a crime victims' rights activist and formed a national association of crime victims, of which he became the chairperson to assist victims in gaining the cooperation of other crime victims and survivors, some of which were high profile (National Association of Crime Victims and Surviving Families (NAVS), 2000).

The Japanese government, in keeping with changes in the domestic issues, had established the Automobile Liability Security Act and created a provision for protecting witnesses in the Penal Code, etc. during the 1950s, and established the Act on Payment of Benefits for Crime Victims enacted in 1981 after the Mitsubishi Heavy Industries Building bombing took place in 1976. In 1990, the Japanese Society of Victimology (now Japanese Association of Victimology) was established (Japanese Association of Victimology, 2016). In the following year, at the symposium of the 10th anniversary of establishment of the Act on Payment of Benefits for Crime Victims, a courageous mother whose son was killed by a drunk driver stood up, talked about her experience as a crime victim, and craved a need for establishing a system of victim assistance. The statements she made influenced the criminal justice professionals, especially bureaucrats of the National Police Agency (NPA) and law enforcement officers who were involved with victim service provision, and journalists. A group of scholars with the cooperation of authorities in the criminal justice system began conducting nationwide surveys on the status of crime victim issues one year later. In the same year, a counselling room for crime victims was established in an academic institution in Tokyo, which invited the establishment of the National Network for Victim Support in 1998. Journalists continued to cover the victim issues.

Meanwhile, the NPA had launched comprehensive support measures for crime victims in 1996 based on the Basic Policy Concerning the Measures for Supporting Crime Victims, and in 2000 established the two laws for protecting crime victims which provided consideration and protection in criminal procedures. However, crime victims continued to express complaints about insufficient economic support, medical and welfare services, and during criminal procedures with secondary victimization included, insufficient support systems, including those in the private sector. In 2003 and 2004, pursuing the goal of realization of the criminal justice system for crime victims, with victim participation and incidental suit included, members and supporters of the National Association of Crime Victims and Surviving Families chaired by Mr. Okamura took part in a signature-collecting campaign on the streets of Japan. The Association collected more than 550,000 signatures as a result (Cabinet Office, 2010).

The establishment of the Basic Act on Crime Victims

As the time was ripe for the government to respond to the demands by crime victims and others who requested comprehensive services for crime victims, the Basic Act on Crime Victims was established in legislation by house members in December 2004. And, in 2005, when the Basic Act on Crime Victims was put in force, the Office for Policies on Crime Victims was established in the Cabinet Office, which had been established in 2001 in order to strengthen the function of the Cabinet of the central government of Japan, headed by the Prime Minister, which supports the Cabinet in formulating important policies as well as overall coordination among Ministries and Agencies (Cabinet Office, 2004).

Article 1 provides the purpose of this Act, which is to promote measures for crime victims comprehensively and systematically, and to protect crime victims' rights and their interests, by clarifying the Basic Principles, specifying the responsibilities of the State, local governments, and fellow citizens, and defining contents that would be the foundation for the Measures for Crime Victims. In the Basic Act on Crime Victims, the rights of crime victims are clearly stipulated, and the spirit of mutual assistance is included (Cabinet Office, 2004).

Article 2 defines the term 'Crimes' as used in this Act as crimes and equivalent acts that have caused emotional or physical harm to the victim. And, the term 'Crime Victims' is used in this Act to mean persons, family or bereaved family members who have suffered damages from these crimes. The term 'Measures for Crime Victims' as used in this Act will mean the process of providing Crime Victims with the proper care and assistance in order for them to alleviate and recover from the suffering they have incurred as fully as possible, and for them to participate in the process in order to live as best as possible (Cabinet Office, 2004).

Article 3 of the Basic Act, states that all Crime Victims' individual dignity will be respected and the appropriate measures of treatment will be taken accordingly. And, the Measures for Crime Victims are to consider the cause and circumstances of the crime, and take appropriate action according to the Crime Victims' situation and other external factors (Cabinet Office, 2004). In addition, the Measures for Crime Victims are to begin from the time the crime victims need assistance directly following the crime, until they are restored to their normal lives again.

Based on the Basic Act, the Office for Policies on Crime Victims has been developing and implementing comprehensive measures by steering the Investigative Commissions, formulating 'The Model Handbook of Assistance to Crime Victims' developing a 'Model Training Curriculum', conducting model projects by regional organizations so as to build understanding about crime victim support, as well as holding the annual Central Public Meeting during 'Crime Victims' Week'. At the same time, the Cabinet Office and local authorities cooperated to host local conventions in three or four prefectures annually.

In Fiscal Year 2013, measures for crime victims included improving crime victim support corresponding to the individual victim's circumstance (guide to problem-solving, anxiety about security, physical and mental problems, lifestyle problems, and offender punishment) and concrete measures for crime victims and their progress (efforts to recover the victim's damages and to provide them with economic support, efforts for the victims to recover from or to prevent mental and/or physical damage, efforts to broaden opportunity for victims to participate in criminal procedures, efforts to improve the system to support crime victims, and efforts to foster understanding among citizens and to earn their consideration and cooperation).

In Fiscal Year 2014, provisions were added calling for support with comprehensive cooperation among institutions, associations and groups concerned, cooperation to prevent re-victimization, and to support victims of sexual violence, child victims, victims of traffic crashes and accidents, and concrete measures for crime victims and their progress.

Case workers engaging in the frontline of assistance and protection of victims and their accompanied family members at Spousal Violence Counselling and Support Centers are those who give substantial influence to them typically right after their re-victimization. Historically speaking, the Women's Consultation Offices (WCOs) were originally established based on the 1956 Anti-Prostitution

Act. Case workers at WCOs in those days used to take a leading role in protecting women and assisting them as they recovered from their trauma. Now the State designates each WCO to function as a hub in the prefecture assisting and protecting victims of spousal violence. Moreover, one of the case workers on the front line of supporting those victims informed the present author that case workers have to deal with homeless women, women who are being stalked, and human trafficking victims as well. Their workload responsibilities have been expanded based on the creation and amendment of Acts having to do with women's welfare without additional personnel. Clients have a variety of needs. Case workers are responsible for almost all the clients' needs. They help victims complete official documents, and communicate with the police, courts, municipal offices, hospitals, schools, family and kin. They are overworked with heavy burdens that are not justifiable. Multi-disciplinary teams consisting of nurses, teachers, study guidance teachers, psychologists, social workers, and case workers are needed at WCOs so as to alleviate the stress of case workers.

Knowledgeable individuals and key figures are well aware of women's issues; not merely those of domestic violence but also those of poverty, physical handicaps, mental disorders, etc. must be taken into consideration in order to make a drastic change, and they would like to legislate rules tentatively called an Act on Women's Welfare Support added to the Basic Act. We will wait and see what will happen in the near future.

References

Bureau of Citizens and Cultural Affairs, Tokyo Metropolitan Government. (1998). *Research report on violence against women.* Tokyo Metropolitan Government, Tokyo. Retrieved from www.seikatubunka.metro.tokyo.jp/en/.

Cabinet Office. (2001). The Cabinet Office's role in the cabinet/structure. Retrieved from www.cao.go.jp/en/pmf/pmf_about.pdf.

Cabinet Office. (2004). The Basic Act on Crime Victims. Retrieved from http://www8.cao.go.jp/hanzai/kihon/hou.html.

Cabinet Office. (2010). NAVS (National Association of Crime Victims and Surviving Families). Retrieved from http://www8.cao.go.jp/hanzai/report/h21-3/pdf/chap5-1.pdf.

Gender Equality Bureau Cabinet Office (GEBCO). (2001). Act on the Prevention of Spousal Violence and the Protection of Victims. 17 April 2016. Retrieved from www.gender.go.jp/english_contents/about_danjo/lbp/index.html.

Gender Equality Bureau Cabinet Office (GEBCO). (2006). Summary of survey on violence between men and women. (内閣府男女共同参画局(2006).男女間における暴力に関する調査)報告書＜概要版＞) Retrieved from www.gender.go.jp/policy/no_violence/e-vaw/chousa/pdf/chousagaiyou.pdf.

Gender Equality Bureau, Cabinet Office (GEBCO). (2008). To victims of spousal violence. Retrieved from www.gender.go.jp/english_contents/about_danjo/lbp/index.html

Gender Equality Bureau, Cabinet Office (GEBCO). (2015). Data on violence from spouse. Retrieved from www.gender.go.jp/english_contents/about_danjo/lbp/index.html.

Kaino, T. (Ed.). (2001). Source 1 Act on the Prevention of Spousal Violence and the Protection of Victims. In *Anti-Domestic Violence Law* (in Japanese) (pp. 282–289). Shogakusha. Retrieved from *www.shogaku.com/.*

Kojima, T. (2002). *Law on Domestic Violence* (in Japanese). Shinzannsha Shuppan. (小島妙子ドメスティック・バイオレンスの法　信山社出版). Retrieved from *www.shinzan-sha.co.jp/*.

Japanese Association of Victimology. (2016). Introduction of the Association. Retrieved from www.victimology.jp/introduction.html.

Ministry of Justice. (2016). Major Human Rights Problems. Retrieved from www.moj.go.jp/ENGLISH/HB/hb-03.html.

National Association of Crime Victims and Surviving Families (NAVS). (2000). Introduction of the NAVS. Retrieved from www.navs.jp/introduction/introduction.html.

National Coalition Against Domestic Violence (NCADV). (2016a). What is Domestic Violence? The National Coalition Against Domestic Violence. Retrieved from www.ncadv.org/need-help/what-is-domestic-violence.

National Coalition Against Domestic Violence. (NCADV). (2016b). Domestic Violence National Statistics. Retrieved from http://ncadv.org/files/National%20Statistics%20Domestic%20Violence%20NCADV.pdf.

National Police Agency. (2016). The Basic Act on Crime Victims. Retrieved from www.npa.go.jp/hanzaihigai/kihon/hou.html.

Sato, Hideo. (1978). Impulsive Murder. Chuo-koron-sha. The 10th Session of the Diet, Committee on Judicial Affairs No. 29, 2 July 1975 (Wed.) (第075回国会　法務委員会　第29号　昭和五十年七月二日　(水曜日) Retrieved from http://kokkai.ndl.go.jp/SENTAKU/syugiin/075/0080/07507020080029c.html.

United Nations. (1995). Beijing Declaration and Platform for Action. p. 11. Retrieved from *www.un.org/womenwatch/daw/beijing/pdf/BDPfA%20E.pdf*.

Yunomae, T. (2001). Anti-domestic violence movement in Japan. In T. Kainou (Ed.), *Anti-Domestic Violence Law* (in Japanese). (pp. 162–186) Shougakusha (ゆのまえ知子　日本における先駆的反DV運動 (戒能民江 (編著) ドメスティック・バイオレンス防止法) 尚学社).

9 The Vietnamese police response to domestic violence against women

The family unit under pressure

*Mike Perkins, Louise Cotrel-Gibbons,
and Huong Thu Nguyen*

Introduction

Domestic violence (DV) in Vietnam has been outlawed by the Law on Domestic Violence Prevention and Control (hereby referred to as the Domestic Violence Law) since 2007. This legislation broadly defines domestic violence as 'purposeful acts of certain family members that cause or may possibly cause physical, mental or economic injuries to other family members' (National Assembly, 2007, Law No. 02/2007/QH12, Article 1.2).

However, rates of domestic violence remain high, with evidence overwhelmingly demonstrating that domestic violence is often normalised, 'brushed under the carpet', or considered an issue which must be resolved in the interests of maintaining family harmony, rather than by what is best for the survivor. Current interventions by law enforcement are often focused on the reconciliation of the family unit, rather than prioritising the protection of the survivor or penalising the perpetrator (UNODC, 2011a). This reconciliation process is often referred to other community organisations, rather than dealt with directly by the police.

The Domestic Violence Law (National Assembly, 2007) acknowledges that domestic violence can occur between any member of the family. In Vietnam, families and households are traditionally multi-generational, housing grandparents, parents, and adult children, who remain in the household until they marry. Sons (particularly the eldest) are expected to remain in the family home with their parents even after marriage. Women, when they marry, will move in with their husband's family and care for their parents-in-law. The various relationships which may involve domestic violence are therefore numerous.

However, it is generally accepted that, due to gender inequalities within Vietnamese society, communities and households (and indeed throughout the world), women are more often subject to domestic violence than men (UN, 2014). Discussion, research, and legal action on domestic violence in Vietnam generally focuses on violence experienced by women from their husbands or partners, within the cultural norm of heterosexual, cis-gendered relationships. Violence between married or partnered men and women falls under various categories which are commonly, and often interchangeably, used throughout the domestic violence literature, including intimate partner violence (IPV), violence against women (VAW) and gender-based violence (GBV). The *Handbook for Legal Aid Providers in Domestic Violence Cases* (UNODC, MOJ & VLA, 2011), explains that in Vietnam:

> domestic violence against women is often referred to as 'gender-based violence' because it partly evolves from women's subordinate gender status in society. In most cultures, unequal power relationships between women and men created and maintained by gender stereotypes is the basic underlying cause of violence against women.
>
> (UNODC & MOJ, 2011, p. 7)

Therefore, without discounting the fact that domestic violence is also experienced by men, by women and men within same-sex relationships, and by transgender individuals, and is also committed by various other family members, this chapter will focus on violence experienced by women by male husbands or partners. Due to differences in how legislation and law enforcement tackles child abuse, this chapter also specifically excludes any examination of violence against children by family members, although this is also legally classified as domestic violence. It is also worth noting that domestic violence research in Vietnam is also limited with regards to examining the situation of those that belong to populations which are isolated, vulnerable or experiencing social stigma and discrimination (Gardsbane, Vu, Taylor & Chanthavysouk, 2010), including remote ethnic minority communities;[1] this chapter is therefore only able to provide an overview of the situation in Vietnam, rather than detailed disaggregation.

This chapter will therefore progress as follows: first, we briefly outline the prevalence of domestic violence in Vietnam, before examining possible underlying reasons behind this level of prevalence. We will then examine how domestic violence against women is tackled by the police, drawing links between the cultural perceptions of domestic violence and both the official protocols for law enforcement and the reality in practice. Finally, we present several recommendations for the improvement of the police response to domestic violence in Vietnam.

How prevalent is domestic violence in Vietnam?

The *National Study on Domestic Violence Against Women* (GSO, 2010) was the first nationally representative study in Vietnam to address violence against women, focusing on violence perpetrated by husbands or partners. In alignment with the Domestic Violence Law, the quantitative survey focused on physical, sexual, emotional and economic abuse, experienced by 4,838 women aged 18–60 years old. The study found that over 58 per cent of ever-married women have experienced sexual, physical or emotional violence (or a combination of these types of violence) from their husbands or partners at some point during their lifetime; 27 per cent reported experiencing violence within the previous 12 months. Qualitative interviews also conducted as part of the study revealed that other family members, particularly in-laws, were sometimes complicit or did not support the survivor, contributing to the continuation of the violence.

Thirty-two per cent of women surveyed had experienced some form of physical violence by a husband or partner, and the majority of these women reported experiencing at least one instance of 'severe violence'.[2] The results indicated that physical violence is likely to occur early in a relationship and continue throughout its course, although decreasing in prevalence as time goes on. Conversely, women's experiences of sexual violence[3] did generally not decrease with time, but were instead sustained throughout the relationship. The survey found that almost 10 per cent of ever-partnered women had experienced sexual violence from a husband or partner. Of the 900 survivors of domestic violence[4] interviewed as part of a study into law enforcement's response to domestic violence (UNODC, 2011a), 95 per cent experienced violence from their husbands: 90 per cent had been hit, slapped or kicked, and 36 per cent had been forced (or attempted to be forced) to engage in sexual intercourse.

Emotional violence is often an integral part of both physical and sexual violence, but is harder to categorise and is highly subjective. For this reason, the GSO survey (2010) allowed a wide definition of emotional violence. Fifty-four per cent of participants reported experiencing emotional violence at some point in their lives, and 24 per cent reported that they are currently experiencing emotional violence. Thirty-three per cent of women in the UNODC (2011a) study reported receiving threats related to harming or killing children or someone close.

Economic abuse, defined in the GSO (2010) survey as either taking a woman's savings or earnings against her will, or refusing to give her money for household expenses even when it is available, appears to be less prevalent than other types of abuse, at 9 per cent. Qualitative evidence from the survey also highlighted other forms of economic abuse, including husbands forcing wives to work harder than they are able, forcing every household expense to be documented with the threat of physical violence, or refusing to contribute money to the household.

The survey also demonstrated, unsurprisingly, that there was significant overlap between women's experience of the different types of violence.

Why does domestic violence in Vietnam continue to be so prevalent?

Understanding domestic violence in Vietnam, and how the police respond to it, requires an awareness of the wider cultural concepts which dictate how people live their lives, and how these relate to the causes and perceptions of domestic violence within Vietnamese society.

Vietnamese culture (for the majority Kinh population) is traditionally dictated by a complex doctrine which combines elements of Confucianism, ancestor worship, Taoism, Buddhism and animism (Nguyen, 1985). Whilst these ideologies have differing origins and complexities, each, and especially the first three, have specific principles which dictate the nature of relationships between men and women.

Confucianist principles are a set of ethics and morals which provide the foundation of Vietnamese society. They promote patriarchal hierarchies, prioritise patrilineal descent, and dictate that a woman's place is within the home. It is a responsibility to ensure a successful family life (Gardsbane et al., 2010; Vu, 2008). This is also linked to the common practice of ancestor worship, which is traditionally patrilineal, and thus prioritises producing sons instead of daughters in order to have offspring to pray for you in the afterlife. Ancestor worship also traditionally reveres a sense of place and homeland, which is one of the reasons why sons, rather than daughters, remain in the family home and inherit family land (UNDP, 2013); they must be available to pray for their ancestors. Family is therefore an extremely important concept in Vietnam, not just in this life but also in the next. The family unit as the foundation of Vietnamese society is formally enshrined in the constitution (National Assembly, 1992, Article 64); we will see later how this has a profound impact on the police response to domestic violence.

Confucianism dictates that women should aspire to the '*tam tòng, tứ đức*' (three obediences and four virtues): obedience to their fathers during childhood, to their husbands when married and to their sons in widowhood; and the virtues of diligence, good manners, proper speech, and morality (Taylor & Choy, 2005). These ideals give men the perceived 'right' to 'discipline' or 'educate' their wives, using various types of violence if necessary. Evidence shows that men in particular see violence as justified, if the woman has done something 'wrong' (GSO, 2010; Duc, Le, Trung & Kanthoul, 2012), for example:

> Men have more knowledge than women do and women are often mean and often fuss about small things. That is why violence occurs. The main cause of conflict in the family is from women.
>
> (Male group discussion in Ha Noi, GSO, 2010, p. 75)

However, studies by UN Women (2015) and others find that these views permeate through Vietnamese society and are also perpetuated by women:

> As a wife, women should know how to balance domestic finance and put things in order, but many are lazy and incapable. Thus, they are scolded or shouted at by their husbands.
>
> (Focus group participant, UN Women, 2015, p. 40)

In Vietnamese society, violence is therefore often accepted as a normal burden to bear for women, and one which she can only avoid if she crafts a harmonious home life, which appears to be her responsibility alone: 'A wife should meet her husband's [in this case sexual] requests to maintain family happiness' (UN Women, 2015, p. 40).

Linked to these issues of obedience and discipline is the concept of 'saving face', which is an extremely strong and important cultural practice in Vietnam (Nguyen, Terlouw & Pilot, 2005). 'Saving face' means not revealing mistakes or weaknesses to others, or receiving criticism in front of others. To lose face can be a very shameful and embarrassing experience. According to accounts in the GSO (2010) study, a wife cannot point out her husband's mistakes, or do anything which may cause him embarrassment, or she is likely to encounter violent consequences.

Showing strong emotions is linked to losing face (Nguyen, 1985). Should issues occur within the household, a virtuous Vietnamese woman is one who can 'endure'; she can deal with these issues without challenging her husband, or escalating disagreements:

> A: ... we just saw a husband beat his wife and never saw a wife beat her husband ...
>
> Q: What do you think the wife in the above [latter] situation should do? What would people say about her – she is wise or she is dumb?
>
> A: I think she is good wife. It means she knows to listen to her husband and to endure him.... Enduring is good. Vietnamese women often endure.
>
> (Male Group Discussion in Hanoi, GSO, 2010, p. 77)

The acceptance within Vietnamese society of the marked differences in the roles and rights of men and women is also linked to elements of Taoist philosophy (Endres, 2015). For example, the principle of *Yin* and *Yang* (*âm* and *dương*, in Vietnamese); the concept that two opposites make a balanced whole. *Dương/Yang* is the male element, and is linked to the sun and with characteristics such as heat, activity, rigidity and conformism. *Âm/Yin* is female, associated with the earth, and is cool, passive, and flexible (Nguyen, 1985; Endres, 2015). These concepts of gendered differences which are intended to balance each other can be equated to men and women's justification of domestic violence (Rydstrom, 2003). Negative events or issues such as domestic violence, occur as a result of an imbalance between these two elements, and within the family. As the cool, passive and flexible half, *Âm*, women are expected to yield to the hot, rigid *Dương* men in order to maintain a harmonious balance. Qualitative interviews undertaken as part of the *National Study on Domestic Violence Against Women* (GSO, 2010) revealed that the majority of participants felt that the 'natural order' of things dictate that men and women deal with anger differently; men find it difficult to control their anger, and also have a right to express it, whilst women are expected to not react to anger, and to help men calm down.[5]

> I think it is right that when my husband is angry I keep silent. It would be strange if a wife was angry and shouted while the husband said nothing. Women should be more gentle.
>
> (Woman in Ben Tre, *National Study on Domestic Violence Against Women*, GSO, 2010, p. 76)

Participants, especially women, also believed that men have 'hot blood' which causes them to be uncontrollably violent (GSO, 2010). The attribution of violent tendencies to biological characteristics naturalises domestic violence between men and women and absolves the perpetrators of responsibility.

The principles of *Âm* and *Dương* can also be seen to have an influence on cultural constructions of sexuality in Vietnam; women are seen to have a naturally low sex drive and thereby are sexually inferior to men, who are expected to possess a naturally strong sexual desire (Nguyen & Harris, 2009). This male sexual desire is perceived, by both men and women, to be satisfied at all costs; with their wives, or with other women (GSO, 2010). Women therefore feel that they must accept all sexual advances in order to prevent their partners from having affairs: 20 per cent of the women who participated in the quantitative survey in the GSO (2010) study agreed with the statement 'the wife has the obligation to have sex with her husband even if she does not feel like it' (p. 7).

> If we want to keep family happiness, we should at all time create happy and comfortable situations and we have to respond to men's [sexual] needs so they would not go out and find other women.
>
> (Commune officer in Ben Tre, *National Survey on Domestic Violence Against Women*, GSO, 2010, p. 77)

This naturalisation of gendered differences with regards to sex, alongside the Confucianist teachings on women's obedience, forms the basis of a justification mechanism for sexual violence. The GSO (2010) study highlighted that although the majority of participants believed that it is unacceptable for a man to force anyone, including his wife, to have sex, participants simultaneously held the view that women did not have the right to refuse sex except for a few certain circumstances.[6] Physical violence is thus not necessarily required to enforce sex, as women do not feel they have the right to refuse.

Rydstrom (2010a, 2010b) argues that the combination of philosophies and logics which are the foundation of Vietnamese society not only legitimises the violent behaviour of a husband, but also puts the woman at the risk of being criticised for her failure to maintain household harmony. These factors contribute to a lack of reporting of domestic violence in Vietnam. Domestic violence survivors may fail to recognise incidents as illegal acts of violence, believing that abuse is a natural part of family life or somehow their fault. Even if they do not think the violence is just, they may fear (violent) reprisal by their families or partners (due to causing them to 'lose face'). A woman may also be concerned about losing face or causing her family or children to lose face, believing that others in the community will think that they have done something wrong, and will judge them: 'I wanted to save my children's faces, so I did not report to the police' (Victim L, UNODC, 2011a, p. 37). They may also fear the impact which reporting domestic violence may have on their marriage, the stigma of divorce, and the financial challenges in bringing up children alone (Kwiatkowski, 2010). The financial challenges in particular are exacerbated by patrilineal approaches to land ownership and inheritance, which may leave a divorced woman without a home or much financial support.

Whilst domestic violence is a crime which is generally under-reported to the police in all societies, the reporting rate in Vietnam is particularly low (UNODC, 2011a). Data from the national survey on domestic violence (GSO, 2010) indicate that 87 per cent of all Intimate Partner Violence (IPV) cases reported that they had never sought help from any source at all, and in the UNODC 2011a) study only 43 per cent of the cases discussed had been reported to the police. In this latter study, when the 57 per cent of survivors who had not reported their experience of violence to the police were asked why (they were able to give multiple reasons), 65 per cent responded that the incident was a family matter, or better dealt with privately by the woman, and 30 per cent downplayed the incident, stating that is was not serious enough to warrant reporting to the police. Similarly, in the GSO (2010) study, when asked to provide reasons as to why this was the case, the most common reason offered was that women considered what was happening to them 'normal, and not serious', regardless of the level of violence being experienced. Thirty per cent of participants also did not want anyone else to know about the incident, whilst approximately 20 per cent cited 'shame, embarrassment' as a reason for not reporting domestic violence. Qualitative research from the same study showed that survivors were concerned that the community would believe that they had done something wrong which caused their partner to be violent towards them.

We have demonstrated above how certain principles and beliefs within Vietnam affect the relationships between men and women and can contribute to the perception of domestic violence as normal, natural, justified or as result of the woman's own failings. These beliefs, teamed with a reluctance or fear of others finding out about domestic violence and speculating on the causes, contribute to a lack of reporting of domestic violence. However, the study by UNODC (2011a) also found that a small percentage (around 9 per cent) cited a reason for not reporting violence is because they felt that the police would not, or could not act. We now explore how police respond to incidences of domestic violence in Vietnam and explore why this belief amongst some women may exist.

The police response to domestic violence

The focus on the family unit as the foundation of Vietnamese society and morality has also had a strong influence on the legislation relating to domestic violence. It is frequently implemented with the end goal of maintaining the 'happy family', focusing strongly on reconciliation rather than prosecution of perpetrators, or protective measures for survivors (UNODC, 2013). Law enforcement officers themselves have also been socialised within these same principles. By upholding socio-cultural norms and operating within this legislative framework, they become key actors and enforcers of these principles. As seen in the above section, the police response to domestic violence is also limited by the impact of survivors' perspectives of domestic violence; how can the police enact significant change in a community if the violence is normalised and not reported?

The DV Law, approved in 2007, provides a clear definition of domestic violence, and the parameters of arrestable and prosecutable offences. Several acts are specifically defined within the law as domestic violence, including:

1   corporal beating, ill-treating, torturing or other purposeful acts causing injuries to one's health and life;
2   insulting or other intended acts meant to offend one's human pride, honour and dignity;
3   isolating, shunning or creating constant psychological pressure on other family members, causing serious consequences;
4   preventing the exercise of the legal rights and obligation in the relationship between grandparents and grandchildren, between parents and children, between husbands and wives as well as among brothers and sisters;
5   forced sex;
6   forced child marriage, forced marriage or divorce and obstruction to free will and progressive marriage;
7   appropriating, demolishing, destroying or other purposeful acts to damage the private properties of other family members, or the shared properties of family members;
8   forcing other family members to overwork or to contribute more earnings than they can afford; controlling other family members' income to make them financially dependent; and
9   conducting unlawful acts to turn other family members out of their domicile.
(National Assembly, 2007, Law No. 02/2007/QH12, Article 2.1)

If an incidence of domestic violence occurs and is reported to the police, the following process should be followed, according to (UN Women, 2014):

1   An initial report of domestic violence is made, either by the victim themselves, a family member or by another party such as the Women's Union. The report can be made in person, by calling the local police station or by calling the national emergency number 113. In cases where a formal complaint is being made by the survivor of domestic violence, this must be done by filing a written complaint.[7] If they withdraw the formal complaint, they must waive their right to bring the complaint again in the future.[8]
2   After receiving the report of the incident, the investigating officer in charge is to question the victim or family members of the victim about the incident, facilitate a preliminary medical examination for the victim, and ascertain the relationship between the victim and the suspect.[9]
3   Once a legitimate complaint is established, the commune police unit who received the case are responsible for immediately forwarding the incident to the district level investigative unit by letter.
4   After receiving the report at the district level, the investigative unit have a period of 30 days (up to a maximum of two months in a case deemed to be highly complicated) in order to decide whether or not to initiate criminal

proceedings and proceed with the investigation. This extensive time period creates a large degree of leeway and the potential for manipulation of the case.

Whilst the above process is what *should* happen, the reality of the situation can be very different. In the UNODC (2011a) investigation, in 83 per cent of the cases the police visited the house of the victim, but 34 per cent of the incidents were dealt with by the police suggesting that the victim solve the problem herself within the family, and 15 per cent by the police suggesting the survivors themselves contact another agency (such as the Women's Union or reconciliation team), rather than filing the paperwork related to opening an investigation with the relative authorities (as laid out in law). According to research (UNODC, 2011b), the majority of domestic violence cases reported to the police are actually diverted to reconciliation. The focus on reconciliation as a primary tool for dealing with domestic violence is due to the strong legal focus on reconciliation and 'happy families' within the legal framework of Vietnam. For example, Article 3.1 (Principles of domestic violence prevention and control) states:

> ... special attention paid to communication and education on family values, counselling and reconciliation in line with the fine traditional and cultural practices of Vietnam.
>
> (National Assembly, 2007, Law No. 02/2007/QH12, Article 2.1)

This Article, amongst others, highlights the legal stance on encouraging reconciliation and counselling of domestic violence within the family and communities, as opposed to further police investigation. This focus coupled with the cultural attitudes of both the survivors of domestic violence and the police officers involved, often results in incidents of domestic violence which are made known to the police being referred to community organisations such as the Women's Union, rather than police action being taken.

Chapter IV of the Domestic Violence Law sets out the specific responsibilities of families and communities in reconciling conflicts and disputes amongst members of the community. Whilst the law specifically states that this reconciliation process should not take place when domestic violence (as specified by the Domestic Violence Law) has taken place (as opposed to family conflicts or disputes) it stresses the reliance on the community in interpreting what is, or is not, domestic violence and how to deal with it appropriately. If there is a lack of understanding as to the specifics of the Domestic Violence Law by either the victim, the community, or even the police themselves, this could result in issues being 'reconciled' when they should have in fact been dealt with through the criminal justice system.

This focus on reconciliation both by the police, and within the legal framework, has in the past led to tragic results. In a case reported in person to one of the co-authors by a female social worker of the Hanoi-based Peace House shelter in 2014:[10]

There was a married couple in province A with two children. It was reported that the woman was frequently subjected to being physically abused by the husband. After a significant period of this abuse continuing, she sought help from the local women's union. The women's union representatives reported the case to the local authorities who issued a no-contact order. The couple were temporarily separated, however, after several days, both were invited to come to the local authority where representatives of the reconciliation unit met and talked separately with both parties. During the consultation, the husband expressed his regret for his abusive behaviours. He wished to be granted an opportunity to talk to his wife privately. Both reconciliation representatives and the police thought that the husband might have been regretful and thus acquiesced to the husband's request, leaving the couple to talk privately in the room. The husband then killed the wife with a knife that he had secretly brought to the meeting.

This focus on reconciliation, coupled with the cultural attitudes of both the survivors of domestic violence and the police officers involved, means that incidents of domestic violence reported to the police are often referred to community organisations such as the Women's Union, rather than further police action being taken. Despite reconciliation being the primary method used by the police of Vietnam for dealing with incidences of domestic violence, according to UNODC and MOJ (2009), 77 per cent of reconciliation cases did not produce the expected outcome, resulting in continued violence against the survivor. Reconciliation cannot fix the underlying cause behind why the violence occurs, or provide an adequate solution for survivors (Gardsbane et al., 2010; UNODC, 2013).

Aside from reconciliation, the police can respond to reported incidents of domestic violence in five main ways:

1   Order the offender to write a self-criticism addressed to the authorities.
2   Place the offender in public criticism in front of the local community.
3   Give the offender an administrative punishment [a fine].
4   Place the offender in a re-education facility.
5   Bring the case to court, where the perpetrator can be sentenced to imprisonment.

(UNODC, 2011a, p. 44).

In the UNODC (2011a) study, only 28 per cent of offenders were fined and in only 12 per cent of the cases did the perpetrators have charges brought against them. The fact that so few measures are taken against offenders sends a signal to both survivors and offenders that domestic violence is not an act that will be taken seriously by the judicial system as a whole, and may serve to increase revenge acts against the survivor for raising the incident to the police in the first place.

Under the law, police can only pursue a criminal case of physical domestic violence against an offender if the 'rate of infirmity' is more than 11 per cent. If the rate of infirmity is lower than this, the matter would be dealt with administratively (without the courts) or through reconciliation. If the rate of infirmity is more than

31 per cent then the police can pursue a criminal case without the permission of the survivor.[11] If the severity of the injuries is between 11 and 31 per cent, the survivor must give their permission for a case to be taken through the judicial system. As we have seen earlier in this chapter, domestic violence survivors may apply a variety of reasonings as to why a criminal case should not be pursued. This can mean that the police are restrained from effectively dealing with offenders due to a lack of consent from the survivor, even if this is due to coercion by the perpetrator. This allows for the cycle of domestic violence to continue unaided by the criminal justice system. The police in Vietnam are also limited in their ability to deal effectively with domestic violence by the tight boundaries of trust which enclose the family unit and the local community in Vietnam (McKernan & McWhirter, 2009). For example, victims who withdraw their complaint due to not wishing to have the police involved with what they consider to be a family matter, or witnesses who provide very vague testimony, limit the ability of the police to carry out a full investigation of reported cases of domestic violence.

This caveat surrounding the prosecution of criminal domestic violence cases is especially concerning when we consider psychological, economic or sexual violence, which (and in particular the first two) may not result in physical evidence, thus leading to difficulties in opening a prosecutable case of domestic violence against the offender.

In the previous section we discussed some of the socio-cultural factors which may lead to a lack of reporting of domestic violence. Evidence has also shown that the actions of the police themselves can lead to a lack of reporting and thus the perpetuation of violence. When a report is made to the police, the decision as to whether or not the case will be handled is not simply based on the rule of law. There is generally a degree of flexibility by the officer, due to focus on mediation and reconciliation that is part of both the culture, and the law. In reality, the police response to an initial report of any incident may be shaped by the impression the officer has of the person making the report with regards to their wealth, place of residence, family background, education and employment status, and the type of emotion being displayed by them (Nguyen, 2011), or whether or not the officer has a personal relationship with the offender (UNODC, 2011a). In the UNODC (2011a) study, survivors of domestic violence were asked about their experiences reporting incidents to the police. Whilst 65 per cent had an 'easy experience', 16 per cent of the respondents classified their experience as 'troublesome', primarily due to the attitudes of the police. It is well established that the attitudes which the police display when dealing with members of the public have an impact on the trust and confidence which the public hold in these officials (Perkins, 2016; Weitzer & Tuch, 2005; Skogan, 2006; Myhill & Bradford, 2012) and it is possible that a preconceived belief in how the police would deal with the individual's situation may have resulted in a lower reporting rate of domestic violence within Vietnam. This mis-trust in the police will affect survivors of domestic violence disproportionately, with one of the stated reasons in the UNODC study (2011a) for non-reporting of DV incidents being 'I did not think the police would/could do anything'.

Incidences of bribery amongst law enforcement agencies within Vietnam have also been reported, either to avoid the arrests or accusations of suspects, the changing of investigative results or the prosecution of both criminal and civil cases in favour of the briber (Dao, 2010; UNODC, 2013). In cases of domestic violence this could have significant impacts on both the reporting of incidents to the police, and how these are dealt with by officials. This may serve to explain the reluctance by some officials to follow the official procedures laid out above, and instead suggest reconciliation by other parties.

Whilst we have explored a number of issues in this section, the social attitudes and norms which exist in both Vietnamese law and the wider society, and the focus on reconciliation in an attempt to ensure a 'happy family', appear to be the major driver explaining the police response to domestic violence in Vietnam. These both combine to limit the efficacy of the police response in these cases, and go some way towards allowing for an understanding as to why the majority of domestic violence cases are not punished as seriously as they could be under the laws of Vietnam.

Policy recommendations

The effective improvement of the police response to domestic violence against women by their husbands or partners in Vietnam requires both short-term practical measures to deal with and prevent violence, and long-term cultural and behavioural change to change police and public perceptions of domestic violence and work towards its elimination.

Evaluations of current methods of responding to domestic violence and acquiring justice for survivors should be conducted (UN, n.d.a), alongside increased research into the prevalence, nature, and drivers of domestic violence, to gain better understanding and develop (new or improved) appropriate and effective police responses. At present, data is limited, with official statistics already several years old and studies conducted by civil society more difficult to publish and to access, due to the sensitive nature of the topic.[12] Comprehensive data which recognises differences in cultural factors related to the prevalence of and police response to domestic violence amongst different regions, ethnic groups and socio-economic backgrounds is also required to ensure that data gathered from one group is not considered as representative of the entire population. Further investigation in Vietnam into domestic violence committed by women towards men, through other family relationships, within same-sex relationships, and which affects transgender people is required, particularly as new gender roles and LGBT individuals continue to become increasingly recognised and accepted in Vietnam. Official statistics which are accurate and adequately address diversity are needed to motivate and substantiate policy changes.

The implementation of current laws and policies needs to be improved, through the capacity building of relevant stakeholders and duty-bearers, including local police, Vietnam Women's Union officers, and representatives of the justice system. Law enforcement officers on the ground must develop greater awareness of the current Domestic Violence Law and the measures that it does already provide; for example, it enables police to prohibit perpetrators to contact survivors. This can be supported through cost-effective measures such as distributing information materials to local police officers (UNODC, 2011a).

Police capacity should be built to enable local officers to take an approach which focuses on the rights and protections of the survivors of violence, and to broaden interventions to include early detection of situations within families and communities which may lead to violence. The United Nations Office on Drugs and Crime (UNODC, 2011a, 2013) suggests developing a pilot model of specialised police officers or units with a specific mandate to address violence against women. These units should include a high ratio of female police officers; the police themselves have said that they need more female police officers to tackle domestic violence cases as female survivors often feel more comfortable talking to another woman (UNODC, 2011a; UN Women, 2015). Understanding of the need for and investment in long-term multi-sector approaches in order to effectively deal with domestic violence is also required. For example, the health sector, as often one of the first points of contact in the event of violence, should also be supported to develop appropriate responses and referrals to law enforcement, as well as support systems for survivors of violence (GSO, 2010; UNODC, 2011a; MOLISA & UNFPA, 2014; UN, n.d.a;).

For the time-being, multilateral non-governmental development agencies continue to be mobilised in supporting the improvement of the police response to domestic violence in Vietnam; for example, UNODC (2011a) have previously issued a number of Training of Trainers manuals and have also provided training in the use of this manual to the People's Police Academy. However, the changing development-funding climate in Vietnam must be recognised, and any future efforts by development agencies must focus on supporting the Government of Vietnam to integrate and scale-up successful measures, in order to ensure sustainability.

The police can only operate to the best of their ability within the existing legal framework. Throughout the entire process of reporting and enduring a criminal, investigative or reconciliatory investigation of domestic violence within Vietnam, the responsibility to drive this process lies almost entirely with the survivor (UNODC, 2013). Evidence provided by the survivor both in the form of a written statement and any physical evidence, is critical in building a case against the perpetrator. This responsibility should instead lie with the police and the judicial system (United Nations General Assembly, 2011). The police should be able to build a case without the permission or testimony of the survivor, as over-reliance on the written statement provided by the survivor of domestic violence may result in weaker police investigations (Coordination Action on Human Rights Violations, 2008).

Acts which relate to domestic violence are also not adequately dealt with by law, preventing the police from taking effective action. Marital rape remains an administratively punishable offence despite its obvious severity (UNODC, 2013), stalking is not covered by any law in Vietnam, and all acts under the

Domestic Violence Law are only punishable under criminal law if they can be shown to cause physical injury. Based on evidence from within Vietnam but also by drawing on international best practice and experiences, the Penal Code needs to be revised in order to ensure clearer definitions of criminal acts of domestic violence, which enable law enforcement to more easily prosecute offenders without the responsibility of the success of the case falling on the survivor. Developments in policy and legislation must also be effectively communicated to local law enforcement to ensure that law enforcement officers are able to utilise the law fully to eliminate domestic violence in their communities, and offer suitable protection and support for survivors.

However, all of the above recommendations serve only to address the superficial issues which have an impact on the ability of the police to address domestic violence. They do not tackle the drivers of violence, or the 'underlying norms and attitudes that normalise GBV and make disclosure, law enforcement, reporting and successful prosecution more difficult' (UN, 2014, p. 40). Long-term change can only come about if deep-seated norms and attitudes, which form gender roles, responsibilities and cultural tendencies, are challenged and shifted amongst the public, police and policy-makers. These changes can take many years or even numerous generations to take root. The debate on how to instigate and sustain cultural changes is wide-ranging and continually ongoing, but it is clear that a long-term multi-faceted approach is required. Practical initiatives may include strengthening education policies which encourage positive conceptions of masculinity and femininity (UN, n.d.b; GSO, 2010), pre-marital coaching for couples (MOLISA and UNFPA, 2014), and behaviour change communications and media messages which reconceptualise gender (UN, n.d.a; UN, n.d.b; UN, 2014). Behaviour change campaigns which aim to reduce the stigma of reporting domestic violence are also vital to enable survivors to come forward but also to gain an accurate picture of domestic violence (MOLISA and UNFPA, 2014). In order to react to budgetary constraints, interventions should be prioritised in areas and communities where the risk of domestic violence is highest (MOLISA and UNFPA, 2014).

Conclusion

On 1 December 2015 at the National Meeting for the International Day for Elimination of Violence Against Women and Girls (VAWG) Deputy Minister Bui Van Nam of the Vietnam Ministry of Public Security (MPS) remarked that

> Over the past years, the people's public security forces have been actively collaborating with relevant agencies for the prevention and combating of domestic violence against women and girls all over the country.
>
> (Duc Mung, 2015)

The use of these terms within his speech, as opposed to the use of stronger terms such as elimination (which would reflect more precisely the spirit and commitments of the international community in eliminating VAWG globally) echo the long-standing cultural views within Vietnam which suggests domestic violence is an inevitable occurrence; an important issue to be tackled, but not expected to be stopped outright.

We have demonstrated in this chapter how these underlying cultural principles of Vietnam, alongside the social attitudes and norms, appear to be the major driver in explaining both the prevalence of, and the police response to domestic violence in Vietnam. These combine to allow for the culturally acceptable stigmatisation of women who report incidents of domestic violence, the normalisation of male violence towards spouses or partners and also affect the manner in which the police carry out investigations relating to domestic violence.

Whilst Vietnam is making large strides in relation to changes in the legislation relating to domestic violence, the underlying cultural elements will likely serve as a strong barrier to allowing for major changes in this area to be affected anytime soon. Only when Vietnamese society as a whole, from the general public, to law enforcement and policy- and law-makers, no longer accept domestic violence on any level and come to support the wellbeing of the survivor above the preservation of the family unit and all other cultural codes of conduct, will the police response to domestic violence in Vietnam be able to become truly effective.

Notes

1 There are 54 ethnic groups in Vietnam. The Kinh is the majority group, representing 86 per cent of the population (GSO, 2009).
2 'Severe violence' is categorised in the survey as being hit with a fist, kicked, dragged, threatened or injured with a weapon, choked or purposely burned.
3 Definitions of sexual violence in the survey included being physically forced to have sexual intercourse, having sexual intercourse out of fear of what would happen if she refused, or being forced to perform sexual acts which she finds degrading or humiliating.
4 Nine hundred respondents from Hanoi, Phu Tho, and Thai Nguyen provinces in the North; Da Nang, Gia Lai, and Ninh Thuan provinces in the Centre; and Ho Chi Minh, An Giang and Can Tho provinces in the South. All were already in contact with the authorities regarding domestic violence.
5 The interviews also revealed that this was also a protective strategy to avoid violent consequences.
6 Such as pregnancy, menstruation or illness.
7 This requirement to submit a written report can, in itself, prevent the reporting of domestic violence due to a lack of awareness of the process, lack of access to a police station, lack of financial resources (UNODC, 2013).
8 This does not mean that the victim cannot raise a separate complaint of domestic violence relating to a different incident against their attacker, however, it does raise questions of the possibility of a victim being pressured by their partner, family or community to withdraw the complaint and deal with it themselves.
9 In practice, 'immediately' usually appears to be around 24 hours.
10 This study was undertaken as part of a postdoctoral research project on 'social perceptions and judicial representations of rape: the cases of Vietnam and the Philippines' (grant number 2013-ey-12), funded by the SEASREP foundation.
11 National Assembly, Penal Code, No. 15/1999/QH10, 21 December 1999: Article 104.

12 NGOs, like all private enterprises within Vietnam, can only operate in the country with the explicit permission of the Government. For these organisations to be effective in serving their beneficiaries, they must be able to have a presence within the country, and they are therefore very cautious when it comes to researching and reporting on issues that the Government of Vietnam considers to be of a sensitive nature.

References

Coordination Action on Human Rights Violations. (2008). *Gendering human rights violations: The case of interpersonal violence, Final report 2004–2007.* Luxembourg: Office for Official Publications of the European Communities.

Dao, L.T. (2010). *Bribery crimes under Vietnamese criminal law in comparison with Swedish and Australian criminal laws.* PhD thesis, Hanoi Law University and Lund University.

Duc Mung. 2015. Nhiều giải pháp ngăn chặn, đẩy lùi bạo lực gia đình [Many solutions for domestic violence prevention and combating]. General news in the web portal of the Ministry of Public Security. Retrieved 10 January 2016 from www.mps.gov.vn/web/guest/ ct_trangchu/-/vcmsviewcontent/GbkG/2004/2102/33546)

Duc, D.T., Le, H.C., Trung, H., & Kanthoul, L. (2012). *'Teach the wife when she first arrives': Trajectories and pathways into violent and non-violent masculinities in Hue City and Phu Xuyen district, Viet Nam.* Hanoi, Vietnam: UN Viet Nam.

Endres, K.W. (2015). Imperious mandarins and cunning princesses: Mediumship, gender, and identity in urban Vietnam. In K. Atsufumi (Ed.), *Weaving women's spheres in Vietnam: The agency of women in family, religion and community* (pp. 193–217). The Netherlands: Brill.

Gardsbane, D., Vu, S.H., Taylor, K., & Chanthavysouk, K. (2010). *Gender based violence: Issue paper.* Hanoi, Vietnam: United Nations Population Fund Viet Nam.

GSO. (2009). *The 2009 Vietnam population and housing census: Completed results.* Hanoi, Vietnam: General Statistics Office

GSO. (2010). *Results from the national study on domestic violence against women in Vietnam.* Hanoi, Vietnam: General Statistics Office.

Kwiatkowski, L. (2010). Dịch Chuyển Xuyên Quốc Gia và Bạo Lực Giới: Định Vị Những Diễn Ngôn về Bạo Hành Gia Đình ở Việt Nam [Transnationalism and gender violence: Locating discourses of domestic violence in Viet Nam]. In V.H. Luong (Ed.), *Hiện Đại và Động Thái của Truyền Thống ở Việt Nam: Những Cách Tiếp Cận Nhân Học [Modernities and dynamics of tradition in Vietnam: Anthropological approaches]* (pp. 477–500). Ho Chi Minh City, Vietnam: Vietnam National University Publishing House.

McKernan, H., & McWhirter, D. (2009). Policing communities in Vietnam: Intercultural lessons for community policing with Vietnamese Australians. Proceedings of 'The Future of Sociology', the Annual Conference of the Australian Sociological Society (TASA 2009), Canberra, ACT, Australia, 1–4 December 2009.

MOLISA and UNFPA, (2014). *Why do some women experience more violence than others? Summary Report: Results of the analysis of risk factors for violence by husbands.* Hanoi, Vietnam: UNFPA in Viet Nam.

Myhill, A., & Bradford, B. (2012). Can police enhance public confidence by improving quality of service? Results from two surveys in England and Wales. *Policing and Society, 22*(4), 397–425.

National Assembly. (2007). Law on Domestic Violence (Law No. 02/2007/QH12).

National Assembly. (1992). Constitution of the Socialist Republic of Viet Nam.

National Assembly. (1999). Penal Code, No. 15/1999/QH10: Article 104.

Nguyen, K.L., & Harris, J.D. (2009). Extramarital Relationships, Masculinity, and Gender Relations in Vietnam. *Southeast Review of Asian Studies*, 31, 127–142.

Nguyen, M.D. (1985). Culture shock – A review of Vietnamese culture and its concepts of health and disease. *Western Journal of Medicine*, *142*(3), 409–412.

Nguyen, P.M., Terlouw, C., & Pilot, A. (2005). Cooperative learning vs Confucian heritage culture's collectivism: Confrontation to reveal some cultural conflicts and mismatch, *Asia Europe Journal*, *3*(3), 403–419.

Nguyen T.H. (2011). *Rape experiences and the limits of women's agency in contemporary post-reform Vietnam*. Unpublished PhD dissertation, University of Amsterdam, The Netherlands.

Perkins, M. (2016). Modelling public confidence of the police: How perceptions of the police differ between neighborhoods in a city. *Police Practice and Research*, *17*(2), 113–125.

Rydstrom, H. (2003). Encountering 'hot' anger. Domestic violence in contemporary Vietnam. *Violence Against Women*, *9*(6), 676–697.

Rydstrom, H. (2010a). Introduction. In H. Rydstrom (Ed.), *Gendered inequalities in Asia: Configuring, contesting and recognizing women and men* (pp. 1–18). Singapore: NIAS Press.

Rydstrom, H. (2010b). Compromised ideals: Family life and the recognition of women in Vietnam. In H. Rydstrom (Ed.), *Gendered inequalities in Asia: Configuring, contesting and recognizing women and men* (pp. 170–190). Singapore: Nias Press.

Skogan, W.G. (2006). Asymmetry in the impact of encounters with police. *Policing & Society*, *16*(2), 99–126.

Taylor, R., & Choy, H. (2005). *The illustrated encyclopedia of Confucianism – Volume 2.* New York: Rosen.

UN. (n.d.a). *Issue paper: The cost of domestic violence against women in Viet Nam.* Hanoi, Vietnam: UN Viet Nam.

UN. (n.d.b) *Issue paper: Redefining masculinity: The role of men and boys in preventing GBV and SRB imbalance in Viet Nam.* Hanoi, Vietnam: UN Viet Nam.

UN. (2014). *From domestic violence to gender-based violence: Connecting the dots in Vietnam: A UN Discussion Paper.* Hanoi, Vietnam: UN Viet Nam.

UN Women. (2014). *Report on the policing and prosecution of sexual violence 2014.* Hanoi, Vietnam: UN Women Vietnam.

UN Women. (2015). *Study report: Access to justice in the plural legal system in Viet Nam: A case study of women domestic violence survivors.* Hanoi, Vietnam: UN Women Viet Nam.

UNDP. (2013). *Women's access to land in contemporary Viet Nam.* Hanoi, Vietnam: UN Viet Nam.

United Nations General Assembly. (2011). *Resolution A/RES/65/228: Strengthening crime prevention and criminal justice responses to violence against women.* Retrieved 10 January 2016 from www.un.org/ga/search/view_doc.asp?symbol=A/RES/65/22

UNODC. (2011a). *Research on law enforcement practises and legal support to female victims of domestic violence in Vietnam: Working paper.* Hanoi, Vietnam: UNODC Viet Nam.

UNODC. (2011b). *Research on the quality of criminal justice services available to victims of domestic violence in Viet Nam: Working paper.* Hanoi, Vietnam: UNODC Viet Nam.

UNODC & MOJ. (2009). *Summary of the assessment of current practices of administrative punishment and the use of reconciliation/mediation teams when dealing with cases of DV in Viet Nam.* Hanoi, Vietnam: UNODC Viet Nam.

UNODC, MOJ & VLA. (2011). *Handbook for legal aid providers at local level to provide legal aid in domestic violence cases.* Hanoi, Vietnam: UNODC Viet Nam.

UNODC. (2013). *Assessment of the situation of women in the criminal justice system in Viet Nam.* Hanoi, Vietnam: UNODC Viet Nam.

Vu, S. (2008). The harmony of family and the silence of women: Sexual attitudes and practices among rural married women in northern Vietnam. *Culture, Health and Sexuality*, 10, 163–176.

Weitzer, R. & Tuch, S.A. (2005). Determinants of public satisfaction with the police. *Police Quarterly*, *8*(3), 279–297.

10 Domestic violence in Australia

A wicked problem

Sedat Mulayim, Mervyn Jackson, and Miranda Lai

Introduction

Interpersonal violence is a universal problem affecting people, mostly women and girls, in all countries of the world (VicHealth, 2014a; WHO, 2005, p. vii). According to the World Health Organization (WHO, 2016), recent global prevalence figures indicate that, worldwide, almost one third (30 percent) of women who have been in a relationship report that they have experienced some form of physical and/or sexual violence perpetrated by their intimate partner. As many as 38 percent of murders of women around the world are committed by an intimate partner. WHO (2016), therefore, regards violence against women, particularly intimate partner violence and sexual violence, as major public health problems and violations of women's human rights.

Australia is no exception. Domestic Violence (DV) in Australia is common and widespread (Mitchell, 2011). Contrary to popular belief, DV is not confined to low-socioeconomic groups, nor to certain cultural or ethnic backgrounds. It is not limited to heterosexual relationships (Flood & Fergus, 2008). In its extreme form, DV results in the tragic loss of human life. In the Australian Institute of Criminology's National Homicide Monitoring Program 2010–2012 report (AIC, n.d.), there were 479 homicide incidents in the period, resulting in a death toll of 511 people, of whom 187 were classified as domestic homicides. Close to 60 percent ($n=109$) of these domestic homicides were perpetrated by intimate partners, and 76 percent ($n=83$) of the victims were females. Statistics collected/collated/gathered by community organizations in 2015 would suggest that 60 percent of murders of women are committed by either a current or an ex-partner (see Figure 10.1).

This chapter provides an overview of the current situation of the problem in Australia, sourcing data from two major recent surveys: one focusing on experience of crime and the other on attitudes toward violence against women, and also offers a synopsis of major policies and initiatives to tackle the problem. The fact that violence against women and negative attitudes to gender equity still exist in all segments of the Australian community despite a range of initiatives and efforts points to the resistant nature of the problem of violence against women. Using Rittel and Webber's (1973) concept of a *wicked problem*, this chapter explores the

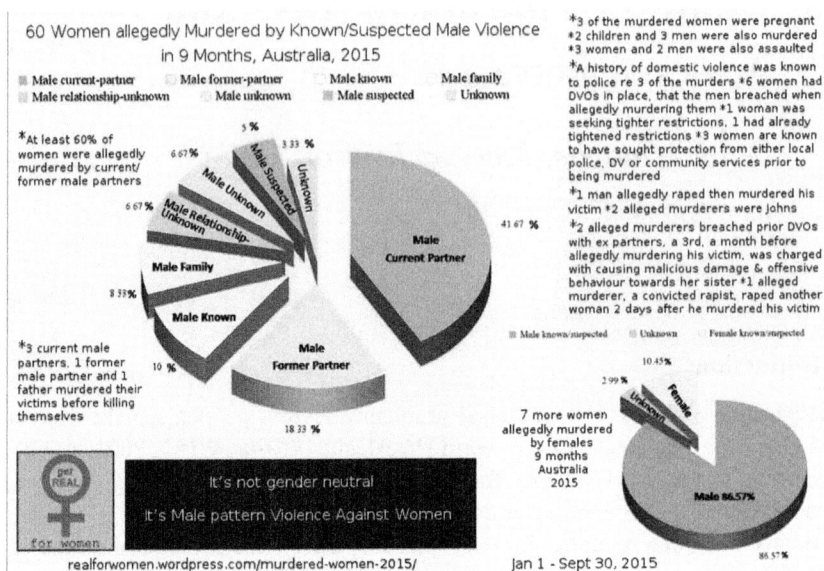

Figure 10.1 60 women allegedly murdered by known/suspected male violence in 9 months, Australia, 2015.

Source: https://realforwomen.wordpress.com/.

complex and resistant nature of DV from the viewpoint that understanding the nature of the problem is part of the solution and is in itself an empowering process. The better all members of society understand the patterns and dynamics of violence, the less likely they are to hold "violence supportive attitudes" (VicHealth, 2014b, p. 37). This chapter concludes with recommendations for further action and research in the light of recent data, while acknowledging limitations.

Current policies and initiatives in Australia

DV and family violence have only recently become issues of national priority in Australia, although there have been initiatives and policies in place since the 1980s to curb violence against women and children (VicHealth, 2014b). The main overarching policy at the national level in Australia is the National Plan to Reduce Violence against Women and their Children 2010–2022, released in 2011 and still currently involves federal, state and territory governments with an aim to coordinate programs and initiatives across the country. The vision of this 12-year plan is that "Australian women and their children live free from violence in safe communities" (COAG, 2011, p. 10). It also aims to fulfill Australia's obligations under the Convention on the Elimination of All Forms of Discrimination against Women (adopted by the United Nations in 1979, and ratified by Australia in 1980)

(Rimmer, 2010, p. 293), the Declaration to End Violence Against Women, and the Beijing Declaration and Platform for Action (UN Women, n.d.). The National Plan is implemented through four three-year action plans, under the titles First Action Plan (2010–2013) "Building a Strong Foundation," the Second Action Plan (2013–2016) "Moving Ahead," the Third Action Plan (2016–2019) "Promising Results," and finally, the Fourth Action Plan (2019–2022) "Turning the Corner" (COAG, 2011). With a wide range of accompanying strategies mapped out for each stage, these plans seek to achieve the following six national outcomes:

1 Communities are safe and free from violence.
2 Relationships are respectful.
3 Indigenous communities are strengthened.
4 Services meet the needs of women and their children experiencing violence.
5 Justice responses are effective.
6 Perpetrators stop their violence and are held to account.

The following performance indicators are established to measure progress according to this 12-year plan:

•   Reduced prevalence of domestic violence and sexual assault.
•   Increased proportion of women who feel safe in their communities.
•   Reduced deaths related to domestic violence and sexual assault.
•   Reduced proportion of children exposed to their mother's or carergiver's experience of domestic violence.

(COAG, 2011, p. 10)

A number of national programs have been rolled out under these plans, including a 24-hour counselling service for victims, respectful relationships education, a social marketing campaign aimed at young people to develop healthy, respectful relationships, specialist training for nurses and Aboriginal health workers in regional and rural areas, funding for the Australian Women Against Violence Alliance and for the White Ribbon Foundation to extend their work to rural practitioners.

Situation on the ground in Australia

To clarify the terminology used in Australia, DV has traditionally been associated with cases of physical violence occurring within intimate relationships, women being the victims in most cases, and in a domestic setting. It is also referred to as partner violence or intimate relationship violence (Morgan & Chadwick, 2009). This definition has now been expanded to include domestic violence that occurs in adults and adolescents, in both heterosexual and homosexual relationships and in married, de facto and separated relationships (Flood & Fergus, 2008). What is interpreted as DV is often confined to physical violence, despite data showing victims are more worried about the emotional suffering such as anxiety and living in fear than physical injuries, and for this reason the phrase "domestic abuse" has recently attracted popular usage. A new term "male pattern violence against women" is also increasingly used in feminist accounts of DV.

Family Violence is also used; however, it is a broader term referring to violence between family members as well as violence between intimate partners. This term also covers a complexity of behaviors beyond that of direct physical violence. The current definition of Family Violence in the Family Law Act 1975 Section 4AB, reads: "family violence means violent, threatening or other behaviour by a person that coerces or controls a member of the person's family, or causes the family member to be fearful" (AUSTLII, n.d.).

Two data sources provide a good insight into the prevalence of and attitudes to DV and family violence in Australia, specifically in relation to violence against women. They are the 2012 Personal Safety Survey (PSS) conducted by the Australian Bureau of Statistics (ABS), and the National Community Attitudes toward Violence Against Women Survey (NCAS) conducted by Victorian Health Promotion Foundation (VicHealth), Melbourne, Australia in 2013.

The Personal Safety Survey (PSS)

The PSS survey provides recent data on the experience of violence in general and especially the experience of partner violence in Australia at a national level. Below are relevant summary data from PSS 2012 to illustrate our discussion of the experience of violence in general and partner violence experienced by women in particular (ASB, 2012).

PSS on prevalence

Thirty four percent (*n*=3,006,100) of women had experienced physical violence and 19 percent (*n*=1,696,100) had experienced sexual violence since the age of 15. However, such experience of violence is not the same across all age groups. Women aged 18 to 24 years had the highest rate of 13 percent, among those who experienced violence in the 12 months prior to the survey, with the next age bracket 25 to 34 years registering a rate of 8.1 percent, and those who were 55 years and over reporting the lowest rate of 1.5 percent.

PSS on perpetrators and the nature of violence

An estimated 36 percent of all women (aged 18 and over) (*n*=3,106,500) in Australia had experienced violence, physical or sexual, at the hands of a known person, compared with 12 percent who had experienced violence at the hands of a stranger. In relation to sexual violence, 16 percent of all women (*n*=1,433,400) suffered violence at the hands of a known person, compared with 5 percent (*n*=462,100) at the hands of a stranger. The most likely type of known perpetrator was a previous partner (15 percent of all women, *n*=1,267,200). However, Mitchell (2011) finds that "most incidents of domestic violence go unreported," and this is supported by Phillips and Vandenbroek's (2014) reference to the fact that less than half of all domestic violence incidents are reported to the police. As opposed to the case of public violence perpetrated against men by men, this makes it difficult to measure the true extent of the problem in such a case of privatized violence against women.

PSS on alcohol and drugs

Alcohol and drug use are considered major contributors to domestic violence (Goodman, 2013; Laslett et al., 2015). Overall, alcohol induced non-domestic violence is more common among male victims, and an estimated 68 percent of these attacks, perpetrated by a male, involved alcohol. More than half of the women (51 percent, $n=1,716,300$) who had been physically assaulted by a male reported that the perpetrator had been under the influence of alcohol or drugs (Laslett et al., 2015). In 2011, a total of 29,684 alcohol-related family violence incidents or domestic assaults were recorded in the states of New South Wales (NSW), Victoria, Western Australia and the Northern Territory. With the exception of NSW, Victoria and Western Australia have experienced steadily rising numbers of alcohol-related family violence incidents (Laslett et al., 2015).

PSS on partner violence

Partner violence here is used synonymously with Domestic Violence and intimate partnership violence (Flood & Fergus, 2008). In order to collect data on experience of violence from respondents who live with or lived, at some point, in a married or de facto relationship with an intimate partner (excluding boyfriends/girlfriends or dates who are non-residing), as opposed to violence in all settings, the PSS also collects data on incidents of physical assaults by a current and/or previous partner. In 2012, an estimated 17 percent of all women (aged 18 years and over, $n=1,479,900$), as opposed to 5.3 percent of all men (aged 18 years and over, $n=448,000$), had experienced violence by a partner since the age of 15. This was very similar to the figure in 2005, indicating continued prevalence. Overall, women comprise the majority of victims of domestic violence (Phillips & Vandenbroek, 2014), and they are not the only victims of the violence. The PSS data show over half (54 percent, $n=128,500$) of the women who had experienced current partner violence had children in their care when the violence occurred, and almost one third of them (31 percent, $n=74,300$) who experienced current partner violence stated that children had seen or heard the violence. This rate was 48 percent with violent previous partners.

PSS on reporting to police

The PSS data reveal that women were reluctant to report violence to the police in Australia. An estimated 80 percent of women ($n=190,100$) who had experienced current partner violence had never contacted the police. Even though the reporting rate improves when it involves previous partners (42 percent were willing to contact the police), it still means that more than half of all DV violence cases against women are not reported to police. Duncan and Western (2011), therefore, further suggest that a more accurate assessment of the violence might emerge on leaving the relationship, with the passage of time and the benefits of safety and hindsight and this may lead to slightly more reporting of violence by previous partners. The lower rate of reporting about current partners may be attributable, according to Duncan and Western (2011), to the fact that women may feel confused, loyal and forgiving about a current partner. Mouzos and Makkai (2004), on the other hand, explain that the lower rates of reporting to police by victims of physical or sexual violence committed by current partners may be because the victims are less likely to perceive the incident as a crime than if it were committed by a stranger. It may also be a manifestation of the victim's belief that the incident is too minor to report, out of shame or embarrassment, a desire to deal with the issue by themselves, fear of the perpetrator or of the consequences of reporting the incident, cultural barriers, or concern about having to relive the event by re-telling the story to multiple parties (as cited in Morgan & Chadwick, 2009). Furthermore, the authors are of the view that partner control and the notion of learned helplessness is another factor – the ultimate example being battered wife syndrome which renders the victim convinced that the batterer is all powerful and results in her repertoire of responses being limited and negligible (Easteal, n.d.). The under-reporting of violence committed by either current or, to a lesser extent, previous partners, on the one hand, shows possible lower awareness of the conception of criminality by the victims, and, on the other hand, manifests a cry for help and protection by services and the police.

These rates of reporting portray a bleaker picture than the ones from the previous report by Michell in 2011, which has 17 percent and 61 percent respectively of violence by current and previous partners. The data from 2012 indicate the channel of communication with the police is still not functioning as well as it could. This is despite significant initiatives such as the Australasian Policing Strategy for Preventing and Reducing Family Violence launched by police commissioners across Australia in November 2008 (Commonwealth of Australia, 2008).

National Community Attitudes toward Violence Against Women Survey (NCAS)

The second recent source of data is the Australia-wide NCAS study conducted by VicHealth in 2013. The survey is unique in the sense that, instead of collecting data on experience of violence, it is designed to track how the population views issues related to violence against women, including their knowledge of what violence means, attitudes toward violence and gender roles, and awareness of sources of assistance (Our Watch, 2013). It was first conducted in 1995, again in 2009 and most recently in 2013 to assess attitude changes over time. The findings in almost all aspects investigated do not indicate significant or extraordinary changes and point to a stable situation. The report finds few differences in attitudes based on demographic factors, i.e., between rural, remote, urban and regional areas, or between states and territories, nor are there differences on the basis of socioeconomic status, although it does record differences between CALD (Culturally and Linguistically Diverse) and non-CALD communities. This is consistent with findings that DV is not confined to any one particular socioeconomic group or ethnic background. The report, however, found the following groups as most likely to endorse violence-supportive attitudes and who have the poorest understanding of what constitutes violence against women:

- men, especially young men and those experiencing multiple forms of disadvantage;
- younger people; and
- people from countries in which the main language spoken is not English, especially those who have recently arrived in Australia.

(NCAS, 2013, p. 7)

Below is a summary of some of the statistically significant findings under the four headings comparing 2009 and 2013 findings. Where relevant, PSS findings with respect to the same issues are added to show a broader picture of the situations in Australia.

NCAS on community knowledge of violence against women

Findings in this section portray a concerning trend, with a decrease in those who recognize that "men mainly or more often commit acts of domestic violence," from 86 percent in 1995, to 74 percent in 2009, and, worryingly, down to 71 percent in 2009, which flies in the face of the finding of the PSS in 2012, in which women (17 percent) were found to be more likely than men (5 percent) to be subjected to violence by a partner from the age of 15 (Phillips & Vandenbroek, 2014). And despite increased focus on DV since 2010 with a national policy, the NCAS report shows a 5 percent drop in the number of people who agreed "violence against women is common," from 74 percent in 2009 to 68 percent in 2013. Again, according to the 2012 PSS, women (62 percent) were much more likely than men (8 percent) to have experienced physical assault by a male in the home. When asked in the NCAS whether the "level of fear is worse for women," the agreement rate slid slightly from 55 percent in 2009 to 52 percent in 2013. Lastly, the report shows that while most Australians recognize that violence against women may cover a wide range of behaviors designed to intimidate and control, e.g., slaps/pushes, forcing partner to have sex, threatening to hurt others and throwing/smashing objects, fewer Australians understand non-physical behaviors also constitute violence against women, e.g., repeated criticism, controls over social life, financial control, and stalking (NCAS, 2013, p. 2).

NCAS on attitudes toward violence against women

Findings particularly worthy of noting relate to justifications for domestic violence. The number of people who agreed violence can be justified if "partner makes him look stupid or insults him in front of his friends" increased from

3 percent in 2009 to 5 percent in 2013. Similarly, agreement rates doubled from 2 percent in 2009 to 4 percent in 2013 with the justification "if ex-partner is unreasonable about property settlement and financial issues." Most worryingly, the agreement rate jumped from 35 percent to 43 percent in answers to the statement "rape results from men not able to control their need for sex," which essentially excuses a rapist and portrays a rapist as someone who is a victim of his body's physical demands. Compared with physical violence and forced sex, the report found that Australians are less inclined to see non-physical forms of control, intimidation and harassment as serious (NCAS, 2013, p. 4). The NCAS report recognizes that a new challenge is to engage the community in responding to such factors for violence as controlling behaviors and disrespect toward women, and holds that preventing violence against women is not simply a matter of changing attitudes, but also involves challenging the social factors that shape such beliefs (Pease & Flood, 2008).

NCAS on attitudes toward gender roles and relations

The survey findings indicate the attitudes about gender roles have not changed for the better since 2009 in Australia. Most notably, those who agreed that "women prefer a man to be in charge of the relationship" remained at the level of more than one in four people (27 percent in 2009 and 28 percent in 2013). Such attitudes supportive of male dominance in decision-making in relationships is identified as a risk factor for partner violence. Agreement rates for the statement that "men make better political leaders" jumped from 23 percent in 2009 to 27 percent in 2013. It is also concerning that statements such as "when jobs are scarce, men have more right to a job than women" and "a woman has to have children to be fulfilled" also recorded slight increases compared with those of 2009. According to Pease and Flood (2008), individuals' evaluations and understandings of men's violence against women are influenced by their attitudes toward the phenomenon. However, Pease and Flood's "critical and social constructionist" (2008, p. 554) inclination also reminds us that attitudes must be recognized as "contingent, contextual, potentially contradictory, having a complex relationship to behavior, and constructed and meaningful only in social contexts" (p. 554). It is, therefore, important to interpret the NCAS responses in the context of Australian social conditions, rather than treating them in isolation.

NCAS on witnessing violence and knowledge of resources

A key action in tackling DV and family violence, especially violence against women and vulnerable people in the family, is to empower them to seek advice and assistance. This last section in the NCAS shows that the number of Australians who knew where to get help decreased from 62 percent to 57 percent, indicating some initiatives to raise awareness may need urgent attention and critical review. With respect to police response times to incident reporting, agreement rates with the statement "police response times have improved" remained the same at 44 percent in 2009 and 2013. This should be assessed in relation to low reporting rates to the police that were revealed in the 2012 PSS. Because police–victim relationships are critical to a reduction in serious harm to victims and their children, the worrying data about reporting incidents and engagement with the police point to a need for further in-depth research into why victims are reluctant and a review of current procedures.

What the data show from the two recent national surveys reported above as well as reports by other agencies such as the Australia Crime Commission and Alcohol and Drug Research Centre is that, despite policies and initiatives at Federal and State or Territory levels in Australia, domestic violence, especially partner violence against women, continues to be a major problem. Key indicators in reducing crime, any crime, such as improving underlying attitudes against crime, developing awareness about different forms of violence and where to get help, and reporting crime to police in a timely manner so perpetrators can be dealt with, appear to be areas remaining unchanged, if not getting worse, based on data from the 2012 PSS and the NCAS in 2013. It is, undoubtedly, proving to be a complex problem, and resistant to change. In the next section we will examine the complexity of Domestic Violence using Rittel and Webber's (1973) concept of a *wicked problem*, which they used in the context of social policy planning.

Conceptualizing the complexity of DV and family violence – a wicked problem

Theoretically, DV and family violence can be narrowly defined as a criminal act and be dealt with as a law enforcement issue employing judicial means. However, as evidenced by the discussions in this chapter so far, DV is a complex social and gendered problem which is correlated with not only individually held attitudes, but also the entrenched nature of society's collective social and cultural norms and ideologies (Pease & Flood, 2008). In light of the breadth of factors, settings, and social forces which contribute to the complexity of the problem, DV can be viewed as what Rittel and Webber call a *wicked problem*. Some authors have linked DV and wicked problems (Laing, Humphreys & Kavanagh, 2013; Stanley, 2015). However, they do not examine in detail what makes DV a wicked problem. We use Rittel and Webber's (1973) concept of a *wicked problem* in the rest of the chapter to examine DV. The term "wicked" is used here not in the sense of evil, rather as an issue highly resistant to resolution (Australian Public Service Commission, 2007).

In discussing a whole range of social planning problems that cannot be successfully solved with traditional linear, analytical approaches, urban planners Rittel and Webber (1973) at the University of California, Berkeley, proposed the term *wicked problems*. The earlier literature on *wicked problems* was on systems design at a "micro" level. However, the concept has gradually gained popularity and been applied to broader social and economic policy problems (Australian Public Service Commission, 2007). Rittel and Webber posit that "social problems are never resolved. At best, they are re-solved – over and over again" (Rittel & Webber, 1973, p. 160). They argue that this is because they are multi-dimensional and often ill-defined and extremely complex. This makes them "wicked," not in the sense of "ethically deplorable" but in the sense that they are "malignant," "vicious," "tricky" and "aggressive" (Rittel & Webber, 1973, p. 160). Rittel and Webber (1973) believe that it is morally objectionable "to refuse to recognise the inherent wicked-ness of social problems" (p. 161), and propose the following 10 distinguishing traits that can be used to identify a problem as wicked:

1   There is no definitive formulation of a wicked problem.
2   Wicked problems have no stopping rule.
3   Solutions to wicked problems are not true-or-false, but good-or-bad.
4   There is no immediate and no ultimate test of a solution to a wicked problem.
5   Every solution to a wicked problem is a "one-shot operation"; because there is no opportunity to learn by trial-and-error, every attempt counts significantly.
6   Wicked problems do not have an enumerable (or an exhaustively describa-ble) set of potential solutions, nor is there a well-described set of permiss-ible operations that may be incorporated into the plan.
7   Every wicked problem is essentially unique.
8   Every wicked problem can be considered to be a symptom of another problem.
9   The existence of a discrepancy representing a wicked problem can be explained in numerous ways. The choice of explanation determines the nature of the problem's resolution.
10   The planner has no right to be wrong.

The traits of a wicked problem can be used to understand the nature and com-plexity of DV and family violence and how this process can then guide efforts to solve the problem. Rittel and Webber (1973) hold that "the challenge of defining a wicked problem *is* the problem" (p. 161). DV is one such problem which is proving to be a challenge to define, as is evidenced by a range of definitions and terms used across jurisdictions, organizations, and stakeholders. This is because, as Rittel and Webber (1973) explain, if a problem could be viewed essentially as a discrepancy between "the state of affairs as it is and the state as it should be" (p. 165), then resolution of a problem starts by identifying the cause of the dis-crepancy. Unlike *tame problems* (Rittel & Webber, 1973) as an opposite notion, which may be technically complex (Australian Public Service Commission, 2007), but are relatively simple and straightforward in the sense that they often have clearly identifiable causes and their solutions have simple criteria for success, the wicked problems have complex, multiple causes and explanations and a whole range of proposals for solutions. The DV literature identifies many causal explanations based on a wide range of theoretical approaches. These include: individual approaches (personality disturbance [psychopathology] and criminogenic factors [violent, crime prone]); family approaches (developmental [role of families]); societal (social psychological [attitudes, stereotypes] and sociological [gender roles, stress]); and, socio-cultural (societal-structural theories [gender income and power inequality] and feminist [male violence to control and limit independence of women]).

How can the effectiveness of DV solutions be assessed? Despite actions and initiatives at national and state levels in Australia, e.g., the National Plan to Reduce Violence against Women and their Children 2010–2022 and the Australasian Policing Strategy on the Prevention and Reduction of Family Violence endorsed by all state police forces in Australia, the problem still remains a serious public issue and a social problem as evidenced by the recent statistics provided earlier. There are no enumerable solutions to tackle these issues, and every "one-shot operation" is undertaken on a trial-and-error basis and every attempt counts, although according to Rittel and Webber (1973), there are no predictable outcomes and the approaches only affect a specifically targeted population in a narrow field for a limited time. In dealing with DV there are many stakeholders that are equally equipped, have a vested interest, and are entitled to judge the success, or otherwise, of solutions. Each of these stakeholders has a different perspective regarding the causes of the problem, and each will use different criteria to judge whether the solution is good (fair) or bad (inadequate) (Rittel & Webber, 1973). Rittel and Webber (1973) postulate that the full consequences of solutions to *wicked problems* cannot be judged until all intended and unintended repercussions have been evaluated. DV affects more people than the direct victim and the perpetrator. Intended or unintended repercussions of any intervention are likely to be at various levels: the individual level, children of partner violence; family level, patriarchal structures; community level (attitudes and gender stereotypes) and society/cultural level (removing gender income and power inequality) (Our Watch, 2013).

This then leads to the conclusion that there can be no guarantee that every viable solution has been identified and considered. In the area of DV, many diverse solutions have been proposed, but there certainly are still more viable solutions to be developed, e.g. in areas such as psychological, legal, sociological, or socio-political and perhaps combinations of strategies from these areas. For instance, along with other initiatives, whether DV laws should be strengthened, and the effect such a strategy would have on the reporting rates of DV and the rates of successful prosecutions of offenders should be explored. What would be the social and financial implications of implementing social policy changes that bring about gender equality in all areas of society? Since there is no definitive (narrow, simple) resolution to DV, then multiple interventions across multiple levels of society will have unknown effects which may change the nature of the problem and may never lead to a complete solution. Resolution of this complex problem will require a myriad of diverse interventions at multiple levels within society, with the requirement of coordinated actions by a diverse range of stakeholders that cover interventions across many distinct government and non-government organizations. All these programs will require on-going independent evaluations with the flexibility to be adapted as time goes by or new factors emerge, as these interventions, in turn, impact and change the parameters of DV.

Rittel and Webber (1973) assert that while *wicked problems* may share similarities with other wicked problems, there will be particular features of each wicked problem that are distinctly different and unique. Among all of DV's features, perhaps the most distinguishing characteristic is that a lot of the time it takes place in the private sphere, therefore making it hard to detect, adding to the complexity arising from the intertwined underlying social, cultural, and gender factors at play. Given these (near) insurmountable challenges, the traditional (conservative) recommendation is typically to advocate a narrow linear approach in an attempt to provide a tame solution to the wicked problem. The most common strategy is to lock down the way the problem of DV is defined. This is achieved by creating a simple sub-problem that has a simple linear solution.

But, on the other hand, it fails to determine first if the non-reporting rate has increased because of increased penalties for DV. This does not mean that the sub-components of DV should not be defined and acted upon, but that these narrow interventions should be part of a holistic view of the broader, more complex (wicked) problem. If we view DV as a symptom, then a number of "higher level" causes need to be resolved, as well as the symptom. If DV is simplistically addressed by increasing punishments for a special category of violent crime, then any higher level causes (psychopathology of the abuser; development and role models in patriarchal society; gender inequality in society) will be ignored and the measure will be potentially self-defeating in terms of effectiveness. Similarly, increasing punishment for DV offenders and removing gender inequality in incomes may possibly not be effective if there is a failure to address mental health problems and socially entrenched attitudes and stereotypes.

Rittel and Webber (1973), therefore, conclude that stakeholders must first see the cause (and thus the solution) within the domain of their control and not as a more realistic multi-causal wicked problem. They also argue that wicked problems, DV being one, are "ill-defined problems" and therefore they have "ill-defined solutions," even though "feasible action plans rely on realistic judgment and trust between the parties" (ibid., p. 164). The data from NCAS indicating recent worsening of attitudes to gender equality, increased rates of justification for DV since 2009, decrease in the number of women who know where to get help, and concerning rates of reporting to police, point to a need for "realistic judgment" by all stakeholders and building "trust" between victims and authorities.

Conclusion

DV has been conceptualized according to many theoretical frameworks (psychological, legal, sociological, feminist) and at various levels within a complex society (individual, relationship, family, community, society-cultural). There is no rule or procedure to determine the "correct" explanation (or combination of explanations). This complexity, combined with the uniqueness of DV and the inability to (safely) experiment, signifies that any choice of the "correct" solution is arbitrary; under such circumstances people choose solutions that are most plausible to them at that moment in time (Rittel & Webber, 1973). To successfully resolve DV and family violence, then, the approach needs to be broad, innovative, flexible and involve interventions at all levels of society. It should involve effective engagement of multiple stakeholders working across diverse organizational boundaries. Given that data show there are worrying trends in attitudes and a tendency to avoid reporting to police for assistance, there is a need to analyze and prioritize specific actions based on data available and realistic judgment. For example, the reasons for not reporting to police and the decrease in the number of women who knew where to get help, need to be illuminated and addressed as a high priority, while evaluating critically other long-term action items such as building trust between victims and authorities and changing the underlying attitudes held individually and collectively, which appear to be resistant to change, or even worsening in some respects in Australia. Finally, all solutions should be critically evaluated for their effectiveness with the ultimate goal of achieving social and economic equality between men and women.

Future research

DV is a wicked problem as there is insufficient understanding of its (real) prevalence, its impact or scope within a community and its causation. Therefore, further data collection and research about practical aspects of services, e.g., accessibility of the police to improve reporting rates, understanding and addressing barriers to reporting, and identifying the reasons for decrease in the number of women who know where to get help, may assist with attempts to reduce serious harm and homicides as well as prevention. Multidisciplinary approaches involving multiple stakeholders in analyzing and identifying solutions should also be explored to address the multi-faceted nature of the wickedness inherent in this societal issue.

References

AIC. (n.d.). *National homicide monitoring program*. Retrieved January 16, 2015 from http://aic.gov.au/about_aic/research_programs/nmp/0001.html

AUSTLII. (n.d.). *Family Law Act 1975 – SECT 4AB*. Retrieved January 16, 2016 from www.austlii.edu.au/au/legis/cth/consol_act/fla1975114/s4ab.html

Australian Bureau of Statistics (ABS). (2012), *Personal safety survey*, ABS Cat. No. 4906.0. Retrieved January 10, 2016 from www.abs.gov.au/ausstats/abs@.nsf/Lookup/4906.0 Chapter1002012

Australian Public Service Commission. (2007). *Tackling wicked problems: A public policy perspective*. Retrieved January 20, 2016 from www.apsc.gov.au/publications-and-media/archive/publications-archive/tackling-wicked-problems

COAG. (2011). *National Plan to Reduce Violence Against Women and their Children 2010–2022*. Retrieved January 16, 2016 from https://www.dss.gov.au/sites/default/files/documents/08_2014/national_plan1.pdf

Commonwealth of Australia. (2008). *Australasian policing strategy on the prevention and reduction of family violence*. Retrieved January 23, 2016 from https://www.police. vic.gov.au/retrievemedia.asp?Media_ID=36290

Duncan, J., & Western, D. (2011). *Addressing 'the ultimate insult': Responding to women experiencing intimate partner sexual violence, Australian Domestic and Family Violence Clearinghouse stakeholder paper, no. 10.* Retrieved January 5, 2016 from www.austdvclearinghouse.unsw.edu.au/PDF%20files/Stakeholder_Paper_10.pdf

Easteal, P. (n.d.). *Battered women who kill: A plea of self-defence.* Retrieved January 23, 2016 from www.aic.gov.au/media_library/publications/proceedings/16/easteal1.pdf

Flood, M., & Fergus, L. (2008). *An assault on our future: The impact of violence on young people and their relationships.* Retrieved January 4, 2016 from www.whiteribbonday.org.au/media/documents/AssaultonourFutureFinal.pdf

Goodman, A. (2013). *Social work with drug, alcohol and substance misusers.* Middlesex University: Sage.

Laing, L., Humphreys, C., & Kavanagh, K. (2013). *Social work and domestic violence: Developing critical and reflective practice.* London: Sage Publications.

Laslett, A.M., Mugavin, J., Jiang, H., Manton, E., Callinan, S., MacLean, S., & Room, R. (2015). *The hidden harm: Alcohol's impact on children and families.* Canberra: Foundation for Alcohol Research and Education.

Mitchell, L. (2011). *Domestic violence in Australia – an overview of the issues.* Retrieved January 10, 2016 from www.aph.gov.au/About_Parliament/Parliamentary_Departments/Parliamentary_Library/pubs/BN/2011-2012/DVAustralia

Morgan, A., & Chadwick, H. (2009). *Key issues in domestic violence*, Summary paper, no. 7. Retrieved January 11, 2016 from www.aic.gov.au/documents/5/6/E/%7B56E09295-AF88-4998-A083-B7CCD925B540%7Drip07_001.pdf

Mouzos, J., & Makkai, T. (2004). *Women's experiences of male violence – Findings from the Australian component of the International Violence Against Women Survey (IVAWS).* Canberra: Australian Institute of Criminology.

NCAS. (2013). *Resource 1: Summary Report.* Retrieved January 21, 2016 from https://www.vichealth.vic.gov.au/media-and-resources/publications/2013-national-community-attitudes-towards-violence-against-women-survey

Our Watch. (2013). *The National Community Attitudes Survey 2013 – key findings.* Retrieved January 21, 2016 from www.ourwatch.org.au/Understanding-Violence/Facts-and-figures

Pease, B., & Flood, M. (2008). Rethinking the significance of attitudes in preventing men's violence against women. *Australian Journal of Social Issues*, 43(44), 547–561.

Phillips, J., & Vandenbroek, P. (2014). Domestic, family and sexual violence in Australia: An overview of the issues. Retrieved January 10, 2016 from www.aph.gov.au/About_Parliament/Parliamentary_Departments/Parliamentary_Library/pubs/rp/rp1415/ViolenceAust

Rimmer, S.H. (2010). Raising women up: Analysing Australian advocacy for women's rights under international and domestic law. In M. Thornton (Ed.), *Sex discrimination in uncertain times* (pp. 291–318). Canberra: ANU E Press.

Rittel, H.W., & Webber, M. (1973). Dilemmas in a general theory of planning. *Policy Sciences, 4*, 155–169.

Stanley, N. (2015). Moving towards integrated domestic violence services. In N. Stanley & C. Humphreys (Eds.), *Domestic violence and protecting children: New thinking and approaches* (pp. 232–252). London and Philadelphia: Jessica Kingsley Publishers.

VicHealth. (2014a). *Australians' attitudes to violence against women. 2013 National Community Attitudes towards Violence Against Women Survey – Research Summary.* Melbourne: Victorian Health Promotion Foundation.

VicHealth. (2014b). *Australians' attitudes to violence against women. Findings from the 2013 National Community Attitudes towards Violence Against Women Survey (NCAS).* Melbourne: Victorian Health Promotion Foundation.

WHO. (2005). *Summary report – WHO multi-country study on women's health and domestic violence agasint women: Initial results on prevalence, health outcomes and women's responses.* Retrieved January 16, 2016 from www.who.int/gender/violence/who_multicountry_study/summary_report/summary_report_English2.pdf

WHO. (2016). *Violence Against Women – Fact Sheet No. 239.* Retrieved January 16, 2016 from www.who.int/mediacentre/factsheets/fs239/en/

11 Domestic violence in South Africa

Christiaan Bezuidenhout and Laetitia Coetzee

Introduction

Domestic violence is the most common manifestation of gender-based violence in South Africa (Geldenhuys, 2014). Although the South African government regularly profess that DV is an unacceptable hideous crime, no effort from their side to curb it seems to work. In addition, most community initiatives seem to serve as a "last resort" initiative, where the victim of DV will only go for help and assistance in the absence of other alternatives. These initiatives seem neutered in the prevention and reduction of DV in South Africa. Moreover, the government has escalated DV to "priority crime" status and specialized legislation has been promulgated. A special police unit has also been established to investigate DV in South Africa, namely the Family Violence, Child Protection and Sexual Offences (FCS) unit of the South African Police Service (SAPS). These initiatives, as well as national projects such as the 16 Days of Activism Campaign which is held from November 25 to December 10 every year, (Kempen, 2006) seem to have very little impact on this crime in South Africa. The year 2016 marks 18 years since the 16 Days of Activism against Women and Children Abuse campaign was adopted by South Africa. Every year South Africans are encouraged to wear a white ribbon during this period and every year DV is condemned in the media by government officials, disc jockeys on radio, journalists, television presenters, celebrities and non-governmental organizations who offer services to victims of DV. All these efforts seem to be fruitless as DV continues unabated. The ongoing and seemingly increasing DV incidents in South Africa reflect the high level of inequality between women and men. This also reflects the attitude many men in South Africa hold toward women, namely that they are the weaker subordinate gender that must serve and satisfy men (Bendall, 2010). In addition, a culture of violence prevails in South Africa. Societies where a culture of violence exists are characterized by the notion that violence is a legitimate avenue that can be used to resolve problems (Burton, 2008; Naidoo & Sewpaul, 2014). This legitimization of violence as recourse to problem resolution is intensified by the fact that South Africans encounter violence on a daily basis during their normal routine activities, or in their domestic environment (De Wet, 2003).

South Africa accommodates a population of about 54 million people and it harbors 11 official languages and a myriad of different cultures and customs that demand special attention in the policing of sensitive crimes such as DV (Bezuidenhout, 2015) (see Table 11.1). Also, approximately 51 percent (approximately 27.6 million) of the population is female (Statistics South Africa, 2014).

Based on the broad diversity, South Africa is globally known as the rainbow nation. According to Bendall (2010) the different cultural and ethnic groups in South Africa also regard the position and role of women differently and in many cases DV is still treated as a private matter. Although most cases of DV in South Africa feature the male as the perpetrator and the female as the victim, males being victims of DV by their female partners has recently been under the spotlight of researchers. In addition, Weideman (2008) indicates that in same sex relationships reporting of DV is escalating as well. Although this chapter will mainly focus on the female victim in a partnership or marital arrangement who suffers domestic abuse, reference will be made to same-sex, child and male victims of DV as well.

Definition of domestic violence

DV is also referred to as family violence, intimate partner violence or spousal abuse. All these concepts are somewhat restrictive to sketch a clear picture of the scope of the problem. The authors will use the concept "domestic violence" throughout with acknowledgment of the extensiveness of the phenomenon. Perilla, Lippy, Rosales and Serrata (2011) also insist that the concept "domestic violence" has a universal meaning to it and encapsulates all types of abuse and violence toward a spouse, partner or child. Violence against women in particular, in a domestic or family set up, as well as in a relationship, is a persistent and universal problem. In addition Bartol and Bartol (2014) state that "a great majority of battered women either remain in lifelong abusive relationships, leave the relationship, or are killed by their abusers."

With regards to South African legislation, the Protection of Family Violence Act 133 of 1993 was revised and replaced with the Domestic Violence Act 116

Table 11.1 Mid-year population estimates for South Africa by population group 2014

Population group	Number	Percentage of population
African (Black)	43,333,700	80.2
Colored	4,771,500	8.8
Indian/Asian	1,341,900	2.5
White	4,554,800	8.4
Total	54,002,000	100

Source: Statistics South Africa, 2014.

Note
Figures have been rounded.

of 1998. The Domestic Violence Act (Act No. 116 of 1998) defines DV as any abusive behavior or violence that occurs within a domestic relationship and compromises an individual's safety, health and/or wellbeing (Artz & Smythe, 2013). A broader discussion of the Act will follow later in this chapter.

Nature and extent of DV in South Africa

Extent of DV in South Africa

The majority of citizens can concur that South Africa is a violent high-risk country where crime flourishes. Murder or homicide rates are extraordinarily high in South Africa and it is assumed that the murder rate is at least five times higher than the global average. South Africa has been in the global top 10 murderous countries for its high murder rate for 13 years out of 15 years between 2000 and 2015. This indicates that since the year 2000 at least 33 or more people are murdered per day per 100,000 of the South African population (Grant, 2015).

International comparison of murder rates

Highly variable data quality means international comparisons can be deceptive, but the best available estimates suggest the highest murder rates today are found in Southern Africa and Central America. Honduras leads the race by a fair margin at about 90 per 100,000 and Venezuela (54), Belize (45) and El Salvador (41) are also considered to have extremely high murder rates. Although not quite at Central American rates, South Africa's rate of above 30 is considered high. Of the roughly 437,000 deaths due to intentional homicide in the world in 2012, about 3.7 percent of them happened in South Africa, even though South Africa's population only comprises about 0.7 percent of the world's population. There is already a large body of research on why South Africa is such a violent society, providing reasons including a history of violence and brutalization, patchy and illegitimate policing, the impact of apartheid on families and the education system, enduring inequality, racism, the availability of firearms, and so on.

Source: Kriegler and Shaw, 2015.

A noteworthy increase in murder occurred in the 2014–2015 financial year in South Africa. A total of 17,805 murders were committed from April 2014 to March 2015, which calculates to nearly 49 murders per day in that financial year, almost rivaling the Central American rates. This rate is significant as South Africa is currently a country not at war. South Africa is creaking as authorities struggle to stem the violent crime sub-culture in South Africa (South Africa "a country at war," 2015). Linking this alarming murder rate to South African women is important. It is estimated that one woman is killed by her intimate partner every six to eight hours, which calculates to a femicide rate of about 8.8 per 100,000 women aged 14 years and older (Modiba, Baliki, Mmalasa, Reineke & Nsiki, 2011; Abrahams, Mathews, Jewkes, Martin & Lombard, 2012). In lieu with this Padayachee and Singh (2003) indicate that, regardless of their race, ethnicity, culture or economic status, approximately 25 percent of South African women are assaulted by their partners every week. This is corroborated by a national sample of males who indicated that 27 percent of them exerted physical violence toward their most recent female partner (Gupta et al., 2008). A survey conducted by the Council for Scientific and Industrial Research (CSIR) with 1000 respondents in six of the nine provinces in South Africa, found that 62 percent of the respondents reported that DV was a common occurrence in their communities and only 24 percent of them did not have friends who were in abusive relationships at the time when the survey was conducted (Weideman, 2008). Another alarming statistic is that the average woman takes 10 years to leave an abusive relationship and it is estimated that during this time, on average, she might be abused 39 times (Padayachee & Singh, 2003). It must, however, be taken into account that a separate category for DV does not exist in South African police statistics and thus one has to rely on other sources such as victim surveys to determine the extent of the crime (Bendall, 2010).

Nature of DV in SA

The authors concur that many factors contribute to domestic violence. Numerous national and international studies also repeatedly report on the same factors that correlate with DV. These include amongst others:

- Personality factors or an underlying pathology (the abuser having a mental or personality disorder [e.g., a psychopath]) (Bartol & Bartol, 2014).
- Social learning and the environment in which you are raised (the son witnesses the father battering the mother and learns this behavior; the daughter see the mother being battered and learns "survival skills" for a future abusive relationship) (Bartol & Bartol, 2014).
- Evolutionary and biological reasons – the male is violent because of a head injury or because of his status as the breadwinner, or the notion that he must retain his female partner at all cost – a strategy Cunningham et al. (1998: i) refer to as the "mate retention tactic." Because of his jealousy and sexual distrust the male endeavors to ensure his partner stays with him. A male that senses that other males give attention to his partner or that his partner attracts other men, tends to become abusive (physically, emotionally or financially) to keep his partner. This links with the Darwinian principle vis-à-vis *survival of the fittest*. In this context the abuser must procreate and show dominance over the female (he feels threatened by other males and to show his prowess and "I am the strongest" status he exerts his dominance in different forms, which include abuse on the partner).
- Exchange principle – partners in a relationship act in certain ways to either earn rewards or to escape punishment. This assumption is in support of the violent abusive cycle supposition of Walker (1979). She contended that the cycle of an abusive situation is divided into three overlapping phases. In

the build-up phase the abuser either emotionally abuses the partner or introduces minor battering incidents which are triggered by imagined or real infractions of rules and expectations laid down by the abuser. The victim often responds serenely trying to reduce the situation, or may attempt to defend themselves against the abusive episode. Both parties may attempt to rationalize the incident and their actions. The victim often believes things will blow over and may even adapt their behavior to prevent a future incident. However, the victim will soon feel tension building (this phase varies in different relationships). As the tension builds, the victim's survival skills may happen to be less effective at preventing the escalating tension. In phase two, known as the acute battering incident, no controls are left and the inevitable result of the escalating tension results in a serious abusive episode – almost overkill in an abusive skirmish. As the victim senses a violent outburst is about to take place, serious tension or anxiety will most probably manifest. In some cases the victim can even attempt to trigger her batterer's violence to "speed up" the inevitable battering incident. In many cases both parties try to minimalize the heavy-handedness and even deny the severity thereof. In phase three, the so-called "honeymoon phase" or respite phase, the abuser often shows signs of distress and becomes a bit benign after the release of tension during phase two. The abuser is apologetic, sometimes buys expensive gifts and promises never to do something like that again. The abuser even promises to go for anger management therapy. However, these promises are empty and transient. In this phase the partner experiences every single positive incident that was anticipated or fantasized about in the initial stages of the relationship. The abuser is kind, soft spoken and treats the partner with a degree of respect. It is difficult to leave a person in this phase as everything is going well. However, the hiatus and respite is short lived and tension will in due course ignite phase one again after a specific trigger, or because of the existing habit. We do want to caution though that not all abusers progress through phases of tranquility, friction and violent behavior similar to this cycle of abuse. Some abusers are blatant, while others use guile and many inconspicuous ways to manipulate or hurt the partner.

- Resource model – the abuser maintains power and dominance in the relationship or family setup by means of DV. The victims (children and partner) become similar to a piece of furniture in the house. They must be there for the benefit of the abuser.
- Cultural endorsement – some cultures allow for the male to dominate and even "discipline" their partners physically (we believe that globally this is probably the most difficult challenge in DV) (Jasinski, 2001).
- Gender roles and masculinity – the two genders view violence and masculinity differently. In many cultural groups males are seen as the provider and in a society of this ilk members endorse the patriarchal system. This attitude could increase the risk of DV as males must maintain their higher relative status compared to females. DV is one tool to keep their "masculinity" in check. In societies of this nature most males adhere to this "masculinity" principle.

- Feminist dogma – DV occurs because societies endorses male-dominated prescripts such as patriarchy and socialization practices that approve male aggression (males must be tough and dominant, while females must be feminine and respectable). In these societies the media and even male peers often support and reinforce the patriarchal values (Jasinski, 2001).
- Social standing and poverty – DV is the result of structural inequality and poverty. In this regard an old nonscientific axiom in South Africa comes to mind: "when poverty walks through the front door love runs out the back door." A male who feels he should be the breadwinner could use violence to rebel against his social standing and he could abuse his partner to resolve conflicts, principally to gain or regain some sense of internal and external locus of control [on the other hand the partner can consistently pressure the abuser to do his masculine duty to protect and provide which in turn can trigger a cyclic abusive connection as illustrated by Walker]. In South Africa this is a significant risk factor pertaining to DV. Musgrave (2015) affirms in this regard "the proportion of the population who are deemed to be living in poverty has increased from 45.5 percent to 53.8 percent. The reason is that the upper-bound poverty line, which measures the income people need for essential items after meeting their basic food needs, was recalculated from R620 (± \$37 USA) a month to R779 (\$47 USA)" (this is equated to a monthly average income per household).
- The culture of violence – many believe that violence is the only way to achieve success or to dominate other individuals. In many cases this perception of violence or sub-culture of violence has been conveyed from generation to generation. It becomes a normal way of life. With cognizance of all of the above factors that correlate to DV we would like to elaborate on the (sub-)culture of violence in South Africa, as it is strongly linked to DV in this country.

The link between the (sub-)culture of violence and DV in SA

To contextualize the nature of violence between partners one should consider the impact of violence in general in South Africa. The sub-culture of violence principle holds that the overt use of violence is generally a reflection of basic values of a sub-culture in a society that stand apart from the dominant culture. This blatant (and often illicit) use of violence constitutes part of a sub cultural normative system that is reflected in the psychological traits of the members of that sub-culture (Wolfgang & Ferracuti, 1967, p. 158; Bezuidenhout, 2011, p. 13). The term "culture of violence" can be used to describe and explain the heightened incidence of violence and more specifically DV in South Africa (Vogelman & Lewis, 1993, p. 41). To understand any form of violent behavior in the South African context the "culture of violence" principle is important. Resolving conflict through violence is part of the historical culture and context of South Africa. In this violent milieu people start associating aspects such as anger, fear and violence as being part and parcel of relationships and this may lead to them being desensitized and not realizing the detrimental consequences of their actions (Naidoo & Sewpaul, 2014, p. 95). Moreover, an adolescent male who witnesses violent interaction, especially directed towards females (e.g., his father beating his mother), might learn that women are seen as inferior to men. In this regard, Petersen, Bhana and McKay (2005, p. 1237) found that from an early age boys are socialized into traditional patriarchal notions of what masculinity entails. These notions usually endorse and legitimize unequal male and female power relations, coupled with violence and intimidation. As a result, the belief that violence and intimidation during interactions with other individuals are normal (as the child forms part of the abusive episode) may have become entrenched. Repeated abuse will impact on the cognitive development of the child. Bartol and Bartol (2014) put it so eloquently – it becomes a cognitive script which in turn becomes a relatively permanent feature of behavior in future.

Victims of crime often become perpetrators of retributive violence or violence in the domestic arena due to displaced aggression (Bezuidenhout & Klopper, 2011, p. 186; Nedcor ISS Criminal Justice Information Centre, 1997). Societies, in which domestic violence and sexual assault are prevalent, are usually characterized by authoritarian actions by males in that society. These societies are also known for their patriarchal attitudes toward domestic relationships. Males usually dominate all relationships and garner all the power in the domestic setup. Furthermore, they believe that violence is a legitimate form of problem solving in domestic relationships (Beckner, 2005; Burton, 2008; Schreiner, 2004).

Some cases of DV (child, partner and/or spouse abuse) can therefore be partly blamed as a by-product of high levels of violence in South Africa. Spouses, partners and children are increasingly becoming victims of abuse in their homes, schools and communities. The young generation is being brought up in a hostile society and they learn that abuse and violence are preferred ways to deal with other human beings. It has become the norm to solve problems and disputes through aggression and violence and this norm is being passed on from generation to generation. Attached to this are the large pockets of poverty amongst the majority of South Africans, where hardship and adversity prevail in many households. In many cases desperation and destitution correlates with DV (Harris, 2009; Maree, 2013; Musgrave, 2015; Van Niekerk, 2006; White, 1995).

In South Africa community violence, sexual violence and violence in the home is an everyday phenomenon and many citizens have accepted violent crime and abuse as "normal." Thus, crime has become a normal everyday occurrence in the home, schools and in society (Bezuidenhout, 2007). Abuse in the domestic sphere has thus become a "normal" occurrence and encompasses all racial, socio-economic and cultural boundaries in South Africa.

Research findings pertaining to the nature of DV in South Africa

In the CSIR survey mentioned earlier 53 percent of the 1000 respondents reported that they were married, or that they had an intimate relationship (22 percent) with the abuser. In addition, it was revealed that 88 percent of the victims of DV had children who were living with them during the abuse. Furthermore, more than a third of the victims reported that they had been victims of DV in more than one relationship, while approximately 18 percent indicated that they were victims of child abuse (Weideman, 2008).

When considering the types of abuse that victims are subjected to, it is significant to note that 90 percent of victims reported being emotionally abused, whereas 76 percent of victims reported being physically abused by their partners. Furthermore, 28 percent of the victims claim that they were abused sexually and 48 percent experienced economic abuse. DV is often a daily occurrence and 83 percent of the abusive incidents occurred in the victim's home (Weideman, 2008). In addition, the Weideman (2008) study reports that perpetrators of DV used a weapon in 50 percent of the incidents. The respondents revealed that the weapon used in 51 percent of the incidents was a knife, a firearm was used in 10 percent of the incidents and in some instances weapons such as sticks, boiling water, axes and pangas (similar to the machete knife – a large cleaver-like knife with a blade length of 30–60 centimeters (12 to 24 inches) long and usually under 2–3 millimeters (0.12 inches) thick). Moreover, it serves to be noted that perpetrators of DV usually do not have a criminal record, but in most instances they have a history of abusive behavior toward previous partners and 30 percent of the victims were aware of their partner's abusive history. Another disconcerting revelation is that in most DV incidents, the abuse was witnessed by other individuals. A minority of 17 percent of the respondents indicated that no one witnessed the abuse and the victims pointed out that even though the majority of witnesses were in a position to render assistance, they failed to do so. Findings from this study contradict the notion that victims of DV are unable or unwilling to speak out about the violence, or that they are unlikely to report it. A majority of the respondents (75 percent) said that they approached various individuals, institutions and organizations. Sixty-two percent of the respondents indicated that they reported the DV to official institutions such as the police, or a legal aid clinic or to individuals such as lawyers, magistrates, court officials or community-based support services. This reporting is in addition to appeals for help extended to friends and family members. The average victim in this survey reported that they sought help five times before they received any assistance. Furthermore, the average time elapsed between an abuse episode and the reporting of the incident was four hours. Nearly half of the respondents (40 percent) had no transportation and walked to the place where they reported the incident. Fifty-two percent of the victims had to rely on public transport and only half of these respondents took less than half an hour to reach their destination (Weideman, 2008). (Many South Africans and immigrants from neighboring countries live in isolated areas or informal poverty stricken settlements on the outskirts of towns and cities.)

High-risk factors contributing to the occurrence of DV

Even though a variety of risk factors can give rise to the occurrence of DV, an overview of the two most prominent risk factors identified within the South African context will subsequently be provided. Ross (2010) is of the opinion that a correlation exists between severe substance abuse and the tendency to abuse an intimate partner. Moreover, the abuse of substances increases the likelihood of becoming a victim of DV. This rings true as individuals who are under the influence of a substance tend to have increased self-confidence, which can manifest in provocative behavior that can be offensive and infuriating, thus increasing the possibility of becoming a victim of an assault (Kaliski, 2006). According to Weideman (2008) substance abuse is correlated with at least 64 percent of the most serious DV incidents and to an excess of 73 percent of overall incidences. The victims of DV report that most of the serious incidents were preceded by the offender's assumption of infidelity, jealousy, the offender's inability to control the behavior or the movement of the victim, or the victim's refusal to have sexual intercourse with the offender. These assumptions or feelings are exacerbated by the use of substances. Moreover, substance abuse highly correlated with male and female offending behavior within domestic relationships, consequently increasing the vulnerability of the partner (Jewkes, Levin & Penn-Kekana, 2002; Padayachee & Singh, 2003).

In 21 percent of the instances aspects such as unemployment, poverty and financial stress were highlighted by respondents as causal factors (Weideman, 2008). A correlation between DV and income inequality within a relationship has been found. Thus, if one of the partners is more financially secure than the other there is an increased chance of the occurrence of DV (Jewkes, 2002). This is exacerbated if both partners struggle to secure some form of income from week to week. Weideman (2008) indicates that 41 percent of the victims are dependent on the offender for housing and the majority of the victims were unemployed at the time of the DV incident.

Male victims of domestic violence

There is a dearth of research pertaining to the prevalence of male victims who are abused by male or female partners. This is exacerbated by the fact that men tend to refrain from reporting the abusive incidents, due to factors such as a fear of secondary victimization, as well as the stigma attached to being a victim of abuse (Artz & Smythe, 2005; Barkhuizen, 2010). Furthermore, society is reluctant to recognize that females can be perpetrators of DV. Barkhuizen (2010) elaborates on this by stating that due to the fact that husband-to-wife abuse is often more aggressive and results in more severe injuries, the focus of most research is on female victimization. This is aggravated by the fact that female victimization is reported more often, which increases its visibility (Coker et al., 2002). Ignorance of the plight of male victims leaves these victims with feelings such as embarrassment, anger and loneliness as well as an increased vulnerability to becoming victims of repeat victimization. Moreover, male victims of DV often report negative perceptions from the criminal justice system as they feel that they are held responsible for being incapable of standing up to the abuse (Barkhuizen, 2014). In one study, approximately 23 percent of males who reside with a male companion reported being physically assaulted, stalked or raped by their partners, while 7.4 percent of males residing with female partners reported victimization (Weideman, 2008).

Same-sex relationships show similar patterns to heterosexual abuse patterns globally. Stiles-Shields and Carroll (2015) cite several studies in the United States of America (USA) that indicate similar abuse patterns in lesbian and gay men's relationships, compared to their heterosexual male counterparts. Bezuidenhout (1995) found that male on male abuse or female on female abuse in same-sex relationships are even more violent in some instances.

South African legislation aimed at regulating domestic violence

Different laws can be used in the legal machinery to address DV. However, legislation specifically aimed at protecting victims of DV in South Africa are the Domestic Violence Act 116 of 1998; the Criminal Law (Sexual Offences and Related Matters) Amendment Act 32 of 2007; the Criminal Procedure Act 51 of 1977; the Children's Act 38 of 2005 and the Constitution of South Africa. With regards to the Constitution, Article 12(c) of the Bill of Rights emphasizes that every South African citizen has the right to freedom from all sources of violence. Furthermore, section 7(2) implies that there is a positive duty on government to protect, promote and fulfill the rights contained in the Bill of Rights, thus implying that government has a legal duty to protect all victims of crime.

The one legal tool that stands out is the Domestic Violence Act 116 of 1998. This Act aims at enhancing all legal services to the victim of DV. In the past, police officials treated DV as a private matter, or often the male abuser convinced police officials it was a domestic quarrel and it would not happen again. Often police will leave the location, only for the abuse to continue. This Act forces police officials to act seriously with every DV complaint. Should a police officer fail to carry out this commitment, the victim can complain to the supervising officer, the station commissioner or the Independent Police Investigative Directorate (IPID). IPID is an agency of the South African government that is responsible for investigating complaints against the SAPS and municipal police services (a watchdog agency). The victim or a concerned acquaintance can report the non-intervention of the police officials involved (Bendall, 2010). Any complaint against a police officer will be logged in a complaints register, stating the name of the member the complaint is related to, the date on which the complaint is lodged and the details of the complaint. If necessary the station commissioner will take disciplinary steps against the member involved. The matter will also be referred to IPID if the complaint was not directly lodged with IPID for their recommendations. Subsequently a short overview of the content of the Domestic Violence Act 116 of 1998 will be given.

To be classified as a domestic relationship existing between the defendant and the complainant according to the Domestic Violence Act 116 of 1998 the following types of relationships are included:

- They are or were married to one another, with reference to marriage according to any law, religion or custom.
- They live or lived together in the nature of marriage, while they were or were not married to one another.
- They are the parents or guardian of a child.
- They are family members, or they are related by affinity or adoption.
- They are or were engaged, in a customary relationship or dating.
- They share or have shared the same residence.

The different actions or behavior that are encompassed in the Domestic Violence Act (Act 108 of 1996) include physical, sexual, emotional, verbal, psychological and economic abuse. This includes behavior such as stalking, intimidation and harassment within domestic relationships. Furthermore, acts such as entering a person's residence without consent, as well as any other form of controlling behavior within a domestic relationship is regulated by the Act (Van der Hoven, 2001; Smit & Nel, 2002).

From the exposition provided above, one can deduce the following regarding DV. Any partner or child who experiences the following in their relationship or marriage is a victim of DV:

- physical abuse or assault (for example, pushing, punching, slapping, biting, kicking, and threats of physical violence);
- sexual abuse (for example, forced sexual activities, rape, demands to participate in unacceptable sexual activities [e.g., bestiality, swinging] – whether you are married to the other person or not);
- emotional abuse (for example, repeated insults, threats, swearing, degrading or humiliating comments or behavior);
- stalking (for example when the partner without consent follows the victim to work or to friends or social events repeatedly);
- other controlling or abusive behavior which poses a threat to your safety, health or wellbeing (for example intentionally over feeding the female partner to ensure she gains weight, or demanding a specific body type and threatening to leave the partner if this is not adhered to);
- damage to property or anything of value to the partner (for example to kill a pet or to damage a vehicle); and
- economic or financial abuse (for example the male partner lies about his financial status, or keeps and or uses money that legally belongs to the female partner or sells the female partner's property without her consent).

One of the main aims of the Domestic Violence Act 108 of 1996 is to reduce the devastating aftermath of DV and to ease the physical, emotional, psychological, spiritual and financial trauma experienced by victims of DV (Artz & Smythe, 2005). Moreover, the Act emphasizes the rights of victims, whilst aiming to hold offenders accountable for their behavior. Furthermore the Act stipulates that the members of the SAPS have a legal obligation to inform victims of their rights when they report a DV case. In addition, the Act enables a police officer to enter a residence where a domestic dispute is taking place, to remove dangerous weapons as a precautionary measure and to arrest an individual when there is a reasonable suspicion of domestic violence (Manamela, Smit & Ngantweni, 2010). The Act also allows the victim the opportunity to obtain a protection order. Details pertaining to what the protection order entail and how such an order is granted will be discussed in the next section. Subsequently a discussion of the effectiveness of the protection order will be provided.

Protection order

A protection order is a legal document which can be issued by the court upon request of the victim of DV. Any victim of DV (children included) can apply for a protection order. The application can also be brought on behalf of the victim by any individual or organization which is acting in the best interest of the victim such as family members, a social worker, teacher, or health service provider, for instance (Bick, 2013). Initially, a temporary protection order may be granted. Such an order is referred to as an interim protection order and once the victim has appeared in the magistrate's court, such an order can be made permanent (Bick, 2013). If the need arises an interim protection order can be issued at any time of the day or night (Bendall, 2010). It serves to be noted that a permanent protection order can be granted in the absence of the offender, as long as the victim or complainant is present for the court procedure (Johnson, 2014). It should be noted that the victim does not need the representation of a lawyer to apply for a protection order (Bendall, 2010). Granting a civil protection order to a victim of DV can protect the victim from further abuse by prohibiting the offender from making contact with the victim, limiting the perpetrator's visitation rights with his children, ordering that the perpetrator must vacate the property, even if it is in his name, requesting the police to accompany the victim when removing personal belongings from the shared residence, ordering the perpetrator to provide emergency monetary relief to the victim and any other actions that can empower the victim (Turvey & Petherick, 2009; Bendall, 2010). In instances where the abusive partner violates the protection order, it needs to be reported to the police, and thereafter an arrest warrant should be released by a magistrate followed by the arrest of the abuser (Peltzer, Pengpid, McFarlane & Banyini, 2013). Unfortunately, the obtainment of a protection order can, however, be a tedious process, varying from two to six weeks. This questions the effectiveness of obtaining a protection order, as numerous acts of abuse can transpire in the interim (Johnson, 2014).

Protection orders are not always effective

Domestic violence-related protection orders – S v Sibiya 2010 (1) SACR 284 (GNP)

In the Sibiya case the accused, a security officer, was prohibited by a protection order from assaulting, threatening or harassing the complainant, his former girl-friend with whom he had a child. However, despite the order, the accused contravened it a week after it had been issued, by harassing the complainant, demanding to see his child and by slapping the complainant twice in the face. Accordingly the accused was convicted in the magistrate's court for the district of Nkomazi of contravening section 17(a) read together with sections 1, 5 and 7 of the Domestic Violence Act 116 of 1998 – contravening any prohibition, condition, obligation or order imposed in a protection order.

He was sentenced to 12 months' imprisonment of which eight months were conditionally suspended for three years. On review before the High Court in Pretoria, the court inter alia reminded that our courts have often emphasized that short terms of imprisonment do more harm than good, of which the present instance is a textbook example. Unfortunately, these admonishments appear to be largely ignored by the turning of a blind eye to the negative consequences that the accused's loss of employment – in these days of dire economic straits – has for the victim and society alike, as a result of the injudicious application of a sentencing option that should be reserved for offenders who are a real threat to society, and not for young hotheads who have not yet learnt to act with restraint.

In the review the conviction was confirmed but the sentence was altered to three months' imprisonment wholly suspended for two years on condition that the accused was not convicted of contravening section 17 of the Domestic Violence Act 116 of 1998; of assault or assault with the intent to cause grievous bodily harm, committed during the period of suspension and for which the accused was sentenced to direct imprisonment. Unfortunately, the accused had served his time which means that the substituted ("new") sentence had no practical effect.

Source: S v Rudolph 2010 (1) SACR 262 (SCA) and S v Sibiya 2010 (1) 284 (GN),
as published verbatim in Lambrechts, 2010.

Therefore from reported case law it appears, *prima facie*, that in some cases the issuing of a protection order can escalate or exacerbate the animosity between the transgressor and the complainant. It often seems to also trigger other comorbid behavioral or even mental disorders (Bartol & Bartol, 2014).

Survey results from the CSIR study revealed that 41 percent of the 1000 respondents acknowledged that they were familiar with the procedures of applying for protection orders. Thirty-one percent of the respondents applied for a protection order and were present in court when the permanent protection order was discussed. Eighty-eight percent of these respondents were successful in obtaining protection orders. Respondents from only one province (Eastern Cape) referred to problematic service delivery, compared to the satisfaction conveyed by respondents from the other five provinces covered in the study. Of those that were granted protection orders, 83 percent reported being satisfied with the order and 8 percent said that it was not too complicated to obtain a protection order. Moreover, more than half of the respondents reported that the protection order brought about positive changes in their lives, a small group of the respondents said that nothing changed after obtaining the protection order and slightly less than half of the respondents claimed that they were worse off after the order was obtained as it probably escalated animosity and abusive behavior from the abuser who was served with the order. In this study 22 percent of the offenders violated the protection order. A worrisome revelation in this regard is that only 27 percent of these violators were arrested (Weideman, 2008).

Victims' perceptions of the criminal justice system and related services

According to Weideman (2008) 63 percent of the 1000 respondents in the study mentioned that they were aware of legal aid clinics or lawyers in the area where they resided, but only 9 percent actually utilized these legal services. Contrary to the views of practitioners and experts in the field, 92 percent of the respondents were satisfied with the attitudes and services provided by magistrates and pro-secutors. Of the respondents who attended court cases, 93 percent testified in court and 88 percent felt that they were heard during the process. Even though 40 percent of the respondents revealed that they did not receive regular updates pertaining to their case, 83 percent of the respondents were satisfied with the service rendered by the courts.

Half of the survey respondents revealed that they contacted the police after the DV took place. Of these, 23 percent phoned the police and 77 percent went to the police station in person. Of those that phoned the police, the police only arrived in time to prevent further abuse in 50 percent of the cases, in 41 percent of the cases it took the police more than 45 minutes to arrive at the scene, while the police did not arrive at all in 13 percent of the cases. Eighty-two percent of the respondents reported that they were attended to in less than 30 minutes at police stations. In addition, more than half of the respondents indicated that they were satisfied with the services rendered by the police (Weideman, 2008). Some of the sentiments shared by the respondents in the previously discussed study were echoed by victims of DV who were approached at a shelter. They conveyed their positive feelings toward the police. One victim stated that the police arrived at the scene of the DV within 10 minutes after the distress call was made and they offered to immediately take her to the police station for support and counseling. Upon her request to rather stay at home and receive counseling there, a counsellor arrived at her home 20 minutes after her request. She described the SAPS's conduct as extremely accom-modating and helpful (Bendall, 2010). Please note that police stations in South Africa are legally and per national instructions from police head office responsible for the implementation of victim-friendly rooms and they must ensure effective victim services at police stations. This includes emotional support, practical support, providing information (e.g., assisting with a protection order), and referral to profes-sional support services (e.g., psychological services or a shelter).

It must, however, be noted that even though there are indications that the service of police officers has improved, some victims still claim that they were not informed of their rights, or of the procedures that should be followed to realize their rights. Furthermore it was revealed that only 44 percent of the respondents were interviewed by a police officer of the same gender. Contrary to policy requirements only 56 percent of the respondents' statements were taken in a private room (victim-friendly room). Of the 37 percent of respondents who required medical attention at the time when they reported the abuse to the police, only 39 percent claim that the police took them to a medical examiner and only 22 percent said that photos of their injuries were taken by the police. In general the respondents (96 percent) were satisfied with the treatment that they received from the district surgeon. Eighty-nine percent of the victims claimed that they were truthful regarding the reason for the injuries while being examined by the medical practitioner (Weideman, 2008).

With regards to shelters or places of safety, 14 percent of the victims indicated that their children were separated from them and were not allowed to stay with them. Twenty-eight percent of the victims reported that shelters only allowed children younger than 14 years old to stay with their mothers in the shelter. This separation created additional trauma for both the mother and the children. Furthermore respondents indicated that they were allowed to stay in the shelters for approximately three months. This is an alarming issue, as 61 percent of the victims indicated that they had no place to stay once they left the shelter and that their only option would be to return to the residence of the perpetrator. Moreover, 74 percent were unemployed or did not have a sufficient income. This explains why 16 percent of the respondents admitted that they left the abuser before, but due to an absence of alternatives they had to return to the abusive situation (Weideman, 2008).

Measures aimed at curbing DV

An important measure taken with the aim of reducing DV is the implementation of the Integrated Victim Empowerment Policy (IVEP). The policy underscores the importance of human rights, whilst taking on a restorative justice approach. It attempts to restore relationships, and aims to protect victims and to eradicate the cycle of violence within the various domestic spheres. Furthermore, the objective of the IVEP is to provide integrated services to victims, enhance the support systems of victims and assist victims in regaining control of their milieus (Kent & McIntyre, 2004). An additional measure taken by government to deal with the occurrence of DV includes the Victim Empowerment Programme (VEP). The purpose of the VEP is to emphasize victim rights, such as the right to be protected, the right to be compensated, as well as the right to receive legal advice. Moreover, the VEP aims to strengthen and coordinate partnerships between government and non-governmental organizations providing services to victims of DV (Van der Hoven, 2001). In addition, the VEP focuses on victim support and empowerment, as well as the prevention of re-victimization (Makofane, 2001). Other important policies pertaining to DV are the Police Framework and Strategy for Shelters for Victims of Domestic Violence in South Africa that was developed in 2003, as well as the Integrated Domestic Violence Training Programme Manual developed in 2004. The purpose of this manual is to provide guidance to individuals who work with DV cases such as police officers, counsellors, prosecutors, magistrates and the like. Practical implementation of the guidelines in this manual takes places in the form of a five-day course focusing on DV, where police officers who attend this course are provided with a detailed discussion of the Domestic Violence Act. Additionally they engage in roleplaying exercises and receive training regarding the completion of relevant documentation, as well as methods to prepare the complainant for court (Bendall, 2010).

There are several South African initiatives focusing on women and children who are victims of DV. In most instances, legislation and governmental strategies mainly focus on reactive measures, in other words focusing on what can be done after the crime occurred. Some non-governmental organizations are, however, involved in raising awareness of the social ill and devastating consequences of DV and have various campaigns focusing on preventative measures. Many of these organizations aim to provide frontline services, but also take on active roles in advocacy aimed at promoting the rights of victims. People Opposing Women Abuse (POWA) is an example of such an organization. POWA deals with the social dynamics of DV, offering services aimed at eradicating violence against women. Another example of a South African initiative is the Support for Abused Women Project, which is coordinated by the National Institute for Crime Prevention and Rehabilitation of Offenders (NICRO). The aim of this project is to provide shelters, and offer counseling, legal advice, as well as education and training to abused women (Van der Hoven, 2001).

Conclusion

As discussed above, numerous policies and strategies aimed at addressing the aftermath of DV have been developed and implemented. Furthermore, great strides have been made in training members of the SAPS, as well as members of the courts dealing with DV pertaining to the best way to handle victims of DV. However, it has to be kept in mind that many victims of DV still regard their victimization as a private matter and thus, they do not report the violence. This necessitates the use of educational programs raising awareness of DV, explaining the legal process pertaining to the serving of a protection order, as well as the influence that the violence has on the broader community and individuals within these communities (Bendall, 2010). The (sub-)culture of violence is a reality in this country as the murder rates serve as an attestation to this. We believe that South Africa experiences some of the most severe cases of DV and that government and the community need to engage in education and victim empowerment. As the late Nelson Mandela stated: "Education is the most powerful weapon which you can use to change the world."

References

Abrahams, R., Mathews, S., Jewkes, R., Martin, L.J., & Lombard, C. (2012). *Every eight hours: Intimate femicide in South Africa 10 years later.* Medical Research Council: Research brief.

Artz, L., & Smythe, D. (2005). South African legislation supporting victims' rights. In L. Davis & R. Snyman (Eds.), *Victimology in South Africa* (pp. 157–159). Pretoria: Van Schaik Publishers.

Artz, L., & Smythe, D. (2013). South African legislation supporting victims' rights. In R. Peacock (Ed.), *Victimology in South Africa.* (2nd ed.) (pp. 47–76). Pretoria: Van Schaik Publishers.

Barkhuizen, M. (2010). *The physical and emotional victimization of a male partner within a heterosexual marriage or cohabiting relationship: An explorative study.* PhD Thesis, South Africa: University of South Africa.

Barkhuizen, M. (2014). Police reaction to male domestic violence: Empathy or perpetuating the myths? *Servamus, 107*(3), 30–31.

Bartol, C.R., & Bartol, A.M. (2014). *Criminal behavior: A psychosocial approach* (10th ed.). Upper Saddle River, NJ: Prentice Hall.

Beckner, H.M. (2005). *Attachment theory as a predictor of female aggression.* Unpublished PhD Thesis, Texas: Texas A&M University.

Bendall, C. (2010). The domestic violence epidemic in South Africa: Legal and practical remedies. *Women's Studies, 39*(2), 100–118.

Bezuidenhout, C. (1995). Attitudes of victims and non-victims of anti-gay violence towards the South African police and the legal system. *Acta Criminologica: Southern African Journal of Criminological, 8*(1), 75–83.

Bezuidenhout, C. (2007). Are we fighting a losing battle against crime? (Editorial). *Acta Criminologica: Southern African Journal of Criminology, 20*(4), i-vii.

Bezuidenhout, C. (2011). Sector policing in South Africa – Case Closed – Or Not? *Pakistan Journal of Criminology, 3*, No. 2 & 3, April–July 2011, 11–25.

Bezuidenhout, C. (2015). Intriguing paradox: The inability to keep South Africa safe and the successful hosting of mega global sporting events. In J.F. Albrecht, M.C. Dow, D. Plecas, & D.K. Das (Eds.), *Policing major events: Perspectives from around the world* (pp. 195–224). FL: USA Taylor and Francis Group (CRC Press).

Bezuidenhout, C. & Klopper, H.F. (2011). Crimes of a violent nature. In C. Bezuidenhout (Ed.), *A Southern African perspective on fundamental criminology* (pp. 182–238). Cape Town: Pearson.

Bick, L. (2013). Protection from harassment. *Without Prejudice, 13*(5), 71–73.

Burton, P. (2008). Learning to fear, fearing to learn: Measuring the extent of school violence. *SA Crime Quarterly, 26*, 15–20.

Coker, A.L., Davis, K.E., Arias, I., Desai, S., Sanderson, M., Brandt, H., & Smith, P. (2002). Physical and mental health effects of partner violence for men and women. *American Journal of Preventive Medicine, 23*(4), 260–268.

Constitution of the Republic of South Africa. (1996). Pretoria: Government Printers.

Cunningham, A., Peter, G., Jaffe, P.G., Baker, L., Dick, T., Malla, S., Mazaheri, N., & Poisson, S. (1998). *Theory-derived explanations of male violence against female partners: Literature update and related implications for treatment and evaluation.* London Family Court Clinic. September 1998.

De Wet, C. (2003). Eastern Cape educators' perceptions of the causes and the scope of school violence. *Acta Criminologica, 16*(3), 89–106.

Domestic Violence Act 116 of 1998. (1998). Published in the *Government Gazette*, (20601). Pretoria: Government Printer.

Geldenhuys, K. (2014). Gender-based violence. *Servamus: Community based safety & security magazine, 107*(8), 10–15.

Grant, L. (2015). *SA's murder statistics in 7 charts.* Retrieved from www.iol.co.za/ news/ sas-murder-statistics-in-7-charts-1.1925800

Gupta, J., Silverman, J.G., Hemenway, D., Acevedo-Garcia, D., Stein, D.J., & Williams, D.R. (2008). Physical violence against intimate partners and related exposures to violence among South African men. *CMAJ, 179*(6), 535–541.

Harris, T.F. (2009). *A psychocriminological investigation into risk factors contributing to youth sex offending.* MA dissertation, Pretoria: University of Pretoria.

Jasinski, J.L. (2001). Theoretical explanations for violence against women. In C.M. Renzetti, J.L. Edleson & R.K. Bergen (Eds.), *Sourcebook on violence against women.* Thousand Oaks, CA: Sage.

Jewkes, R. (2002). Intimate partner violence: Causes and prevention. *Violence Against Women III, The Lancet, 359*, 1423–1429.

Jewkes, R., Levin, J., & Penn-Kekana, L. (2002). Risk factors for domestic violence: Findings from a South African cross-sectional study. *Social Science and Medicine, 55*, 1603–1617.

Johnson, M. (2014). Protection from harassment. *Without Prejudice, 14*(2), 52–53.

Kaliski, S. (Ed.). (2006). *Psycholegal assessment in South Africa.* Cape Town: Oxford University Press.

Kempen, A. (2006). 16 Days of activism campaign for no violence against women and children. *Servamus: Community-based Safety & Security Magazine, 99*(2), 40–43.

Kent, V., & McIntyre, A. (2004). From protection to empowerment: Civilians as stakeholders in the Democratic Republic of the Congo. *Institute for Security Studies Papers, 84*, 1–15.

Kriegler, A., & Shaw, M. (2015). *South Africa's mysterious murder rate.* Retrieved from www.dailymaverick.co.za/article/2015-10-02-south-africas-mysterious-murder-rate/#. VqYD7lJ6-W8

Lambrechts, D. (2010). Ask Pollex. *SERVAMUS Community-based Safety & Security Magazine, 103*(7), 69–70.

Makofane, D. (2001). Process evaluation of the victim empowerment programme for abused women in the Northern Province. *Acta Criminologica, 14*(1), 97–104.

Manamela, M., Smit, J., & Ngantweni, G. (2010). Policing domestic violence effectively at Rietgat police station: An assessment. *Acta Criminologica, 2*, 99–112.

Maree, A. (2013). Criminogenic risk factors. In C. Bezuidenhout (Ed.), *Child and youth misbehaviour in South Africa: A holistic view* (3rd ed.). Pretoria: Van Schaik.

Modiba, L.M, Baliki, O., Mmalasa, R., Reineke, P., & Nsiki, C. (2011). Pilot survey of domestic abuse amongst pregnant women attending an antenatal clinic in a public hospital in Gauteng Province in South Africa. *Midwifery, 27*(6), 872–879.

Musgrave, A. (2015). *More people living below breadline.* Retrieved from www.iol. co.za/business/news/more-people-living-below-breadline--stats-sa-1813099

Naidoo, L., & Sewpaul, V. (2014). The life experiences of adolescent sexual offenders: Factors that contribute to offending behaviours. *Social Work/Maatskaplike Werk, 50*(1), 84–98.

Nedcor ISS Criminal Justice Information Centre. (1997). Victim empowerment. Midrand: Duplico.

Padayachee, A., & Singh, D. (2003). Intimate violence and substance abuse – the correlative relationship. *Acta Criminologica, 16*(1), 108–114.

Peltzer, K., Pengpid, S., McFarlane, J., & Banyini, M. (2013). Evaluation of the effectiveness of protection orders for female victims of intimate partner violence in Vhembe District of South Africa. *Journal of Psychology in Africa, 23*(3), 489–493.

Perilla, J.L., Lippy, C., Rosales, A., & Serrata, J.V. (2011). Prevalence of domestic violence. In J.W. White, M.P. Koss, & A.E. Kasdin (Eds.), *Violence against women and children. Vol. 1. Mapping the terrain.* Washington, DC: American Psychological Association.

Petersen, I., Bhana, A., & McKay, M. (2005). Sexual violence and youth in South Africa: The need for community-based prevention interventions. *Child Abuse & Neglect, 29,* 1233–1248.

Ross, L.E. (2010). *The war against domestic violence.* Boca Raton, FL: CRC Press.

Schreiner, J.A. (2004). *Rape as a human security issue, with specific reference to South Africa.* MA Dissertation, Pretoria: University of Pretoria.

Smit, J., & Nel, F. (2002). An evaluation of the implementation of the Domestic Violence Act: What is happening in practice? *Acta Criminologica, 15*(3), 45–55.

South Africa "a country at war" as murder rate soars to nearly 49 a day. (2015). Retrieved from www.theguardian.com/world/2015/sep/29/south-africa-a-country-at-war-as-rate-soars-to-nearly-49-a-day

Statistics South Africa. (2014). Statistical release P0302: Mid-year population estimates 2014. Retrieved from www.statssa.gov.za/publications/P0302/P03022014.pdf

Stile-Shields, C., Carroll, R. (2015). Same sex domestic violence: Prevalence, unique aspects, and clinical implications. *Journal of Sex & Marital Therapy, 41*(6), 636–648.

Turvey, B.E., & Petherick, W. (2009). *Forensic victimology: Examining violent crime, victims in investigative and legal contexts.* Amsterdam: Academic Press.

Van der Hoven, A. (2001). Domestic violence in South Africa. *Acta Criminologica, 14*(3), 13–25.

Van Niekerk, J. (2006). The often neglected side of the sexual abuse equation – the child sex offender. In Spies, G.M. (Ed.), *Sexual abuse: Dynamics, assessment and healing.* Pretoria: Van Schaik.

Vogelman, L., & Lewis, S. (1993). Gang rape and the culture of violence in South Africa. *Der Uberblick, 2,* 39–42.

Walker, L. (1979). *The battered women.* New York: Harper and Row.

Weideman, M. (2008). *Consolidated report on the nature and prevalence of domestic violence in South Africa.* Retrieved from www.cindi.org.za/files/eNews/ enews13/Consolidated_Report_Domestic_Violence_South%20Africa.pdf

White, J.A. (1995). Violence prevention in schools. *Journal of Health Education, 26*(1), 52–53.

Wolfgang, M.E., & Ferracuti, F. (1967). *The subculture of violence: Towards an integrated theory in criminology.* London: Tavistock Publications.

12 Combatting the menace of domestic violence

The Ghanaian experience

Gerald Dapaah Gyamfi

Domestic violence is a significant family health issue that publicly affects people across the globe with far-reaching consequences (Cronholm, Singh, Fogarty & Ambuel, 2014). Many international bodies, such as the United Nations, have expressed grave concern over the devastating effect of this menace to society. It is considered to be a global problem that many nations are striving to contend with. While many nations have committed resources to fight this menace, statistics indicate that there has been an upsurge in problems associated with domestic violence (Cronholm et al., 2014).

Domestic violence in Ghana

Ghana has long recognized domestic violence as a problem that has social and health implications. Due to cultural and social issues, many domestic violence victims feel reluctant to report such issues to law enforcement agencies in Ghana. Many Ghanaians perceive domestic violence as a family issue and discourage women from reporting the issues to the police and other justice systems. The main aspects of domestic violence discussed in this chapter were found following implementation of a national study on domestic violence in Ghana between 1995 and 2016 by the Gender Studies and Human Rights Documentation Centre in Ghana (GSHRDC) and its partners (including DFID, EU, Global Fund, and Star Ghana). It was revealed that domestic violence causes emotional stress, psychological, physical, and sexual damage to many Ghanaian women, especially those in adolescent and adult age groups. It was shown that one third of Ghanaian women have experienced domestic violence from their spouses or former marriage partners in their lifetime. Many domestic violence victims, especially women, consider domestic violence as part of family life situations that must be tolerated to maintain their homes. Historically, many married women in Ghana consider their spouses as their lords who must be served with dignity and respect and that they must pay obeisance to them. Many women consider their spouses as the breadwinners for the home and consider it as a duty to serve their spouses as masters of the homes. In view of that assertion, most Ghanaian men consider it a part of maintaining the household to molest their spouses if something goes wrong in the home.

Negative stereotypes and norms regarding Ghanaian women stifle their development over time as they come to believe that the abuse is part of their culture and must be endured in order to have a lifetime spousal relationship. Many spouses find it very difficult to report violence meted on them to third parties because the family members or friends also consider it to be a norm, and in most circumstances advise against the victims reporting these incidences to the police or seeking counseling from other third parties (Bhatta, 2014). The victims in most cases try to avoid mentioning the cause of bruises sustained during an attack to their medical doctors as a way of shielding their partners. Most of the victims of domestic violence suffer psychological problems due to emotional impact of the violence directed toward them. The emotional impact results from threatening behaviors including death threats, verbal abuse, discrimination, husbands taking second wives or girlfriends, and husbands refusing to talk to their wives or listen to them (Yi-Hsiu, Jia-Shun & Tsui-Hua, 2014). In some cases, domestic violence leads to destruction of property, husbands refusing to have sex with their spouses, unilateral termination of marriage, false accusations, insults, relegating the women as inferior partners, shaming wives before other people, disrespecting and sometimes confining women to secluded places. The Ghanaian culture, in some situations, permits polygamy (GSHRDC, 2016). Such marriages usually lead to favoritism and subordination of some of the wives. Many children in Ghana suffer from domestic violence resulting from their fathers taking second wives, breaking homes, divorce, and humiliation.

Domestic violence adversely impacts many factors related to the country itself as a developing nation. Many women with youthful exuberance who make contributions to increase Ghana's gross domestic product have been victimized or killed as a result of domestic violence (Ofei-Aboagye, 1994). A report from the Office of the Ministry of Gender, Children and Social Protection (2015) indicates that 68 percent of the female population are illiterate with only 39 percent participating in higher education. This makes it difficult for women to find intellectually productive work. Lamptey (2015) bemoaned how women were portrayed as sex objects in many Ghanaian movies, inculcating into the minds of the men that the women are too weak to resist sexual abuse.

Domestic violence has ramifications on justice, and legal and health concerns. The dire consequences of domestic violence in Ghana include broken homes, isolation from relatives and friends, homelessness, loss of opportunities, low income, poor health, and death. It also leads to some psychological consequences including depression, physical and mental injury/impairment, and low esteem. As a result of domestic violence some women suffer from sexual problems in Ghana, according to some medical experts consulted (Leach & Mitchell, 2006). Most people in marriage, especially women, suffer sexual violence from rape emanating from forced sexual intercourse without the consent of the other party (Santos da Silva et al., 2014).

In certain parts of Ghana, most of the females are forced to undergo genital mutilation where their clitorises are removed using sharp objects which inflict severe pain at their genital region. In some situations the women are forced to refuse any family planning measures to have control over their reproduction. Due to abject poverty some parents push their adolescent daughters into forced prostitution. Some school teachers use psychological means to entice school girls into having sexual intercourse with them. Sometimes these teachers threaten that girls will not perform well academically if they fail to have sexual intercourse with their male teachers. In some situations women seeking jobs are coerced into having sexual intercourse with the officers in charge of the jobs before being offered a job. After being hired, they are often pressured into having sexual affairs with their superiors (Leach & Mitchell, 2006; GSHRDC, 2016).

The Gender Studies and Human Rights Documentation Centre in Ghana (GSHRDC, 2016) and its partners' (including DFID, EU, Global Fund, and Star Ghana) findings revealed that 33 percent of women in Ghana had suffered physical violence in their intimate relationships with men. Two out of three of the women suffered bodily pain and injuries resulting from bruises, broken bones, aches, swollen faces (including eyes), blood from ears, and open wounds. Forty-nine percent of the injuries and pain required medical treatment. Some of the women were slapped and some of the men used objects including belts, canes, chairs, and knives to physically assault the women. Out of the number sent for treatment at medical facilities 16 percent were sent to clinics, hospitals (36 percent), herbalists (6 percent), pharmacies (21 percent), and drug peddlers (21 percent).

Traditional practices in some parts of Ghana humiliate women and inflict emotional and psychological pain, and sometimes sexual damage to females. Bridal dowries paid by men, as customary rites to getting married to a woman, result in men considering their spouses as their property. Widowhood rites include depriving women who have lost spouses of sex for a long time after the death of a husband, as well as cold water bathing, thereby subjecting widows to humiliation (Amoakohene, 2004).

Statistical data on domestic violence from the Domestic Violence and Victim Support Unit (DOVVSU)

A report from the Domestic Violence and Victim Support Unit (DOVVSU) of Ghana Police Service (GPS) indicates that between 1999 and 2010, 109,784 cases of domestic violence were reported with a greater number of the cases perpetrated against women. Records available from the office of DOVVSU in 2015, revealed at the Third Domestic Violence Awareness Workshop, by the Coordinating Director of DOVVSU, Habiba Twumasi-Sarpong, indicated that 84,899 domestic violence cases were recorded by the unit nationwide between 2010 and 2014. The statistical data on domestic violence cases provided for the various years were as follows: 2010, 12,706 cases; 2011, 17,965 cases; 2012, 17,655 cases; 2013, 18,795 cases; and 2014, 17,778 cases. The types of reported cases included defilement, rape, unnatural carnal knowledge, incest, sodomy, and assault. According to the report, 95 percent of the victims were women and children. In 2014, refusal of husbands to contribute money for housekeeping cases reported to DOVVSU ranked highest with 6,158; cases of wife battery was 5,212; assault, 1,667 cases; threat, 1,111 cases; and defilement and rape was 290 cases.

Statistics from one DOVVSU regional office in Ghana revealed that domestic violence cases were the least reported types of cases among the 10 regions of Ghana. Domestic violence cases rose in the second quarter of 2015 as compared to the reported cases in the second quarter of 2014. Assault rose from 31 to 62 cases in 2015, defilement rose from 2 to 9, rape moved from 0 to 3 cases, and reports of threat of harm and death ballooned from 5 to 18.

Interventions to curb domestic violence

Domestic violence has become an issue that many international organizations have considered with much concern. United Nations (1993) embarked on an affirmative action to eliminate domestic violence that includes violence against women by adopting a declaration and the establishment of a special Rapporteur that tackled the issue of violence against women. In the declaration, systematic violence against women was treated as a human rights violation. The detrimental effects of domestic violence have triggered many nations to execute protection powers that prompt the police and the courts to embark on swift actions to protect victims (Griffith, 2014). A study has shown that the actions of domestic violence professionals demonstrating willingness and support fulfill some needs and expectations of many families that are victimized (Santos da Silva et al., 2014). Some cultural practices create a depressing paradigm of gender disparities leading to violence against women and children that must give way to a new cultural paradigm that provides affirmative action towards equity. Affirmative actions that increase educational opportunities, and create consistent seasonal employment and fair treatment to women should be encouraged (Valenzuela & Zincke, 2015).

The analysis of the statistical data provided by DOVVSU over the last 5 years suggests the number of reported domestic violence cases increased from about 40 percent to about 95 percent of the victims being women and children. These data are consistent with other countries across the globe (Pobutsky, Brown, Nakao, & Reyes-Salail, 2014; Johnson & Brown, 2014). In Ghana, due to some cultural and religious beliefs, stigmatization, and family- related reasons, most of the domestic violence cases are not reported to the police and other agencies involved in criminal investigations. In Ghana abuse of women and children has persisted for a long time and it is time swift actions are embarked upon to eliminate the canker. The statistical data from GSHRDC indicates violence against women usually results from cultural and traditional practices, sexual habits, economic factors, misunderstandings, and lack of education. This is an indication that domestic violence in Ghana has far-reaching consequences on families, the communities, and the society in general as revealed from the study by Johnson and Brown (2014).

The findings from GSHRDC also indicate that in some instances domestic violence not only results in physical wounds, but psychological and emotional wounds as well. Sexual neglect can inflict psychological pain when a spouse learns that her partner is having sexual relations with someone else. Young girls made to undergo sexual mutilation suffer lifelong pain inflicted on them by their parents or family relatives; this cultural practice in Ghana is a form of domestic violence that can be avoided.

Ghana has many criminal code provisions to curb domestic violence, but due to attitudinal and traditional problems, many law enforcement agencies under-enforce the codes. Many people in authority traditionally consider domestic violence as a family matter and fail to penalize the perpetrators. Many clergy men and women in Ghana consider marriage as a sacred institution and so reporting spouses to court and the police is seen as tantamount to attempting to break a sacred institution ordained by God, which the clergy abhor and will not encourage. The Ghana government has ratified many international treaties that impose an obligation to take steps to curb the menace but, due to lack of logistics, financial constraints, and political agendas, the enforcement agencies such as the Women and Juvenile Unit (WAJU), DOVVSU of Ghana Police Service, and the Commission on Human Rights and Administrative Justice (CHRAJ) fail to investigate and punish the culprits (Cantalupo, Martin, Pak & Shin, 2006).

Implications for research, policy, and practice

The role of the media in creating awareness about domestic violence against women is highly essential in curbing the menace. The media can be used to educate the masses on how to report and deal with issues involving domestic violence (Amini, Heidary & Daneshparvar, 2014). Pastors, imams, teachers, and leaders of other faith-based organizations can use their platforms to preach against domestic violence and how to avoid, reduce or eliminate the violence from their communities. Financial support from the government to equip the police with the appropriate equipment and procedures is useful for the elimination or reduction of the violence against the most vulnerable groups.

Governments can roll out certain protection powers that support the Judicial Service and the Police Service to act swiftly when dealing with domestic violence, such as using information that relates to an offender's previous abusive behavior (Griffith, 2014; Youngs, 2015). In Ghana, for instance, the 1992 Constitution of Ghana gives equal rights to all Ghanaians, irrespective of gender or age, therefore, enforcement of the rights is guaranteed by the Constitution (1992) and should help reduce domestic violence, especially, violence against women and children. Ratification of international charters relating to domestic violence and enforcement of the rights of the most vulnerable is an avenue that can help curb the incidence of domestic violence. Victims of domestic violence must be supported in order to recover from their traumatic situations during investigations into their cases (Herreira Triguero, Labronici, Aparecida Barbosa, & Raijmondo, 2014). For instance, the state agencies should provide victims of domestic violence with temporary shelter and food in situations where domestic violence renders the victims home-less. The non-governmental agencies as well as governmental agencies, such as the Ministry of Gender, Children and Social Protection, the CHRAJ and GSHRDC should be financially supported by philanthropists and the state to enable them to enhance their efforts in fighting domestic violence.

Intensification of the collaborative efforts among the police, the general public, agencies involved in domestic violence, and the other stakeholders can play major roles in the fight. Formation of community-based combat teams against domestic violence can be a useful weapon to fight the menace (Trevillion, Agnew-Davies & Howard, 2013). Traditionally, chiefs and opinion leaders in charge of communities can help to reduce ethnocentrism and other cultural practices that put women and children at risk of domestic violence (Jeremiah, Gamache, & Hegamin-Younger, 2013). Health entities that receive cases of injuries, trauma, and threats resulting from domestic violence can collaborate with the police and other groups in dealing with the problems (Basu & Ratcliffe, 2014; McGarry, Westbury, Kench & Furse, 2014). Many married women in Ghana depend on their husbands for their eco-nomic upkeep and rely wholly on their husbands for their survival. In view of that, many husbands treat their spouses as people who must be controlled and treated as dependents. Encouraging and enforcing internationally accepted affirmative actions that view women as equals with their male counterparts will contribute to reduce domestic violence.

Conclusion

Domestic violence has significant implications on the health of people in a com-munity and has international ramifications. Countries such as Ghana, where domestic violence is pervasive, have significant obligations to curb the menace. Ghana's domestic violence emanates from several sources, including economic, cultural, educational, and financial issues. Pragmatic steps, involving all stake-holders such as governments, the law enforcement agencies, and non-governmental organizations must be taken to ensure that domestic violence is reduced drastically, if not eliminated.

References

Amini, L., Heidary, M., & Daneshparvar, H. (2014). Mental health and some socio-demographic determinants in women with domestic violence experience. *Journal of Urmia Nursing & Midwifery Faculty, 12*(8), 599–605.

Amoakohene, M.I. (2004). Violence against women in Ghana: A look at women's per-ception and review of policy and social responses. *Social Science & Medicine, 59*(11), 2373–2385.

Basu, S., & Ratcliffe, G. (2014). Developing a multidisciplinary approach within the ED towards domestic violence. *Emergency Medicine Journal, 31*(3), 192–195.

Bhatta, D.N. (2014). Shadows of reproductive violence and extramarital sex cohesion with spousal communication among males in Nepal. *Reproductive Health, 11*, 44.

Cantalupo, N.C., Martin, L.V., Pak, K., & Shin, S. (2006). *Domestic violence in Ghana: The open secret.* Georgetown, DC: Georgetown Law Faculty Publication. Retrieved from http://scholarship.law.georgetown/facpub/433.

Cronholm, I.F., Singh, F., Fogarty, C.T., & Ambuel, B. (2014). Trends in violence education in family medicine residency curricula. *Family Medicine, 46*(8), 820–825.

Gender Studies and Human Rights Documentation Centre (GSHRDC). (2016). *Facts on violence against women in Ghana.* Retrieved from www.gendercentreghana.org/?p=63.

Griffith, R. (2014). Government implementation of domestic violence protection measures nationwide. *British Journal of Community Nursing, 19*(6), 302–306.

Herreira Triguero, T., Labronici L.M., Aparecida Barbosa, M., & Raijmondo, M.L. (2014). The process of resilience in women who are victims of domestic violence: A qualitative approach. *Cogitare Enfermagem, 19*(3), 395–401.

Jeremiah, R.D., Gamache, P.E., & Hegamin-Younger, C. (2013). Beyond behavioural adjustments: How determinants of contemporary Carribbean masculinities thwart efforts to eliminate domestic violence. *International Journal of Men's Health, 12*(3), 228–244.

Johnson, V., & Brown, C. (2014, October-December). Applying the Korem profiling system to domestic violence. *Army Medical Department Journal.* Retrieved August 16, 2016 from *www.ncbi.nlm.nih.gov.*

Lamptey, S. (2015). *Women in Law and Development in Africa.* Accra.

Leach, F.E., & Mitchell, C. (Eds.). (2006). Combatting gender violence in and around schools. Stoke-on-Trent: Trentham.

McGarry, J., Westbury, M., Kench, S., & Furse, B. (2014). Responding to domestic violence in acute hospital settings. *Nursing Standard, 28*(34), 47–50.

Ofei-Aboagye, R.O. (1994, Summer). Domestic violence in Ghana. *Columbia Journal of Gender Law,* 4(1), 1–25.

Office of the Ministry of Gender, Children and Social Protection. (2015). Retrieved August 16, 2016 from *www.ghana.gov.gh.*

Pobutsky, A., Brown, M., Nakao, L., & Reyes-Salvail, F. (2014). Results from Hawaii domestic violence fatalities review, 2000–2009. *Journal of Injury & Violence Research,* 6(2), 79–90.

Santos da Silva, M.R., Silva, P.A, Luz, G.S., Schek, G., da Rosa Silveira Nunes, M.P, & Ciencia, C. (2014). Family need and professional practices in intra-family domestic violence. *Saude, 13*(2), 335–362.

Trevillion, K., Agnew-Davies, R., & Howard, L. (2013). Healthcare professionals' response to domestic violence. *Primary Healthcare, 23*(9), 34–42.

United Nations. (1993, December). Declaration on the elimination of violence against women, GA. Res 48/104UN. GAOR. Retrieved August 16, 2016 from www.un.org/documents/ga/res/48 /a48r104.htm.

Valenzuela, F.A., & Zincke, C.R. (2015). How abuses become "domestic violence": The performance path. *Revista de Estudios Sociales, 51,* 213–226. DOI: 10.7440/res51.2015.16.

Yi-Hsiu, T., Jia-Shun, K., & Tsui-Hua, H. (2014). Using feminist phenomenology to explore women's experiences of domestic violence in pregnancy. *British Journal of Midwifery, 22*(6), 418–426.

Youngs, J. (2015). Domestic violence and the criminal law: Reconceptualizing reform. *Journal of Criminal law, 79*(1), 55–70. DOI: 10:1177/0022018314566746.

Index

Page numbers in *italics* denote tables, those in **bold** denote figures.